# POETRY 2
# ALOUD HERE

# POETRY 2
# ALOUD HERE

## Sharing Poetry with Children

Sylvia M. Vardell

An imprint of the American Library Association
CHICAGO   2014

**Sylvia M. Vardell** is currently a professor at Texas Woman's University in the School of Library and Information Studies, where she teaches graduate courses in children's and young adult literature. She received her PhD from the University of Minnesota in 1983. Vardell has published articles in *Book Links*, *Language Arts*, *English Journal*, *Reading Teacher*, *New Advocate*, *Young Children*, *Social Education*, and *Horn Book*, as well as several chapters and books on language and literature, including *The Poetry Teacher's Book of Lists*, *Poetry People: A Practical Guide to Children's Poets*, and the popular *Poetry Friday* series coedited with Janet Wong. Her current work focuses on poetry for children, including a regular blog, *Poetry for Children*. Since 2006 Vardell has organized and hosted the annual Poetry Round-Up at the Texas Library Association Conference. She recently was coeditor of the international journal *Bookbird* and previously was president of the Children's Literature Assembly and of the United States Board on Books for Young People.

© 2014 by Sylvia M. Vardell. Any claim of copyright is subject to applicable limitations and exceptions, such as rights of fair use and library copying pursuant to Sections 107 and 108 of the U.S. Copyright Act. No copyright is claimed for content in the public domain, such as works of the U.S. government.

Printed in the United States of America
18  17  16  15  14      5  4  3  2  1

Extensive effort has gone into ensuring the reliability of the information in this book; however, the publisher makes no warranty, express or implied, with respect to the material contained herein.

ISBN: 978-0-8389-1177-8 (paper).

**Library of Congress Cataloging-in-Publication Data**
Vardell, Sylvia M.
    Poetry aloud here 2: sharing poetry with children / Sylvia M. Vardell. — Second edition.
      pages   cm
    Updated and expanded edition of: Poetry aloud here! 2006.
    Includes bibliographical references and index.
    ISBN 978-0-8389-1177-8 (alk. paper)
    1. Children's libraries—Activity programs. 2. School libraries—Activity programs.
    3. Poetry and children. 4. Poetry—Study and teaching (Elementary) 5. Language arts
    (Elementary) I. Vardell, Sylvia M. Poetry aloud here! II. Title.
    Z718.3.V37 2014
    372.64—dc23

                                                                                    2013020181

Cover design by Kirstin Krutsch. Image © Shutterstock, Inc.
Text design by Kim Thornton in Adobe Garamond and Brandon Grotesque.

⊗ This paper meets the requirements of ANSI/NISO Z39.48-1992 (Permanence of Paper).

# Contents

# Acknowledgments

**I** AM SO PLEASED TO BE INVITED TO OFFER A SECOND EDITION OF THIS book. That means that poetry may be catching on even more and that this book may be helping in some small way. That makes me very happy! Since writing the first edition of this book, I started a blog, *Poetry for Children*, and maintain it weekly; I started the regular "Everyday Poetry" column for the American Library Association's magazine *Book Links*; and I've kept the Poetry Round-Up of poet readings rolling at the annual conference of the Texas Library Association. All this has put me in touch with many poets and poetry lovers, and what a privilege that has been. It has also fostered the development of many more poetry projects (like my books, *Poetry People* and *The Poetry Teacher's Book of Lists*) and more blogs (like creating "toolboxes" with reader's guides and digital trailers for promoting all the major poetry awards for young people). I've even had the opportunity to collaborate with the poet Janet Wong in publishing the first digital anthologies of original poetry for young people (*PoetryTagTime, P*TAG, Gift Tag*) as well as a massive collection of new poetry for children, a *Poetry Friday* anthology, which has a poem a week for every grade from kindergarten through fifth. And I am not alone in these endeavors, as I rely on the help and support of many people in each and every instance. My heartfelt thanks go to the following:

The generous children's poetry community, which cares so deeply about providing poetry for children and shares so generously with one another

My many colleagues who have shared their ideas, insights, and quotes with me

Current and former graduate students (librarians and teachers) for sharing their thoughts and comments, particularly the practitioners quoted in this book: Kay Hardy, Pam McWhorter, Melanie Letendre, Lauren Yarbrough, Jean Collier, Renee Newry, Nicki Blake, S. Zulema Bewley, Sarah Dornback, Charry Lackey, Bonnie Boyd McCormick, Lindsey Mendrop, Wendy Watson Fox, Jackie Chetzron, Kirsten Murphy, Clarice Howe-Johnson, Rhonda Brockett, Cristal Isaacks, Hilary Haygood, Tracy LaHue, Monica Walker, Kelly Bolden, Diana Ellis, Xelena González, Carol Kolenet, Carol Neeland, Karen McKenzie, Debbie Owen, and Emily Felker

The amazing and generous poets who shared their thoughts, words, and poems in the poet profiles throughout the book: Brod Bagert, Margarita Engle, Douglas Florian, Nikki Grimes, David L. Harrison, Lee Bennett Hopkins, J. Patrick Lewis, Pat Mora, Naomi Shihab Nye, Jack Prelutsky, Joyce Sidman, Marilyn Singer, and Janet Wong

*Book Links* editors Laura Tillotson and Gillian Engberg, for early opportunities and the encouragement to write about poetry for children, and ALA Editions editor Stephanie Zvirin, for her patience and support

My wonderful family, who continues to believe in me and give me time and space away when needed: my patient husband, Russell Vardell; my mom, Ingrid Mergeler; my son, Alex Vardell; and my daughter, Emily Vardell

My husband—believe me, this bears repeating—for leaving me alone when I needed it and not, when he knew better: thank you, sweetheart

# How to Read a Poem Aloud

*by April Halprin Wayland*

To begin,
tell the poet's name
and the title
to your friend.

Savor every word—
let
each
   line
      shine.

Then—
read it one more time.

Now, take a breath—
and sigh.

Then think about the poet,
at her desk,
late at night,
picking up her pen to write—

and why.

1

# Why Make Poetry a Priority?

*We have no borders when we read.*
—Naomi Shihab Nye, poet

**RECENTLY HAD THE OPPORTUNITY TO EDIT A JOURNAL (*BOOKBIRD*)** focused on children's poetry around the world. We included articles that explored the genre in South Korea, Slovenia, Greece, Slovakia, Romania, France, and beyond. One writer discussed images of Africa as they appeared in Slovenian poetry for young people. Another examined Korean picture books featuring traditional songs, labor songs, children's songs, and classic and contemporary poems, and how diverse cultural and linguistic aspects of Korea were revealed. Two major movements in poetry for children in Greece were discussed, with a special focus on poetic themes, forms, and types. Another writer studied the Slovak movement of "nonsense poetry" for children, with a particular focus on the changing historical and political context, and another explored the links between surrealism and the remembrance of childhood. French publisher Alain Serres (Rue du Monde) discussed his goal of sharing poetry from around the world with children of all ages, and the Dutch-based Poem Express, an international poem poster competition for children, was highlighted. The U.S. poet Helen Frost wrote about her experiences as a visiting author in two schools—in Fort Wayne, Indiana, in the United States, and on the Isle of Barra in Scotland—and how students connect with one another through her novel in poems, *The Braid*.

We also featured reviews of global nursery rhymes collected in New Zealand, railroad songs from Canada, poems about the days of the week and months of the year in French, lighthearted German poems by Jürg Schubiger, poems about childhood games and toys of Nicaragua by Oscar Corea, an anniversary collection of poems by Saša Vegri of Slovenia, and the innovative poems of Spanish poet Juan Carlos Martín. Full-text poems by award winners Shuntaro Tanikawa and Tone Pavček were showcased, as was the *Arche Kalender* from Germany, which highlights a children's poem each week of the year in multiple languages. Isn't it fascinating and inspiring to consider how poetry for young people is valued in cultures around the world?

And if you just look around you, you may be surprised at the poetry you'll find right here, too. For example, I encountered the following examples of poetry and poetic language all in a single day:

> I heard a wedding toast (in rhyme) on a morning TV show.
>
> I found a penny on the ground and spontaneously recited the rhyme "see a penny, pick it up, all day long, you'll have good luck" and remembered the teen version that I have seen on a T-shirt and always makes me laugh: "see a penny, pick it up, all day long, you'll have . . . a penny."
>
> I listened to music on the car radio (with rhyming lyrics).
>
> I reviewed a biography of Ben Franklin that ended with one of his proverbs told in rhyme.
>
> I scanned a magazine in a doctor's waiting room and found an ad that used rhyme ("the potion's in the lotion").
>
> I stumbled upon the middle of a movie on cable television, *Desk Set*, in which Katharine Hepburn's character spouts multiple stanzas of several classic poems.
>
> On an electronic discussion list I read a posting about a friend who had a loved one in hospice care who wanted to hear poetry read aloud.

As we stop and think about the language we encounter in our everyday lives, it is interesting to observe how often that language takes poetic form. It may not always be in the form of a published poem on a piece of paper, but the presence of poetry is interwoven throughout our lives and around the world.

## Life without Poetry

To approach things from another angle, the gadfly poet Charles Bernstein shared this opinion about poetry's place in society:

> As an alternative to National Poetry Month, I propose that we have an International Anti-Poetry [M]onth. As part of the activities, all verse in public places will be covered over—from the Statue of Liberty to the friezes on many of our government buildings. . . . Parents will be asked not to read Mother Goose and other rimes to their children but only . . . fiction. Religious institutions will have to forgo reading verse passages from the liturgy and only prose translations of the Bible will be recited, with hymns strictly banned. . . . Poetry readings will be replaced by self-help lectures. Love letters will have to be written only in expository paragraphs. . . . No vocal music will be played on the radio or sung in the concert halls. Children will have to stop playing all slapping and counting and singing games and stick to board games and football. (www.press.uchicago.edu/Misc/Chicago/044106.html)

An interesting prospect . . . Clearly, the world would be far less interesting if poetry were absent!

## What Does Poetry Do?

Poetry is all around us. Published poetry and classic poetry are more present than you might think—and informal verses and rhyming language are so ubiquitous that we take them for granted. We have experienced a renaissance in poetry publishing in recent years, with greater general interest in poets, poetry books, poetry jams and slams, poetry websites, National Poetry Month, and the like. Why? What does poetry do for us? In her essay "Spiral Staircase," the poet Naomi Shihab Nye wrote, "Poetry wasn't trying to get us to DO anything, it was simply inviting us to THINK, and FEEL, and SEE" (2005, 253). Booth and Moore put it this way:

> Like film makers or photographers, poets manipulate our ears and eyes at the same time, using close-ups, long shots, slow motion, fast forward,

and soft focus; they juxtapose sound and image to make new meanings; they weave in subplots and overlap scenes; and they do it at lightning speed, in a few lines, in one word. (2003, 12)

First Lady Michelle Obama, an avid poetry lover, reminds us:

Think about how you feel when you read a poem that really speaks to you, one that perfectly expresses what you're thinking and feeling. When you read that, you feel understood, right? I know I do. You feel less alone. I know I do. You realize despite all our differences, there are so many human experiences and emotions that we share. . . . And even if you don't grow up to be a professional poet, I promise that what you learn through reading and writing poetry will stay with you throughout your life. (www.whitehouse.gov/the-press-office/2011/05/11/remarks-first-lady -poetry-student-workshop)

Through the ages, great minds have hypothesized where the power of poetry lies. The words? The sounds of words? The structure and shape? Meaning? Emotion? Effect? The philosopher Plato wrote, "Poets utter great and wise things which they do not themselves understand." The poet Robert Frost noted, "Poetry is the renewal of words forever and ever. Poetry is that by which we live forever

**PRACTITIONER PERSPECTIVE**

*Although my first experiences with poetry were positive, I often felt inept in high school and college as we were forced to dissect, analyze, and memorize poems. Invariably, my analyses were different from those of my teachers or professors. While some instructors were flexible and open to discussion, others were dogmatic and thought that what was written in the teacher's guide was the only correct response. My own negative experiences with inflexible teachers have caused me to be open to all responses from students. They often think in new and creative ways that open new vistas for me.*

Hilary Haygood, librarian
San Andres Elementary School, Andrews, Texas

and ever unjaded. Poetry is that by which the world is never old." Years later, at the dedication of a library named for Robert Frost at Amherst College, President John F. Kennedy said:

> When power leads man towards arrogance, poetry reminds him of his limitations. When power narrows the areas of man's concern, poetry reminds him of the richness and diversity of his existence. When power corrupts, poetry cleanses. For art establishes the basic human truth which must serve as the touchstone of our judgment. (www.arts.gov/about/Kennedy.html)

Whatever the reasons, our human capacity for language has long manifested itself in poetic expression.

---
**POET PROFILE**
---

## Why I Write Poetry: A Really Good Poem Can Reach Kids in Wondrous and Unexpected Ways

### BY JOYCE SIDMAN

People often ask me—in a slightly mystified tone of voice—why I write poetry. I know what they're thinking: poetry is a bit outside the mainstream; many readers don't seek it out, and some avoid it. So why deliberately choose it?

In some ways, I think poetry chose me. I've loved it right from childhood, drawn to those tiny sculptures of words on the page. The words themselves enchant me: so vivid, so concise, so rich and full of allusion. I love the music in them—so satisfying to the ear. I love the way a really good poem explodes inside of me, taking the "top of my head off," as Emily Dickinson so famously wrote. There's great power in poetry, and great mystery. It's not easily pinned down, and its allure is difficult to explain. Why do I embrace it? And why do I believe it is absolutely essential for children? Allow me the old Zen trick of answering questions with stories.

## Story No. 1: Capturing the Moment

My husband and I have been hiking all morning in the fall sunshine. We reach a beautiful open field, where we decide to eat lunch (hurrah!). Lake Superior glitters in the distance. Bright scarlet sumac leaves dot the undulating grass.

Overhead, an aspen gleams yellow against a blindingly blue sky. Heaven. As we drowse in the sunlight, a single raven soars over the field. I've just been studying ravens, and I was hoping to see one on this trip! It spots us, does a flip in the air, warbles, burbles, rasps, and carries on a comical conversation with itself before disappearing.

For me, this is a moment of pure happiness. One that will stick in my brain . . . until, eventually, it's relegated to the trash heap of all my memories. Unless I write a poem about it, which I immediately start to do in my head. Poetry can capture a moment—its sights, sounds, smells, feelings—so vividly, it's like you're back inside it. "Think you'll always remember what it's like to be ten years old?" I ask students in schools I visit. "You won't. Write a poem about your life right now, and you will have it forever."

## Story No. 2: Everything Is Connected

I'm walking with my six-year-old nephew along a sunny beach. We dance in and out of the waves. The tide has strewn shells across the sand, and he pounces on them, one after the other. "Look!" he cries out. "This shell's like a hat!" He holds it triumphantly. "And this one looks like a fish! And this one's a hammer!" He dashes about, consumed by his discovery both of the individuality of each shell and of its link to something else in his life. Using his eyes and imagination, he's making sense of what he sees—and taking delight in it. This power, which we call metaphor, is at the heart of poetry.

Aristotle said that "ordinary words convey only what we know already; it is from metaphor that we can best get hold of something fresh." Comparing one thing to another—"fear is a spider web in the heart," as one of my students once wrote—creates a new and flexible understanding of both things. Children are natural metaphor makers, but research has shown that they lose this capacity as they grow older, probably from learning more linear ways of thinking. Poetry—both the reading and the writing of it—creates links back to that more imaginative, explosive, creative way of thinking. The whole world is connected, says Poetry. It's up to you to figure out how.

And so, why do I write poetry? For the chance to feel connected to everything around me. For the chance to capture a moment of joy. For the chance to ease the heart. And why do I encourage children to write poetry? To watch them take a crisp, clean dive into the mysteries that confront them every day, find what glitters beneath the surface, and emerge triumphant. Try it. You'll see.

*Excerpted from "Why I Write Poetry: A Really Good Poem Can Reach Kids in Wondrous and Unexpected Ways," by Joyce Sidman. School Library Journal, April 1, 2012. Used with permission.*

## This Book
*by Joyce Sidman*

Small. Square.
Opens, shuts;
this eye
with cardboard lids.
This tree
of milk-white leaves.
This stack of wings.
This trick window.

This escape route,
travel-pouch,
dream-pillow.

This treasure.
Open it.

*From Joyce Sidman's website: www.joycesidman.com/bookmark.html. Used with permission.*

**CLASS EXERCISE** You will also find this poem formatted as a bookmark on Sidman's website. Make a list of the metaphors for *book* that are found in this poem, such as *eye, tree, stack of wings, window, escape route, travel-pouch,* and *dream-pillow.* Then brainstorm a new list of words or phrases that could describe a book and create a group-made poem variation on her theme using some of those new words and phrases. Create a bookmark out of the children's new poem, too.

---

## Reclaiming Poetry

What is it about life's big and little moments that calls for a poem? At weddings. At funerals. On greeting cards. In church. On the radio. At moments of great happiness or deep sadness. At beginnings and endings. Cullinan, Scala, and Schroder remind us that "poetry is a shorthand for beauty; its words can cause us to tremble, to shout for joy, to weep, to dance, to shudder or to laugh out loud" (1995, 4). Poet Emily Dickinson wrote, "If I feel physically as if the top of my head were taken off, I know that is poetry." And actress Helena Bonham Carter, who served as a narrator for the first poetry app for children, iF Poems, observed:

> There is little that is as deeply satisfying as the apt poem. It's like chocolate for the soul. Except less fattening. It resolves the nervous system, captures the elusive experience of being alive so we may always have it and never lose it. Give your child an appetite for poems and they will never be bored . . . with poems in your pocket, you'll be armed with beauty and food for the soul and you will never be lonely. (http://ifpoems.com/#iF+Poems+App)

Professor and author Charlotte Huck wrote, "Fine poetry is the distillation of experience that captures the essence of an object, feeling, or thought" (2003, 359). Poetry is brief and full of interesting language, but it is the capture of emotion or experience in a nutshell that gives poetry its power. And amazingly, poetry does this in fewer words than any other genre. And unlike with other genres, we often return to the same poems over and over and over again. We can cherish one poem throughout a lifetime, gaining new meaning from it as life experiences color our perceptions and understanding. Research commissioned through the Poetry Foundation noted that most poetry readers (80 percent) first encounter poetry as children, at home or in school; 77 percent of all readers were read nursery rhymes as children; 45 percent of current poetry readers also had other forms of poetry read to them as children.

If this is so, why is there often such a disconnect when the topic of poetry comes up in our work life? Even the word *poetry* puts off many adults. It reminds them of forced memorization, searching for hidden symbolism, or counting meter for iambic pentameter. So many adults have had negative experiences that keep them from sharing poetry with children. Children then grow into a similar dislike or apathy for poetry. Maybe we need to remodel our poetry memories. Sara Holbrook in her book *Practical Poetry* (2005) writes:

> I believe in functional poetry. Much like functional pottery, this is poetry that holds water. It makes sense to keep it around. It does something for us. Makes a connection. It doesn't just sit there on the shelf and look mysterious. Art for art's sake is a silly philosophy that relegates us to that room down the hall in which we run the risk of losing our connection to the real world. I would argue that art is for the sake of everyone. Art, poetry included, should be an intramural event, not simply a spectator sport. (xvi)

If we think about poetry in this way, we may begin to see both the beauty and the utility in this form of literature. We can reclaim poetry as something new.

## The Value of Poetry for Children

Why make poetry a priority when our shelves are full of many choices and our days are full with many tasks? Scholar Lissa Paul makes a case for the importance of children's poetry, from traditional verse to more literary poetry, in her introduction to "Verse" in the seminal work *The Norton Anthology of Children's Literature: The Traditions in English*. She reminds us that "the history of poetry written for children begins in oral tradition" (Zipes et al. 2005, 1132) and includes lullabies, baby songs, nursery verse, riddles and wordplay, playground verse, nonsense, and standard poetry collections. It is a rich tradition that has stood the test of time and has nurtured us from the cradle onward. It is also a shared experience that brings adults and children together by virtue of its oral dimension. Poetry for children begs to be heard, to be shared out loud, to be talked about. It is a social connection as well as a language experience.

**POET PROFILE**

## Exploring the Self

### BY PAT MORA

Opportunities prompt creativity. I grumbled when I was a student and had to write essays, poems, or book reports; but when I finished, I had written what would probably never otherwise have arrived on the page. I'm grateful to my friend Sylvia Vardell for inviting me to write about sharing poetry aloud. I like Sylvia so much that I told her that even if I had no writing implements and had to carve the poem with a stick or rock, I'd be happy to try.

Poems incubate. I knew I had this "assignment" and wanted to write a poem that might be useful for teachers and librarians working to excite students about presenting poems, theirs or poems written by others. When I was in elementary school in El Paso, Texas, we memorized many poems, but we really didn't experience the pleasure of investing ourselves in sharing them. In high school and college, I competed in oral interpretation. I'd prepare poems I liked to share with an audience. I never thought about sharing my own poems.

In New York recently, accompanied by Sylvia's request, I just let the possibilities simmer. I love museums and folk art, so I returned to the American Folk Art Museum, where I discovered *Self and Subject*, self-portraits by folk artists. "Hmmm," I thought as I strolled. "Animal self-portraits by children." The tradition of the animal spirit within is an old and complex one. It's always fun to ask children (and adults), "What animal would you like to be?" but the structure of the poem below lures the reader beyond wishing to feeling, to exploring within.

In some indigenous communities in Mexico and Central America, there's the belief that at birth every infant is given a *nagual*, a guardian animal spirit. My anthropologist husband remembers that we were once in Chiapas, Mexico, and heard someone talk about how family members in such communities would search outside for animal footprints when a baby was born. If many different kinds of footprints were found, the child was assumed to be a shaman, a human with many guardian spirits. In my adult Halloween poem to my three children, "Mama Spell" (*Agua Santa/Holy Water,* 1995), I write to my son, "Discover your hidden *nagual*, pan, pan / Come, dance in the fright of the moon."

All those ideas and images simmered inside me, though not necessarily in an intellectual manner. Yes, I wanted to write a poem that would be both fun and intriguing to children and young people, that would prompt them to ponder and then to create on the page. Yes, I wanted an approach that would lend itself to presentations and dramatizations, to giggles and growls. And yes, I wanted to create an opportunity for you, teachers and librarians, to explore your inside selves, too, and to explore creating an affirming atmosphere that would allow all kinds of spirits to reveal and revel.

'Tis true, and yet, and yet when I wrote the poem, I was too busy playing to be that premeditated. I was exploring possibilities, images, sounds, echoes. I hope you and your students do the same.

## Who's Inside?
*by Pat Mora*

Are you a lumbering bear, *un oso*,
shoving your big ole paw
into a honey hive and licking that gold
sweetness with your thick tongue,

(continued)

or are you a cheetah racing
with the wind, running so fast you

       fly,

your spots, streaking black stars?

Are you *un águila*, an eagle screeching,
"Eeek eeek," over mountaintops,
each wing stretched wide to touch blue
sky, your shiny eyes roaming,

or are you a giraffe, *una jirafa*,
looking
down
     down
         down
at us with round, brown eyes
and long, smiling lashes?

Listen.
Who's inside your skin?

With your magic wand, draw
that inside self, write
your inside poem, the song
of a bear, cheetah, eagle, *jirafa*,
or maybe a manatee, grazing
on grasses all day, all night;
rolling in water all day,
rolling in glimmering stars all night.

**CLASS EXERCISE** Read "Who's Inside?" out loud one or more times. Because the poem mentions many animal movements and sounds, it is ideal for children to act out through pantomime. In addition, children may enjoy animal face painting or making paper-plate masks for the bear, eagle, cheetah, giraffe, manatee, or other inner animal.

---

Poetry forms a bridge from children's oral language development to their first steps in reading and writing language (Hadaway, Vardell, and Young 2001). It helps children move forward in their literacy development. Indeed, children's book author and literacy expert Mem Fox has noted, "Rhymers will be readers; it's that simple. Experts in literacy and child development have discovered that if children know eight nursery rhymes by heart by the time they're four years old, they're usually among the best readers by the time they're eight" (2001, 85).

Poetry does so much for children still developing their language skills:

- It introduces new vocabulary and figurative language.
- It reinforces word sounds, rhymes, and patterns (think phonics!).
- It provides practice for word recognition and word pronunciation.
- It provides examples of synonyms, antonyms, puns, wordplay, and the coining of new words and expressions.
- It is rich in imagery and stimulates the imagination.
- It can provide sensory experiences, giving children the sense of touching, feeling, smelling, and seeing.
- It is an important part of our literary and cultural heritage. Remember Beowulf? The Psalms? "Twinkle, Twinkle, Little Star"? "Hold Fast to Dreams"?
- It is meant to be heard and shared, and thus it provides practice for oral language development, listening, oral fluency, and choral reading and performing.
- It is accessible to a wide range of reading abilities and language learning skill levels.
- It has many pedagogical uses across the curriculum, for building

science concepts, reinforcing historical themes, adding motivation to math lessons, as a "sponge" activity in transition times, and so forth.

Poetry has value for any of us at any age, but for children it offers even more specific benefit. As children are growing in their knowledge of language and literature, poetry is just right for their developing minds and hearts. Poetry is primal: it speaks to a basic human need for expression and is made from the basic building blocks of language.

## Learning through Poetry

Poetry is one of the first forms of literature children experience, albeit often in oral rather than printed form. Mother Goose nursery rhymes are often the first experience a child has with literature of any kind. "Their compact structure, lyrical rhythm and rhyme, colorful characters, and clever titles not only captivate young children but also reinforce key reading skills, such as phonemic awareness and word recognition" (Cullinan 1999, 55). From an early age, children love the rhythm and rhyme of poetry and increase their knowledge of language and its conventions without even realizing it. When we consider the recent emphasis on developing phonemic awareness, on the sound and rhythm of words and the importance of words' beginnings, endings, and middles, we see that that

**PRACTITIONER PERSPECTIVE**

*I am tutoring a child learning English this summer. Since we started, I have been using poems and some of the strategies I have read about. I can already see his confidence and his fluency improving as he reads aloud. The flow of the words, the repetition, and the introduction to new vocabulary have helped with his various reading needs. He has been more willing to read as a result. It has been a short time, but I believe that we will see great results with this child. Today we were calling out sentences about things we like. He yelled out, "I like poems!" and "I like homework!" His homework this week was to read my selected poems. What a joy! I cannot wait to share these strategies with my teachers, especially those who teach English as a second language.*

Renee Newry, library media specialist
Evelyn T. Clifton Early Childhood School, Irving, Texas

**PRACTITIONER PERSPECTIVE**

*What is so fascinating about a poem is that it can have a different meaning for each of us. Poetry that touches one person may have no effect on another. Or, two persons may come away with different impressions after reading the same poem. That is why I think it is so important to let poetry speak to children.*

S. Zulema Bewley, librarian
Harry Shimotsu Elementary School, Mission, Texas

is exactly what children learn by experiencing and enjoying poetry and verse (Bryant et al. 1989).

A first-grade teacher uses poetry to introduce sight words—high-frequency words taught explicitly (Burleson 2002). She chooses poems and nursery rhymes on the basis of the sight-word vocabulary that appears in them and then introduces each poem with the sight words highlighted. Teacher and class enjoy reading the rhymes out loud together and talk about the new words they encounter. Students get their own copies and practice the poem at home and in class and add it to their poetry anthologies at the end of the week. This provides practice with learning vocabulary in the context of poems that are appealing, memorable, and worth revisiting. Thus, children learn both words that are phonetically significant and words that may be phonetically irregular through the rhyme as well as the meaning of poetry.

The use of poetry capitalizes on "the magical moment when children fall in love with words: they notice that the sounds of language fall gently on the ear, they discover double meanings, and they notice the playfulness of language" (Cullinan, Scala, and Schroder 1995, xiii). In a brief interview at Art Arena, a website focused on Persian art, history, and literature, Mahmud Kianush, regarded as the founder of children's poetry in Iran, said, "Poems for children are like toys that are made of words, and these words give wings to their imagination. Children want to sing them, to dance with them, and to play with them" (www.art-arena.com/cpoetry.html). Through poetry, children internalize word sounds and meanings in the most playful, magical contexts, from classic poems like Laura E. Richards's "Eletelephony" to contemporary gems like Douglas Florian's "The Daddy Longlegs."

But in addition to all these cognitive benefits, exposure to poetry also provides emotional benefits. Sharing poetry can reduce stress, increase laughter, provide comfort, offer inspiration, give relief, mirror emotions, and reinforce identification—even for adults. For example, a school librarian, Gail Bush (1997), initiated the Random Acts of Poetry program during the month of April. For each staff member, she chose several poems that would have special meaning. Then, each day throughout the month, she placed some of the poems, one at a time, in the mailboxes of their intended recipients. Typically, those who received poems were so pleased that they spontaneously shared the verses with their students and others, and those who did not receive poems looked forward to when they would. Needless to say, the program was a big success.

## Teaching about Poetry

Where do we begin as we start to share poetry with young people? "As librarians and teachers, we need to set this pattern. Don't analyze it [poetry] too much, but rather enjoy it for what it is—a unique presentation of timeless and universal topics. Think of it [poetry] as psychology without the guilt, songs without the music, art without the illustration" (Korbeck 1995, 44). Poet Lee Bennett Hopkins says, "Don't dissect poetry, enjoy it . . . every day! There shouldn't be a day without poetry—it fits into every area of the curriculum, every area of life" (qtd. in Raymond 1999, 59).

Pauline Harding, a homeschooling colleague, asked her own homeschooled ten-year-old son why we should study or learn about poetry. He said, "We shouldn't." She continued:

> That kind of threw me, since he loves poetry, and we do tons of it. So I asked him to explain. "Learning poetry would be dead boring." Aha— he means "doing poetry as school." He said we should read poetry, and buy poetry books, and listen to poetry on books-on-tape, and snuggle up on winter mornings and take turns reading poems to each other, and memorize poems we like 'cause we feel like it, and have poetry readings at our co-op, but we should NOT "learn" poetry, in the sense of doing worksheets about it or having to analyze it and so on. (Personal communication, September 10, 2005)

**WAYS TO TEACH KIDS TO HATE POETRY**

- Read children sentimental poems that you think are wonderful.
- Make the entire group memorize the same poem, and then make each child recite it in front of the class.
- Tediously analyze the rhyme scheme of each poem read.
- Discuss a poem until everyone in the class arrives at the same interpretation that you have predetermined.

**WAYS TO ENCOURAGE KIDS TO LOVE POETRY**

- Keep in mind that children have different tastes in poetry, and allow them to help you select the poems to share.
- Ask children to respond to poetry, but avoid picking each line apart.
- Allow listeners to express their own interpretations.
- Keep a variety of poetry books available at all times.

Source: Based on Nancy A. Anderson, *Elementary Children's Literature: The Basics for Teachers and Parents*, 2nd ed. (New York: Pearson, 2006), 310–11.

Clearly, there is a message here. What this ten-year-old may not recognize, however, is that reading poetry, listening to poetry, sharing poetry—this is all part of "learning" poetry. We do not have to "butcher" poems for instructional value via lecture and exposition when poems themselves can teach us so much. Involving children in just reading, listening to, performing, and responding to poetry offers rich learning experiences in and of itself. In fact, in this context, thoughtful discussion and critical analysis often emerge quite naturally as children begin to notice patterns, new words, interesting ideas, and powerfully expressed emotions.

## How to Begin

How do we begin? In their literature textbook *Children's Literature, Briefly,* Jacobs and Tunnell (2004) give very clear-cut advice on how to create a community of readers. I find their list of tips for learning from motivated readers particularly intriguing and applicable to promoting poetry. Specifically:

- Be an adult who reads poetry.
- Make poetry books accessible (at arm's length, if possible).
- Put poetry books and poems on the agenda every day.
- Model joy and enthusiasm for poetry.
- Begin where the children are, with their interests, concerns, and experiences.
- Provide opportunities for choral reading and active participation.
- Feature notable poets and access to quality poetry books.
- Focus on meaning, cross-curricular connections, and children's responses.

These variables remind us of what is important in any attempt to encourage reading in any genre. Typically, we are fairly diligent about using these strategies to promote the reading of fiction: we read aloud, display books, share booklists, and develop programs. How often do we apply this same full-court press to promoting poetry for children? What would happen if we gave poetry this same royal treatment?

This book is intended as a guide for librarians, teachers, and others who want to share poetry with children in ways that are inviting, meaningful, and participatory. It is drawn from my experiences with librarians and teachers who agree that young people should be introduced to poetry they will enjoy but whose own familiarity with poetry is often limited to a handful of poets and poetry books, and only a few strategies for presenting those materials. My approach is focused on helping adults share a variety of poetry with children between the ages of five and twelve years in innovative ways in an atmosphere that encourages participation and exploration. Grounded in the current renaissance of interest in poetry and spoken-word events evidenced by the growing celebration of National Poetry Month, this book offers an overview of major poets writing for children, an update on the latest poetry books published for children, an outline of effective poetry promotion activities, a tool kit of poetry presentation strategies, and a repertoire of follow-up possibilities.

Although the last chapter includes several ways to involve children in brief poetry-writing exercises, this book is not about poetry writing per se. Child writers need ongoing time and support to draft and revise their poems, and there are many excellent resource books on how to guide children through the process of writing original poetry. Instead, the emphasis of this book is on the oral dimensions of poetry, on sharing poems out loud and reveling in the spoken word. If you work primarily with teens or with preschoolers, you will have to be somewhat creative in adapting these ideas for your audience. However, you will find a wide continuum of poetry included in the lists and examples provided, from light verse to serious poetry, from nonsensical rhymes to ageless classics. Fortunately, poems are generally less age-bound than any other genre, and you should find poems cited here that children (and adults) across the spectrum will enjoy. I am never too proud to share an odd nursery rhyme with teens or a favorite classic with kindergarteners!

In these pages you will find noteworthy quotes about poetry, perspectives from practitioners in the field, and poet essays and original poems generously shared by well-known poets writing for young people, including Brod Bagert, Margarita Engle, Douglas Florian, Nikki Grimes, David L. Harrison, Lee Bennett Hopkins, J. Patrick Lewis, Pat Mora, Naomi Shihab Nye, Jack Prelutsky, Joyce Sidman, Marilyn Singer, and Janet Wong. Children who are immersed in poetry and poets, hear poems read aloud every day, jump in and participate in poem read-alouds, experience poetry in all curricular subjects, and talk about and share their responses to poetry will quite naturally engage in a great deal of verbal interaction, higher-level thinking, and critical analysis. They may even unknowingly memorize favorite poems that they have asked to hear again and again. But analysis and memorization are not my primary focus. My approach is to provide children access to poetry in all its variety, hoping that everyone will find poems that become a special part of his or her literate life.

*Every poet is a big child.*
*And every child is a little poet.*
*Childhood is the poetry of life.*
*Poetry is the childhood of the world.*

—Boris Novak, poet

## 2

# Which Poets Are Popular?

*There's no money in poetry, but*
*there's no poetry in money either.*
—Robert Graves, poet

HICH POETS ARE WORTH KNOWING ABOUT? IN THIS
chapter we look at the leading awards given to poetry
for children, the classic poets and poems still worth
sharing, notable anthologists, and poets from many
cultures. We briefly consider nearly seventy contemporary poets who write for young people, and we dis-
cuss the value of websites and biographical resources that can help provide background information as well as strategies for promoting poets.

Poetry award winners are certainly a good place to begin, but they are not the
only poets children will enjoy. We can also rely on classic poets whose work has
stood the test of time. And reputable anthologists can be relied on for thematic
collections. But there are many other wonderful writers creating poetry for
young people today, including many poets from different cultures and countries
around the world. Try to discover as many new names as possible as you choose
poems to read and share with children. The past twenty years have been a golden
age for publishing poetry for children, with more variety of poets and poetry formats than ever (Barton and Booth 2004). Today's selection of poetry for young
people is so varied, with styles, topics, themes, and names ranging from Shel

Silverstein to Valerie Worth, from girl bullies (in "The New Kid on the Block," by Jack Prelutsky) to racism ("The Incident," by Countee Cullen). Every reader can surely find poems that speak to him or her, given the proper introduction.

That is the key: providing open access to poetry, free from the roadblocks of formal analysis. Opportunity for in-depth responding and understanding can follow when we create an environment for spontaneous pleasure in poetry. Poet and teacher Georgia Heard puts it this way: "Kids need to become friends with poetry as well. They need to know that poems can comfort them, make them laugh, help them remember, nurture them to know and understand themselves more completely" (1999, 20).

## Poetry Awards
How do we identify which poems are the best for children and young adults? One of the best places to begin is by looking at award winners.

### *Children's Poet Laureate*
The Children's Poet Laureate was established by the Poetry Foundation in 2006 to raise awareness of the fact that children have a natural receptivity to poetry and are its most appreciative audience, especially when poems are written specifically for them. The Children's Poet Laureate receives a $25,000 cash prize and a medallion that includes the inscription "Permit a child to join," taken from an Emily Dickinson poem. The Children's Poet Laureate serves as a consultant to the foundation for a two-year period and gives at least two major public readings for children and their families, teachers, and librarians during his or her term. The Children's Poet Laureate also serves as an adviser to the Poetry Foundation on children's literature and may engage in a variety of projects and events to help instill a love of poetry among the nation's youngest readers.

### Recipients
2013  Kenn Nesbitt
2011  J. Patrick Lewis
2008  Mary Ann Hoberman
2006  Jack Prelutsky

## *The NCTE Award for Excellence in Poetry for Children*

The National Council of Teachers of English (NCTE) gives another major award for poetry. This award is given to a poet for her or his entire body of work in writing poetry for children. Thus there is name recognition—you can bet that any book of poetry by one of these award winners will be well worthwhile.

The NCTE established its Award for Excellence in Poetry for Children in 1977 to honor a living American poet for his or her lifetime achievement in works for children ages three to thirteen years. The award was given annually until 1982, at which time it was decided that the award would be given every three years. In 2008 the Poetry Committee updated the criteria and changed the time frame to every other year.

The NCTE strives to recognize and foster excellence in children's poetry by encouraging its publication and by exploring ways to acquaint teachers and children with poetry through such means as publications, programs, and displays. As one means of accomplishing this goal, the NCTE established its Award for Excellence in Poetry for Children to honor a poet for his or her aggregate work. More than a dozen leading poets have since been recognized. Each met the following criteria:

Literary merit (art and craft of aggregate work)
- Imagination
- Authenticity of voice
- Evidence of a strong persona
- Universality; timelessness

Poet's contributions
- Aggregate work
- Evident potential for growth and evolution in terms of craft
- Excellence

Evolution of the poet's work
- Technical and artistic development as evidenced in the poetry
- Evidence of risk, change, and artistic stamina
- Evidence of different styles and modes of expression

Appeal to children
- Evidence of childlike quality, yet poem's potential for stirring fresh insights and feelings should be apparent. Although the appeal to children of a poet's work is an important consideration, the art and craft must be the primary criterion for evaluation.

## Recipients of the NCTE Poetry Award

| | |
|---|---|
| 2013 | Joyce Sidman |
| 2011 | J. Patrick Lewis |
| 2009 | Lee Bennett Hopkins |
| 2006 | Nikki Grimes |
| 2003 | Mary Ann Hoberman |
| 2000 | X. J. Kennedy |
| 1997 | Eloise Greenfield |
| 1994 | Barbara Esbensen |
| 1991 | Valerie Worth |
| 1988 | Arnold Adoff |
| 1985 | Lilian Moore |
| 1982 | John Ciardi |
| 1981 | Eve Merriam |
| 1980 | Myra Cohn Livingston |
| 1979 | Karla Kuskin |
| 1978 | Aileen Fisher |
| 1977 | David McCord |

Look for *Another Jar of Tiny Stars: Poems by NCTE Award-Winning Poets*, edited by Bernice Cullinan and Deborah Wooten, an anthology of poems by NCTE Poetry Award recipients (up to the year of the book's publication). It is an excellent resource, based on children's votes for their favorite poems by each award winner. It is a very child-friendly collection of some of the best poetry by some of the best poets who have ever written poetry for children. Plus, it includes biographical information about, sketches of, and quotations from the award-winning poets.

## *The Lee Bennett Hopkins Promising Poet Award*

Other sources of quality poetry for children are books by recipients of a fairly new award that is given to up-and-coming poets. The Lee Bennett Hopkins Promising Poet Award was established in 1995 by Lee Bennett Hopkins, himself a poet and anthologist, in cooperation with the International Reading Association to encourage new poets in their writing. Although the award winners cannot have published more than two books, their work has already proved to be of high quality.

As the award's website reports, the Lee Bennett Hopkins Promising Poet Award is a monetary prize given every three years to a promising new author of poetry for children and young adults up to grade 12 who has published no more than two books of children's poetry (www.reading.org/resources/AwardsandGrants/childrens_hopkins.aspx). The winning poet or anthologist receives a handsome plaque and a $500 honorarium, made possible by Hopkins. A book-length single poem may be submitted. Children's poetry is defined as poetry rather than light verse, and the award is for published works only. Readers, besides enjoying the award winners' current titles, should watch for their future works.

### Recipients of the Lee Bennett Hopkins Promising Poet Award

2013   Guadalupe Garcia McCall, for *Under the Mesquite*
2010   Gregory Neri, for *Chess Rumble*
2007   Joyce Lee Wong, for *Seeing Emily*
2004   Lindsay Lee Johnson, for *Soul Moon Soup*
2001   Craig Crist-Evans, for *Moon over Tennessee: A Boy's Civil War Journal*
1998   Kristine O'Connell George, for *The Great Frog Race and Other Poems*
1995   Deborah Chandra, for *Rich Lizard and Other Poems*

## *The Lee Bennett Hopkins Award for Children's Poetry*

As we seek out new books of poetry, it is helpful to know about awards for specific titles. The Lee Bennett Hopkins Award for Children's Poetry, established in 1993, is presented annually to an American poet or anthologist for the most outstanding new book of children's poetry published in the previous calendar year. The award is made possible by a gift from Lee Bennett Hopkins himself and is administered by the Pennsylvania State University College of Education and the Pennsylvania State University Libraries. The winning poet or anthologist receives a handsome plaque and a $500 honorarium. In recent years, the committee has also cited several honor books each year. As specified on the award's website, the award shall be granted annually to an anthology of poetry or a single-volume poem published for children in the previous calendar year (per copyright) by a living American poet or anthologist. The criteria state the following:

> Good poetry is imaginative. It deals with emotion and has significance beyond the act of creation. It uses figurative language, yet is compact in thought and expression. Good poetry has an element of beauty and truth which appears unstable outside of the poem. The book which wins the Lee Bennett Hopkins Award for Children's Poetry must be accessible to children and its presentation must serve the poem or poems in an attractive and appropriate manner. (www.pabook.libraries.psu.edu/activities/hopkins/)

## Recipients of the Lee Bennett Hopkins Award for Children's Poetry

2013 *Water Sings Blue: Ocean Poems,* by Kate Coombs

2012 *Won Ton: A Cat Tale Told in Haiku*, by Lee Wardlaw

2011 *The Ink Garden of Brother Theophane*, by C. M. Millen

2010 *Button Up! Wrinkled Rhymes*, by Alice Schertle

2009 *Diamond Willow*, by Helen Frost

2008 *Birmingham, 1963*, by Carole Boston Weatherford

2007 *Jazz*, by Walter Dean Myers

2006 *Song of the Water Boatman and Other Pond Poems*, by Joyce Sidman

2005 *Here in Harlem: Poems in Many Voices*, by Walter Dean Myers

2004 *The Wishing Bone and Other Poems*, by Stephen Mitchell

2003 *Splash! Poems of Our Watery World*, by Constance Levy

2002 *Pieces: A Year in Poems and Quilts*, by Anna Grossnickle Hines

2001 *Light-Gathering Poems*, by Liz Rosenberg

2000 *What Have You Lost?*, by Naomi Shihab Nye

1999 *The Other Side: Shorter Poems*, by Angela Johnson

1998 *The Great Frog Race and Other Poems*, by Kristine O'Connell George

1997 *Voices from the Wild*, by David Bouchard

1996  *Dance with Me*, by Barbara Esbensen
1995  *Beast Feast*, by Douglas Florian
1994  *Spirit Walker*, by Nancy Wood
1993  *Sing to the Sun*, by Ashley Bryan

For activities and ideas for promoting these award and honor books, go to the Lee Bennett Hopkins Poetry Award Teaching Toolbox here: http://leebennett hopkinsaward.blogspot.com.

## *The Claudia Lewis Award*

One other well-known poetry award recognizes a single title each year: the Claudia Lewis Award, given by Bank Street College in New York. Presented for the first time in 1998, this award honors the late Claudia Lewis, a distinguished children's book expert and longtime member of the Bank Street College faculty and Children's Book Committee. According to the award's website, Lewis conveyed her love and understanding of poetry with humor and grace, and the award is a tribute to her legacy. The award is presented annually for the best poetry book of the year. Given Bank Street College's long and distinguished history in teaching and literature, this award is worth noting.

### Recipients of the Claudia Lewis Award

2013  *The National Geographic Book of Animal Poetry*, edited by
     J. Patrick Lewis
2012  *Emma Dilemma: Big Sister Poems*, by Kristine O'Connell George, and
     *The Watch That Ends the Night: Voices from the Titanic*, by Allan Wolf
2011  *Guyku: A Year of Haiku for Boys*, by Bob Raczka
2010  *Red Sings from Treetops: A Year in Colors*, by Joyce Sidman
2009  *The Surrender Tree*, by Margarita Engle
2008  *Here's a Little Poem: A Very First Book of Poetry*, edited by Jane Yolen
     and Andrew Fusek Peters
2007  no award given
2006  *A Kick in the Head: An Everyday Guide to Poetic Forms*, edited by Paul
     B. Janeczko
2005  *Here in Harlem: Poems in Many Voices*, by Walter Dean Myers

2004 *The Way a Door Closes*, by Hope Anita Smith

2003 *Little Dog and Duncan*, by Kristine O'Connell George

2002 *Love That Dog*, by Sharon Creech, and *Amber Was Brave, Essie Was Smart*, by Vera B. Williams

2001 *Mammalabilia*, by Douglas Florian

2000 *Stop Pretending: What Happened When My Big Sister Went Crazy*, by Sonya Sones

1999 *I, Too, Sing America: Three Centuries of African American Poetry*, edited by Catherine Clinton

1998 *The Invisible Ladder: An Anthology of Contemporary American Poems for Young Readers*, edited by Liz Rosenberg

For activities and ideas for promoting these award and honor books, go to the Claudia Lewis Poetry Award Teaching Toolbox here: http://claudialewispoetry award.blogspot.com.

## The Lion and the Unicorn Award

The Lion and the Unicorn Award for Excellence in North American Poetry, established in 2005, focuses on North American poetry for young people and carries on the prior tradition begun by the British journal *Signal*: to "instigate, provoke, and sustain a conversation about poetry published for children." Recipients are now from both the United States and Canada. In addition, the Lion and the Unicorn Award includes an essay that discusses the award winners and speculates on issues unique to writing and publishing poetry for children, thus "painting a picture of that year in children's poetry" (http://lionandunicorn poetryaward.blogspot.com).

## Recipients of the Lion and the Unicorn Award

2012 *Roots and Blues, A Celebration*, by Arnold Adoff

2011 *Nest, Nook, and Cranny*, by Susan Blackaby

2010 no award given

2009 *A Voweller's Bestiary, from Aardvark to Guineafowl (and H)*, by JonArno Lawson

2008 *Tap Dancing on the Roof: Sijo (Poems)*, by Linda Sue Park

2007   *Black Stars in a White Night Sky*, by JonArno Lawson
2006   *Jazz A·B·Z: An A to Z Collection of Jazz Portraits*, by Wynton Marsalis
2005   *Fortune's Bones: The Manumission Requiem*, by Marilyn Nelson

For activities and ideas for promoting these award and honor books, go to the Lion and Unicorn Poetry Award Teaching Toolbox here: http://lionandunicorn poetryaward.blogspot.com.

---

As we strengthen the poetry holdings in our library collections, one extra step that may help patrons find more award-winning poetry is to note the awards a title has received on its circulation records. Such notations can also assist us in compiling bibliographies and recommended reading lists.

As we seek out the best new poetry books for children each year, other sources of recommendations can also be helpful. For example, you can count on the annual *Horn Book* Fanfare List to identify the poetry titles that the magazine's judges have selected as the year's best in children's literature. The Cybils Award was established in 2006 to recognize the role of bloggers in the "kidlitosphere," the online children's literature world. Cybils, an acronym for "Children's and Young Adult Bloggers' Literary Awards," are given annually in a variety of genre and format categories, including poetry. The Centre for Literacy in Primary Education in England initiated a new prize for children's poetry in 2003, hoping that "the Prize will place children's poetry firmly in the literary limelight, imbuing it with some long overdue prestige and encouraging the growth of a knowledgeable, critical, enthusiastic poetry readership of the future." Those are worthy goals for all of us who care about children's poetry. Other local and regional organizations offer poetry prizes of one kind or another from time to time, too. In fact, there is no reason you can't initiate your own local celebration and recognition of new poets and poetry books—and even involve children in voting for their favorites.

## Classic Poets

When we look for poetry to share with children, we often remember the poems of the past that were shared with us in our own childhoods. Many of us have fond memories of hearing classic poems read aloud by loving family members. We may even be able to recite "Jabberwocky," by Lewis Carroll, or "The Swing," by Robert Louis Stevenson, or "Eletelephony," by Laura E. Richards, without missing a beat. Or we may recall the poetry anthologies of Walter de la Mare, Robert Graves, or Charles Causley with great fondness. These are further reminders of how powerful an enthusiastic model of reading can be in fostering a love of poetry. Unfortunately, the opposite is also true. For some people, classic poems conjure up memories of forced memorization or puzzled analysis. Classic poems may seem abstract or old-fashioned. But this need not be the case. For example, books such as A. A. Milne's *When We Were Very Young* and Robert Louis Stevenson's *A Child's Garden of Verses* are still in print and include poems of childhood experiences and musical language that kids today can still relate to.

## Classic Poems Worth Sharing

Many classic poems are still popular with young people. The subject matter, language, rhythm, and imagery of these poems are still inviting for today's readers and listeners. Most of the selections that follow continue to be included in current anthologies of popular children's poetry.

### Twenty Classic Poems Not to Be Missed

Cecil Frances Alexander, "All Things Bright and Beautiful"
Gwendolyn Brooks, "We Real Cool"
Lewis Carroll, "Jabberwocky"
Emily Dickinson, Poem No. 288, "I'm Nobody! Who Are You?"
Eugene Field, "Wynken, Blynken, and Nod"
Robert Frost, "Stopping by Woods"
Langston Hughes, "Dreams"
Rudyard Kipling, "If"
Edward Lear, "The Owl and the Pussycat"
Henry Wadsworth Longfellow, "Paul Revere's Ride"
A. A. Milne, "If I Were King"
Clement Moore, "A Visit from St. Nicholas"
Ogden Nash, "The Tale of Custard the Dragon"
Laura E. Richards, "Eletelephony"
Christina Rossetti, "The Wind"
Carl Sandburg, "Fog"

Robert Louis Stevenson, "My Shadow"
Edna St. Vincent Millay, "Afternoon on a Hill"
Ernest Thayer, "Casey at the Bat"
Walt Whitman, "O Captain! My Captain!"

Classic poems are often available in picture-book format, which can provide fresh, new interpretations of these familiar verses and make them even more accessible for younger readers. Susan Jeffers, for example, illustrated the Robert Frost poem "Stopping by Woods" in a beautiful picture book. The Thayer poem "Casey at the Bat" has been illustrated several times over, most recently by Christopher Bing, whose version won Caldecott honors. Both Jan Brett and James Marshall created unique visions of Lear's "The Owl and the Pussycat" in picture-book form. Quentin Blake reinterpreted Ogden Nash and Lewis Carroll, among others, in *The Penguin Book of Nonsense Verse*. Many, many versions of "A Visit from St. Nicholas," often known as "The Night before Christmas," are available from a variety of illustrators and retellers. Kids Can Press offers its graphic Visions in Poetry series, "classic verse through the eyes of outstanding contemporary artists in handsomely bound collectable hardcover editions," beginning with *Jabberwocky*, illustrated by Stéphane Jorisch.

As much as I enjoy many classic works, I admit that I do not usually choose them first when I introduce poetry to children. It may seem counterintuitive since we usually begin with what we are familiar with, but I have found that

**PRACTITIONER PERSPECTIVE**

*My oldest son is ten and he's extremely shy. It usually takes him until March to open up and converse with his teachers. He's been watching me read poetry books and I've even read several aloud to him. (He really likes Jack Prelutsky). Earlier this month, he won a poetry competition in the local newspaper. I had no idea that he had submitted anything. When I read it, I was absolutely beside myself as something had finally broken through his shy veneer. I was soooo proud, but even better, he was so very proud of himself. Just this week, he IM-ed his dad with a poem he had written! I wholeheartedly believe that shy children can benefit from poetry.*

Kelly Bolden, elementary school librarian
Killeen, Texas

children respond more immediately to the humor and relevance of contemporary poetry. I find that once I lay the groundwork with poems about school, homework, siblings, and the like, the door is open to a greater and greater variety of poetic styles, formats, and voices.

## Anthologists

Knowing which individual poets to look for is very helpful, but in this genre, anthologies have also been essential, particularly for showcasing the work of new, up-and-coming poets whose work may not yet be published individually. Poetry anthologies have long been a staple of libraries, enabling us to use a single resource for a variety of purposes. In the past, anthologies were often large collections of three hundred pages or more, full of poems in small print, with few or no illustrations. They were often intended for adults to read out loud to children and not for children themselves. That has changed. A few comprehensive anthologies still offer a wide-ranging poetry smorgasbord like *Julie Andrews' Collection of Poems, Songs, and Lullabies*, *The Bill Martin Jr. Big Book of Poetry*, and *Forget-Me-Nots: Poems to Learn by Heart* (edited by Mary Ann Hoberman), but in most cases the poetry anthologies published today are slimmer volumes gathered around topics of particular interest to children and are richly illustrated.

Several anthologists have established excellent reputations for compiling numerous high-quality collections of poetry for children. Most have also published volumes of their own poetry and are known as both poets and anthologists. The popular Jack Prelutsky has compiled several anthologies in addition to volumes of his own work, including the very successful *Random House Book of Poetry for Children*. *Knock at a Star*, a combination poetry anthology and instructional guide by husband-and-wife team X. J. Kennedy and Dorothy Kennedy, is considered a standard. Former English teacher Paul B. Janeczko has created many anthologies particularly for teens, as well as several excellent guidebooks for aspiring poets, such as *Seeing the Blue Between*. Lee Bennett Hopkins may be the most prolific anthologist of all, winning a Guinness World Record for creating more anthologies of poetry for children than anyone—ever. His work includes an incredible variety of on topics interesting to kids (e.g., *Dinosaurs*) and friendly to teachers (e.g., *Marvelous Math*). Even multicultural and international poetry anthologies are available, compiled by such stellar names as

Arnold Adoff, Joseph Bruchac, Ashley Bryan, Naomi Shihab Nye, Neil Philip, and Michael Rosen. Each of these anthologists has created several outstanding poetry collections full of the work of many different poets. Such books provide a helpful assortment of many poems in one spot and can lead to more in-depth study of individual books by individual poets.

**Major Poetry Anthologists**
 Arnold Adoff
 Joseph Bruchac
 Lori Carlson
 Ruth Gordon
 Georgia Heard
 Lee Bennett Hopkins
 Paul B. Janeczko
 Caroline Kennedy
 X. J. Kennedy and Dorothy Kennedy
 Bruce Lansky
 Naomi Shihab Nye
 Elise Paschen
 Neil Philip
 Barbara Rogasky
 Michael Rosen
 Liz Rosenberg
 Charles Sullivan
 Patrice Vecchione
 Laura Whipple

## Poets from Many Cultures

In the United States today, more poetry is being published for young people by a larger variety of poets than at any time in the past. Not only is poetry experiencing a publishing renaissance, but also the field's openness to new voices has encouraged multicultural poetry to flourish. A quick survey of recent poetry titles will turn up at least fifty notable poets of color who are writing for children today, representing most of the main microcultures within the United States. And more and more international poetry is finding its way into libraries and classrooms in the United States as well.

The diverse viewpoints reflected in the poetry of parallel cultures enable us to show children firsthand both the sameness and the differences that make the human landscape so dynamic and fascinating. Poets of color are using the language, experiences, and images of their cultures in ways that are fresh and powerful (Vardell 2005). In addition, the special succinctness of poetry provides young people with an appealing introduction to other cultures. Powerful points about prejudice, identity, and cultural conflict can sometimes be made in a very few words. Consider Janet Wong's poem "Speak Up," from *Good Luck Gold and Other Poems*, whose language and structure suggest the playground taunting of a child who appears different. In addition, we can often rediscover our universality in the words and feelings of poems that cross cultural boundaries. Langston Hughes's poems in his classic work *The Dreamkeeper and Other Poems* show human emotions and experiences that are real and vivid, no matter what color a person's skin is. I have found that young people of all colors enjoy the writing of poets from many parallel cultures. That is to say, poets do not speak only to readers from their own cultures. Asian American readers have understood "I, Too," by Langston Hughes, an African American poet, and Native American readers have related to "Speak Up," by Janet Wong, an Asian American poet. The fact that cultural heritage and the distinctiveness of language are addressed through poetry is interesting and important to all young people. Fortunately, more and more excellent examples of multicultural poetry are available for sharing.

### African American Poetry for Young People

Although rarely anthologized in the past in collections of poetry for children, African American poets like Langston Hughes, Lucille Clifton, Countee Cullen, Paul Laurence Dunbar, Nikki Giovanni, Gwendolyn Brooks, Marilyn Nelson, and others are regularly featured in collections of American poetry for young people today. Poets also share powerful visions of African American history in *Roots and Blues: A Celebration*, by Arnold Adoff; *Never Forgotten*, by Patricia McKissack; *We Are America: A Tribute from the Heart*, by Walter Dean Myers; and *Remember the Bridge: Poems of a People*, by Carole Boston Weatherford.

More and more African American poets are gaining widespread recognition and praise. Eloise Greenfield won the National Council of Teachers of English Poetry Award for her lifetime contribution to poetry for children, including the popular collection *Honey, I Love*. Nikki Grimes, another NCTE Poetry Award recipient, creates an unforgettable modern heroine in the Danitra Brown poetry books. Charles R. Smith Jr. showcases athletes and heroes from the African American community in his raplike poem picture books, and Hope Anita Smith tells raw family stories in her poetry. These poets speak of their lives, of their color, of their humanity, of their humor. Some write in dialect, some use rhyme, some focus on racial pride, some share emotional universals. Children of all cultural backgrounds deserve to know their names and hear their words.

### Latino and Latina Poetry for Young People

Poems, rhymes, songs, and chants are also an important part of Hispanic American or Latino (Latina) children's literature. There are also more and more

**PRACTITIONER PERSPECTIVE**

*I think that of all the varieties of multicultural poetry, Hispanic and Latin American poetry have to be my favorites. I do not know if it is the poetry's language, or its take on life, but it is so vibrant! I also think that it is vital to use bilingual poetry in our classrooms—whether you teach Spanish speakers or not. The two-way writing in Spanish and English that is available in most Spanish poetry books is a great way either to introduce something new and different to English-only speakers or to help ease an otherwise rocky transition for Spanish speakers. Many teachers I know hesitate to read the Spanish versions aloud for fear that they will mess up. However, when I taught in a bilingual classroom (and no, my Spanish is not proficient), I loved trying to read Spanish the best I could. The kids would very willingly help me out with words I could not pronounce. Then we would switch roles and I would help them get through the English translation. So, if you are slightly leery of bilingual books and poetry or do not think that you have a place in your class or library curriculum for them—take a chance! If you yourself are uncomfortable reading Spanish poetry aloud, invite fluent Spanish speakers, whether they are older kids, parents, or friends, into the classroom or library as guest readers. Everyone will benefit!*

Lauren Yarbrough, reading specialist
Calvin Bledsoe Elementary School, Frisco, Texas

published collections of Latino poetry for children from which to share. Gary Soto, for example, has several collections of poetry suitable for children and teens, such as *Worlds Apart: Fernie and Me*. His work may already be familiar to children who have read his picture books and novels. In addition, many Latino poets tackle powerful social themes about identity, language, and culture, as in the historical novels in verse by Margarita Engle or the poem biographies by Carmen T. Bernier-Grand. There are also several bilingual and interlingual (with Spanish words interspersed) collections of poetry available by poets such as Francisco X. Alarcón (e.g., *Animal Poems of the Iguazú / Animalario del Iguazú*) and Pat Mora (*Confetti, Yum! Mmmm! ¡Qué rico! Americas' Sproutings*), as well as *The Tree Is Older Than You Are*, edited by Naomi Shihab Nye. If you are a Spanish speaker or work with Spanish-speaking children, reading poems aloud in both Spanish and English can be very inviting and empowering. Several collections of children's nursery rhymes and songs in English and Spanish are available for sharing with young children. They include multiple works by Alma Flor Ada and Isabel Campoy, as well as by José-Luis Orozco. The verses in their books such as *Ten Little Puppies / Diez perritos* and *Diez deditos / Ten Little Fingers* incorporate music and movement that invite children to participate. Look for Rose Treviño's excellent resource book *Read Me a Rhyme in Spanish and English* for more ideas and recommendations. What an opportunity to introduce poetry, language, and culture all at the same time!

---

**POET PROFILE**

# In Her Own Words

## MARGARITA ENGLE

I am haunted by stories about people who make hopeful decisions in situations that seem hopeless. The verse novel form allows me to distill complex historical situations down to their emotional essence. I need to learn the facts and figures of history, but I don't want to clutter my books with information. My goal is an uncrowded page that flows easily and quickly, without intimidating reluctant readers. . . . Researching real people and historical events requires obscure references. I start with recent publications and work my way back in time by searching for references listed in bibliographies. When I find a diary, I feel like I've won a prize, because first-person accounts offer emotional aspects along with the details of daily life.

Giving voices to characters I admire feels natural, but it's a struggle to let the ones I detest have their say. When I wrote *The Surrender Tree*, I really didn't want to let the slave hunter speak. I had to force myself to write his voice, but he was part of the story, so it had to be done. I also wrote a shorter novel in verse with only one voice, inspired by stories my grandmother told me about her childhood. She struggled with dyslexia, so I dedicated the book to reluctant readers.

My parents met, fell in love, and got married without speaking the same language. I was born and raised in my father's hometown of Los Angeles, but my Cuban mother taught me Spanish while I was little, and when we spent summers in Cuba, I was immersed in Spanish. Growing up bilingual was a formative experience. I am always aware of the different ways of thinking that come with a language. For instance, in Spanish we say we dream "with" someone, instead of dreaming "about" them. In English we say we "fly" from coast to coast, but in Spanish people can't fly. They have to "go by airplane." Language is a magic window. It lets you glimpse the human mind.

I exist in the space between two hostile countries, Cuba and the United States, so the interface between cultures fascinates me. . . . Tropical landscapes are constantly bursting with life and death. Everything grows fast, and everything rots. It's a setting filled with fragrance and stench. It can only be described with all five senses on high alert. . . . For centuries, Cuban writers have portrayed a striking blend of natural beauty and moral corruption. It may seem surrealistic, but it's actually a completely realistic image of life in the tropics.

## Caribbean Windows

*by Margarita Engle*

They are always open
rectangles of air
instead of glass.
They might as well be doors.

*(continued)*

Dragonflies and mystery birds
zoom into my thoughts.

Each daydream
invites the sea breeze
to lift me away
then carry me back
across the quiet space
where long-ago ancestors
were young,
gazing through windows
of wonder.

*Copyright © 2012 Margarita Engle. Used with permission.*

**CLASS EXERCISE** Invite children to talk about what they daydream about. If you have access to a pile of out-of-date magazines, encourage them to browse and select and cut out a daydream image or images (or use the Internet to research images). Glue the picture(s) to a sheet of construction paper, one per child. Then cut out another sheet of construction paper to resemble a window frame and glue one on top of each sheet of images. Post them on a wall all together, one next to the other, along with the poem, creating a giant window of daydreams.

## Asian–Pacific American Poetry for Young People

When it comes to sharing poetry by Asian–Pacific American writers, there are also several choices. Asian and Asian American poets often express a deep appreciation for nature in much of their poetry for young people. Other poems explore the tensions between traditional and modern ways. Family traditions and beliefs are also the focus of many poems by contemporary Asian American writers. For example, Janet Wong's collection *Knock on Wood* looks at superstitions across cultures, including in her own Korean and Chinese heritage and Linda Sue Park explores the Korean poem form of the *sijo* in *Tap Dancing on the Roof: Sijo (Poems)*. Minfong Ho shares ancient Chinese poetry in the beautifully illustrated collection *Maples in the Mist: Poems for Children from the Tang Dynasty*, which is also available in a bilingual edition; and Kam Mak offers a culturally rich poem memoir in *My Chinatown: One Year in Poems*. Recent novels in verse offer insight on growing up Asian in America in Joyce Lee Wong's *Seeing Emily* and Thanhha Lai's *Inside Out and Back Again*, for example. Although most of these particular Asian and Asian American poems are not rhyming, young readers are drawn to their simplicity and clarity.

### Native American Poetry for Young People

In many Native American or American Indian cultures, the rituals and traditions, stories, and songs of everyday life are often expressed poetically. Many contemporary Native American poets consider their poetry a continuation of the oral narrative tradition of their people and heritage. This can be seen in many Native American poems about the seasons, historical events, and the like. Joseph Bruchac, for example, published several poem collections that capture elements of land, animals, and nature, such as *The Earth under Sky Bear's Feet* and *Thirteen Moons on Turtle's Back*. Bruchac tries to incorporate Native words (from the poet's root culture) within the translated poems to provide some of the music and rhythm of the original language for the non-Native speaker. Bruchac often performs these poems aloud to the beat of a drum—a powerful auditory experience. Native poetry can include a variety of poetic forms, including rhymes, free verse, chants, charms, prayers, blessings, lullabies, warnings, eulogies, wishes, prophecies, healings, war chants, songs, night songs, medicine songs, mother-child poems, and more. John Bierhorst compiled several collections of Native poetry, including *On the Road of Stars: Native American Night Poems and Sleep Charms*. Other examples of authentic voices can be found in Hettie Jones's classic collection *The Tree Stands Shining: Poetry of the North American Indian* and Virginia Driving Hawk Sneve's seminal work, *Dancing Teepees: Poems of American Indian Youth*. Three resources of contemporary Native poetry include *Rising Voices: Writings of Young Native Americans*, *Walking on Earth and Touching the Sky: Poetry and Prose by Lakota Youth at Red Cloud Indian School*, and *Night Is Gone, Day Is Still Coming: Stories and Poems by American Indian Teens and Young Adults*. Just a reminder: some Native poetry may be presented in translations filtered through a non-Native perspective, so seek out works by Native poets whenever possible.

## International Poetry for Young People

Translation is also an issue in international poetry for young people. More and more international poets are now being published in the United States and translated into English. Remember, however, that poems that may have rhymed in German, for example, may no longer rhyme in their translated English versions. Or the translator may have opted to create rhyming patterns in English that affect the meaning in the original language. Thus, translated poems may not be as rhythmic and musical as the rhyming English poems children are used to. For more strongly rhythmic poetry, start with our neighbors to the north and south. There are several collections of poems from the Caribbean available by poets such as Monica Gunning, Lynn Joseph, John Agard, and Grace Nichols that are very appealing. The humorous work of Canadian poet Dennis Lee (e.g., *The Ice Cream Store*) is often compared to that of Shel Silverstein, and other popular Canadian poets include JonArno Lawson and Pamela Porter. Looking farther abroad, one finds that Michael Rosen has compiled many collections of British and other verse from a variety of countries (e.g., *The Kingfisher Book of Children's Poetry*), as have Graham Denton and Liz Brownlee. Australia gives us Steven Herrick and his many engaging novels in verse, such as *Naked Bunyip Dancing*. And Naomi Shihab Nye has gathered anthologies of international poetry with English translations, such as *This Same Sky: A Collection of Poems from around the World* and *The Space between Our Footsteps: Poems and Paintings from the Middle East*. Jan Greenberg offers the ekphrastic international collection *Side by Side: New Poems Inspired by Art from around the World*. For bilingual Japanese-English poetry, look for the lovely collections by Michio Mado, *The Animals* and *The Magic Pocket*, both illustrated with traditional cut-paper art. Sharing such rich and varied poems from around the world can help bring us all a little closer together.

Multicultural poetry, much like all forms of literature, is written as an individual response to personal, social, economic, or environmental conditions. It reflects a distinct point of view as well as a specific time and place. And, from a personal perspective, multicultural poetry offers each of us the opportunity to connect: to connect to the poem, to connect with the poet, and to connect with one another as readers. The best approach is to infuse all our poetry sharing with multicultural and international poets whenever and wherever the theme, subject, style, form, or topic suggests a connection. Multicultural poems are not just for cultural history months or special occasions; they speak to every possible moment.

## Meet the Poets: Sixty-Six Names to Know

In survey after survey, we find that nearly every library holds multiple copies of Shel Silverstein's poetry collections. His work is a staple of children's poetry and has been enjoyed by several decades of children. Jack Prelutsky follows as a close second in most library collections. His zany humor and musical rhythms continue to engage children. But that is where the list often stops. In my research on the poetry holdings of school and public libraries, I have found that poetry collection development is often spotty and inconsistent. Many people are unfamiliar with poetry awards, with contemporary poets writing for children today, and with multicultural poets in particular. What follows is a brief introduction to sixty-six poets whose work for children is worth buying, reading, collecting, and sharing. Just a bit of background information is shared along with a sampling of their work. Most of these poets have personal websites, and more poets' sites are added regularly. And of course, new poets are emerging all the time. Once your radar is tuned to poetry, you will find wonderful poetry books and poets popping up in many places.

### ARNOLD ADOFF                                  *www.arnoldadoff.com*

Arnold Adoff became the eighth winner of the NCTE Award for Excellence in Poetry for Children in 1988 and is recognized as a champion of multiculturalism in American literature for children. His poems are marked by the innovative use of shape, playfulness with the mechanics of language, and frequently strong social conscience, as seen in his groundbreaking anthology *My Black Me: A Beginning Book of Black Poetry* and his own recent work, such as *Roots and Blues: A Celebration.*

### FRANCISCO X. ALARCÓN

Francisco X. Alarcón is probably best known for his four season-based picturebook anthologies in Spanish and English: *Laughing Tomatoes and Other Spring Poems / Jitomates risueños y otros poemas de primavera, From the Bellybutton of the Moon and Other Summer Poems / Del ombligo de la luna y otros poemas de verano*, *Angels Ride Bikes and Other Fall Poems / Los ángeles andan en bicicleta y otros poemas de otoño*, and *Iguanas in the Snow and Other Winter Poems / Iguanas en la nieve y otros poemas de invierno*. His metaphorical poetry captures personal memories as well as childhood experiences.

**KATHI APPELT**                                    *www.kathiappelt.com*

For a unique poetic format, look for Kathi Appelt's book *My Father's Summers: A Daughter's Memoirs*. These sensitive prose poems depict a young girl's experience in a divided family through a scrapbook of photos and poetic vignettes. Her *Poems from Homeroom: A Writer's Place to Start* is also a unique resource for young people who want to know how poets work.

**BROD BAGERT**                                    *www.brodbagert.com*

Brod Bagert is the author of several collections written specifically for children to perform, including *Let Me Be the Boss: Poems for Kids to Perform*, *The Gooch Machine: Poems for Children to Perform*, *Chicken Socks and Other Contagious*

**PRACTITIONER PERSPECTIVE**

*We have several books by Francisco X. Alarcón in our classroom. His books have been exciting to have because, aside from being so beautifully illustrated, they have wonderful poems written in both Spanish and English. I have five students who are learning English. Two of them speak almost no English. Just like the rest of my students, these two boys love to sign up for poetry breaks. For the first several months of school, they could choose a buddy and share a poem in Spanish and then have their buddy read the same poem in English. Now they are familiar enough with the poems that they can read them in English, too. All of the other children in the class enjoy practicing and reading poems in Spanish. Alarcón has a terrific imagination that has been especially appealing to my second and third graders. He writes about tomatoes laughing, chilies that explode, and tortillas that applaud the sun. He also writes about his grandmother's songs, pets he has owned, and children who have worked in the fields. He honors his mother in many of his poems and shares that she is the one who taught him that with hard work and education his dreams would come true. He is definitely one of the favorite poets to read in our classroom!*

Nicki Blake, grades 2–3 multiage teacher
Tapteal Elementary School, West Richland, Washington

*Poems*, and *Shout! Little Poems That Roar*. His outrageous humor and shout-out rhymes from the points of view of children are nearly irresistible.

## CALEF BROWN
*www.calefbrown.com*

Both author and illustrator, Calef Brown's picture-book poem collections are billed as stories and have been compared to the nonsensical narratives of Edward Lear. Look for *Polkabats and Octopus Slacks*, *Dutch Sneakers and Flea Keepers*, *Flamingos on the Roof*, *Soup for Breakfast*, and *Hallowilloween: Nefarious Silliness*.

## JOSEPH BRUCHAC
*www.josephbruchac.com*

Of Abenaki descent, the Native American poet Joseph Bruchac is a storyteller, editor, educator, publisher, and writer of many genres, including poetry for young people. Most notable are *The Earth under Sky Bear's Feet*, *Thirteen Moons on Turtle's Back*, and *The Circle of Thanks*, all richly illustrated picture books with a strong, serious tone.

## JEN BRYANT
*www.jenbryant.com*

A former teacher, Jen Bryant began her career as an author by writing nonfiction and biographies for young people, including the award-winning *A River of Words: The Story of William Carlos Williams*. Since then, she has also branched out into notable novels in verse, including *The Trial*, *Pieces of Georgia*, *Ringside 1925: Views from the Scopes Trial*, and *Kaleidoscope Eyes*. Often historical in scope, Bryant's books capture strong characters caught in fascinating circumstances.

## JOHN CIARDI

John Ciardi became the sixth winner of the NCTE Award for Excellence in Poetry for Children in 1982. His many intelligent and witty poetry books for children include *You Know Who*, *The Monster Den*, and *Someone Could Win a Polar Bear*, each illustrated by Edward Gorey. In studies of children's poetry preferences, children often list Ciardi's poem "Mummy Slept Late and Daddy Cooked Breakfast," from *You Read to Me, I'll Read to You*, as their favorite.

## KALLI DAKOS
*www.kallidakos.com*

The subject of school is the central focus of Kalli Dakos's poetry, and children find the topic equal parts painful and hilarious through her work. In addition,

Dakos employs a great variety of poetic forms and character voices that lend themselves to varied choral performance techniques. See, for example, *If You're Not Here, Please Raise Your Hand: Poems about School*, or her more recent work, *A Funeral in the Bathroom and Other School Bathroom Poems*.

## REBECCA KAI DOTLICH                    *www.rebeccakaidotlich.com*

Rebecca Kai Dotlich's gentle and lyrical collections include *Lemonade Sun and Other Summer Poems*, *When Riddles Come Rumbling: Poems to Ponder*, *In the Spin of Things: Poetry of Motion*, and *Over in the Pink House: New Jump-Rope Rhymes*. Her use of personification, in particular, is fresh and compelling and expressed exactly in terms children understand.

## MARGARITA ENGLE                    *http://margaritaengle.com*

Margarita Engle grew up in Los Angeles, with roots in the lush language and stories of her mother's Cuba. An agronomy professor by training, her writing for young people burst onto the scene with her first novel in verse, *The Poet Slave of Cuba: A Biography of Juan Francisco Manzano*, which earned a Pura Belpré Medal. This was followed by more verse novels and more awards, including a Newbery honor: *The Surrender Tree*, *Tropical Secrets: Holocaust Refugees in Cuba*, *The Firefly Letters: A Suffragette's Journey to Cuba*, *Hurricane Dancers: The First Caribbean Pirate Shipwreck*, and *The Wild Book*.

## BARBARA ESBENSEN

Barbara Esbensen became the tenth winner of the NCTE Award for Excellence in Poetry for Children in 1994. Her poetry collections incorporate strong imagery, fresh perspectives, and deft use of language. Her focus on animals and nature is particularly appealing in such books as *Echoes for the Eye: Poems to Celebrate Patterns in Nature*, *Who Shrank My Grandmother's House? Poems of Discovery*, and *Words with Wrinkled Knees*.

## AILEEN FISHER

Aileen Fisher became the second winner of the NCTE Award for Excellence in Poetry for Children in 1978. For a recent compilation of some of Fisher's most popular poems, look for *I Heard a Bluebird Sing*. This volume features forty-one

Fisher poems chosen by children, along with excerpts of interviews with and articles by Fisher about her life and work. Her simplicity and directness shine through her poems, which often reflect a childlike point of view about the natural world.

### PAUL FLEISCHMAN
*www.paulfleischman.net*

Paul Fleischman is one of the few writers to win a Newbery Medal for a work of poetry, *Joyful Noise: Poems for Two Voices*. This distinctive format was preceded by another collection, *I Am Phoenix: Poems for Two Voices*. Fleischman followed these with a collection of poems for more voices, *Big Talk: Poems for Four Voices*.

### RALPH FLETCHER
*www.ralphfletcher.com*

Ralph Fletcher's recent work, *A Writing Kind of Day: Poems for Young Poets*, offers advice poems for young people who want to express themselves through poetry writing. Pair this with his nonfiction work for young writers, *Poetry Matters: Writing a Poem from the Inside Out*.

### DOUGLAS FLORIAN
*www.douglasflorian.com*

The poems of artist and poet Douglas Florian often focus on the animal world, as in *Insectlopedia* or *Mammaliabilia* or *Dinothesaurus*. However, his longer collections, such as in *Bing Bang Boing* or *Laugh-eteria*, include a variety of topics from the simple to the sublime. He uses large doses of humor for his descriptive poetry as well as very clever wordplay and puns. His growing body of work also includes lovely collections reflecting on the seasons, as in *Autumnblings*, *Winter Eyes*, *Handsprings*, and *Summersaults*.

### BETSY FRANCO
*www.betsyfranco.com*

Betsy Franco has been a primary school teacher, writer, poet, anthologist, educational consultant, and recently an actor. Her work includes more than a hundred books, especially poetry for math and science, like *Mathematickles!* and *Counting Our Way to the 100th Day! 100 Poems*, plus curricular poetry guides; a wonderful professional reference book titled *Conversations with a Poet: Inviting Poetry into K–12 Classrooms*; and anthologies of poetry written for teens, like *Falling Hard: 100 Love Poems by Teenagers*.

**HELEN FROST**                                        *http://helenfrost.net*

In a relatively short time, Helen Frost has created a body of poetry for young people that has garnered several of the most prestigious literary awards, including a Printz honor. In her carefully crafted novels in poems, she even invents new poetic forms and uses existing forms in very creative ways. That impressive repertoire includes *Keesha's House*, *Spinning through the Universe: A Novel in Poems from Room 214*, *The Braid*, *Diamond Willow*, *Crossing Stones*, *Hidden*, and the poem picture book *Step Gently Out*.

**KRISTINE O'CONNELL GEORGE**                    *www.kristinegeorge.com*

Kristine O'Connell George burst onto the poetry scene when she won the Lee Bennett Hopkins Promising Poet Award for her first book, *The Great Frog Race and Other Poems*. She continued to explore the natural world in fresh and playful imagery and rhymes in subsequent works: *Old Elm Speaks: Tree Poems*, *Toasting Marshmallows: Camping Poems*, and *Hummingbird Nest: A Journal of Poems*. A recent work, *Emma Dilemma: Big Sister Poems*, examines the complicated but loving relationship between young siblings.

**NIKKI GIOVANNI**                                 *http://nikki-giovanni.com*

Nikki Giovanni is a poet who has established a notable reputation as a writer for adults, but young people also embrace several of her works. Among those books are *Spin a Soft Black Song*, *Vacation Time: Poems for Children*, and *The Sun Is So Quiet*, each of which addresses issues of race and culture in equal measure with experiences and observations of childhood and family life. She edited the anthology *Hip Hop Speaks to Children*, which includes her own and other contemporary works in this book plus a CD.

**JOAN BRANSFIELD GRAHAM**                         *www.joangraham.com*

Joan Bransfield Graham's poetry books are wonderful examples of shape, or concrete, poetry, in which the words of a poem are laid out on the page to suggest the poem's subject. In both *Flicker Flash* and *Splish Splash*, the graphic illustrations combine with the verbal descriptions of water and light in their many, varied forms.

## ELOISE GREENFIELD

Eloise Greenfield became the eleventh winner of the NCTE Award for Excellence in Poetry for Children in 1997. Her first book of poetry, *Honey, I Love*, has become a modern-day classic. Her poetry reflects the cultural experience of growing up African American, but her themes reach out to all children, as in *Nathaniel Talking*, *Night on Neighborhood Street*, *The Friendly Four*, and *Brothers and Sisters: Family Poems*.

## NIKKI GRIMES                                    *www.nikkigrimes.com*

Born and raised in New York City, Nikki Grimes is the 2006 recipient of the NCTE Award for Excellence in Poetry for Children and the creator of picture-book poetry collections featuring the proud and spunky character Danitra Brown: *Meet Danitra Brown*, *Danitra Brown Leaves Town*, and *Danitra Brown, Class Clown*. Grimes has won Coretta Scott King honors multiple times and has received recognition for works such as *Hopscotch Love*, *My Man Blue*, and *Shoe Magic*, among others. She's also created noteworthy works for tween and teen audiences, including *Bronx Masquerade*, *Dark Sons*, and *Planet Middle School*.

## AVIS HARLEY

Avis Harley specializes in creating unique compilations of poetry known for their diversity and experimentation. She is adept at demonstrating poetic form for children, as seen in her first collection, *Fly with Poetry: An ABC of Poetry*, which set the stage with acrostics, blank verse, cinquain, and more. She added more poetic forms and literary terms in *Leap into Poetry: More ABCs of Poetry*. Later works continue her experimentation with form, as well as her focus on the natural world in *The Monarch's Progress: Poems with Wings* and *African Acrostics: A Word in Edgeways*.

## DAVID L. HARRISON                           *http://davidlharrison.com*

Author of more than eighty books for young people, David Harrison has previously worked as a pharmacologist, an editorial manager, and a business owner, and as a professional musician, music teacher, and symphony trombonist. His poetry for children offers a range of topics, from family time in *Vacation: We're*

*Going to the Ocean* to the natural world in *Bugs: Poems about Creeping Things* and famous figures in history in *Pirates* and *Cowboys*.

### GEORGIA HEARD                                    *www.georgiaheard.com*

A frequent speaker and visiting poet in schools around the world, Georgia Heard writes both insightful professional resources for adults, such as *For the Good of the Earth and Sun: Teaching Poetry* and *Awakening the Heart: Exploring Poetry in Elementary and Middle School,* and distinctive anthologies for young people that use a variety of poetic forms, such as *Falling Down the Page: A Book of List Poems* and *The Arrow Finds Its Mark: A Book of Found Poems.* Her work includes original nature poems, many for two voices, and *This Place I Know: Poems of Comfort,* an anthology created to commemorate the attacks on the United States on September 11, 2001.

### MARY ANN HOBERMAN                          *www.maryannhoberman.com*

In 2003 Mary Ann Hoberman became the thirteenth winner of the NCTE Award for Excellence in Poetry for Children and then in 2008, the second Children's Poet Laureate. Hoberman's poetry often targets our youngest audience with rhythm and repetition and is usually published in picture-book form or as read-aloud rhyming stories, such as in her You Read to Me, I'll Read to You series. Other inviting collections include *The Llama Who Had No Pajama: 100 Favorite Poems* and *All Kinds of Families,* as well as edited anthologies for middle-grade readers, *The Tree That Time Built: A Celebration of Nature, Science, and Imagination* and *Forget-Me-Nots: Poems to Learn by Heart.*

### SARA HOLBROOK                                    *www.saraholbrook.com*

Few poets address the emotional roller coaster of the tween and teen years better than Sara Holbrook in works such as *Weird? (Me, Too!) Let's Be Friends* and *More Than Friends: Poems from Him and Her,* coauthored with Allan Wolf. Her collection *By Definition: Poems of Feelings* pulls from several earlier works about teen angst. In addition, she offers advice to young poem performers in *Wham! It's a Poetry Jam: Discovering Performance Poetry* and *Outspoken: How to Improve Writing and Speaking through Poetry Performance* (with Michael Salinger).

**LEE BENNETT HOPKINS**                    *www.leebennetthopkins.com*

Lee Bennett Hopkins won the NCTE Award for Excellence in Poetry for Children in 2009 and also set a Guinness World Record for the most poetry anthologies for children, with more than 113 books of poetry and books about poetry to his credit as a writer and anthologist. Hopkins has also nurtured many new talents in poetry, commissioning up-and-coming poets to write poems for anthologies he compiles. A few of his recent titles include *Give Me Wings, Behind the Museum Door, America at War, Incredible Inventions, Sky Magic, I Am the Book, Amazing Faces, Sharing the Seasons, Nasty Bugs,* and *City I Love*, the last of which features only his own poetry.

**PAUL B. JANECZKO**                    *www.pauljaneczko.com*

Besides his several guides for aspiring poetry writers, such as *Poetry from A to Z: A Guide for Young Writers* and *Seeing the Blue Between: Advice and Inspiration for Young Poets*, Paul B. Janeczko has also created or compiled many innovative poetry collections focusing on poetic form, such as *A Poke in the I: A Collection of Concrete Poems, A Kick in the Head: An Everyday Guide to Poetic Forms,* and *A Foot in the Mouth: Poems to Speak, Sing, and Shout*. He is also the author of several powerful historical novels in verse, including *Worlds Afire* and *Requiem: Poems of the Terezin Ghetto*.

**ALAN KATZ**                    *www.alankatzbooks.com*

Alan Katz worked as a print and television writer for many years before making his mark with his popular "silly dilly" song-parody picture books, including *Take Me Out of the Bathtub and Other Silly Dilly Songs, Where Did They Hide My Presents? Silly Dilly Christmas Songs, Going, Going, Gone! and Other Silly Dilly Sports Songs,* and *Mosquitoes Are Ruining My Summer! and Other Silly Dilly Camp Songs*, among others. His wacky sense of humor is also evident in two poetry collections, both of which are illustrated by cartoonist Edward Koren: *Oops!* and *Poems I Wrote When No One Was Looking*.

**BOBBI KATZ**                    *www.bobbikatz.com*

Bobbi Katz's long career includes working as an art historian, a fashion editor, a social worker, a radio talk-show host, a teacher, and an editor. Her extensive body of poetry contains her own fresh and engaging work, as well as appealing anthologies of many poets' writing, as in the popular *Pocket Poems* and *More Pocket Poems*. Her own poetry ranges from the fiendishly clever *The Monsterologist: A Memoir in Rhyme* to the insightful, historically focused *We the People* and *Trailblazers: Poems of Exploration*.

## X. J. KENNEDY
*www.xjanddorothymkennedy.com*

X. J. Kennedy became the twelfth winner of the NCTE Award for Excellence in Poetry for Children in 2000. Kennedy, known for his cagey sense of humor and witty wordplay, writes poems that are fun to read out loud to eager audiences. His collection *Exploding Gravy: Poems to Make You Laugh* is a compilation of a quarter century of some of his most humorous poems. He and his wife, Dorothy, compiled a child's guide to poetry, *Knock at a Star: A Child's Introduction to Poetry*, which presents an engaging introduction to the elements of poetry, as well as nearly two hundred poems.

## KARLA KUSKIN
*www.karlakuskin.com*

In 1979 Karla Kuskin became the third winner of the NCTE Award for Excellence in Poetry for Children. Her pictures and poetry are brimming over with the experiences of children growing up in a big city. For a wonderful compilation of poems from several previous works as well as additional poems, look for *Moon, Have You Met My Mother? The Collected Poems of Karla Kuskin*. And if you have a copy of *Dogs and Dragons, Trees and Dreams*, you will see that Kuskin often provided a brief note before a poem to explain where she got her inspiration for writing it.

## J. PATRICK LEWIS
*www.jpatricklewis.com*

J. Patrick Lewis received the NCTE Award for Excellence in Poetry for Children and was named Children's Poet Laureate in 2011. Quite an accomplishment! With nearly one hundred books of poetry in print or coming out soon, J. Patrick Lewis is a prolific specialist in thematic collections in picture-book form. His narrative poems have strong rhythm and clever wordplay. Just a few popular, recent examples include *When Thunder Comes: Poems for Civil Rights Leaders*,

*If You Were a Chocolate Mustache, The Underwear Salesman and Other Jobs for Better or Verse, Countdown to Summer: A Poem for Every Day of the School Year,* and *Spot the Plot! A Riddle Book of Book Riddles.*

## MYRA COHN LIVINGSTON

Myra Cohn Livingston became the fourth winner of the NCTE Award for Excellence in Poetry for Children in 1980. She was a giant in the field of children's poetry who authored many works about poetry writing (e.g., *Poem-Making: Ways to Begin Writing Poetry*) and inspired and taught many of today's emerging poets. Her nurturing of children's sensitivity and awareness of the world around them is apparent in such works as *Calendar, A Circle of Seasons, Celebrations, Festivals,* and *Space Songs.*

## DAVID MCCORD

David McCord was the winner of the first NCTE Award for Excellence in Poetry for Children in 1977. He was noted for his creative, rhythmic, and often whimsical poems. He invented a new style, symmetrics, a five-line verse form attributed to him by the American Heritage Dictionary. He wrote more than five hundred poems, many of which are gathered in his omnibus collection, *One at a Time: His Collected Poems for the Young.* Look for one of his most popular poems for children, "The Pickety Fence," in *Every Time I Climb a Tree.*

## EVE MERRIAM

Eve Merriam was the winner of the fifth NCTE Award for Excellence in Poetry for Children in 1981. Her work is playful and lively and explores language through word origins. Check your library shelves for two of her classic collections, *It Doesn't Always Have to Rhyme* and *There Is No Rhyme for Silver,* as well as more contemporary collections, such as *You Be Good and I'll Be Night,* and many rhyming picture books.

## LILIAN MOORE

Lilian Moore was the winner of the seventh NCTE Award for Excellence in Poetry for Children in 1985. She was a teacher, a reading specialist, and the editor at Scholastic who established the Arrow Book Club. Her accessible poetic work encourages children to wonder and imagine, as in *Mural on Second Avenue and Other City Poems* and *Beware, Take Care.*

## PAT MORA                                                    *www.patmora.com*

Pat Mora is an award-winning author of poetry, nonfiction, and children's picture books. Many of her works are written in two languages (English interwoven with Spanish words and phrases) and draw on themes from her life experience as a bilingual, bicultural woman from the Southwestern desert. She has received critical acclaim for such works as *Uno, dos, tres / One, Two, Three*; *Confetti*; *Yum! Mmmm! ¡Qué rico! Americas' Sproutings*; *Dizzy in My Eyes*; and the compilation *Love to Mamá: A Tribute to Mothers.*

## HEIDI MORDHORST                                      *www.heidimordhorst.com*

Heidi Mordhorst has taught children ages three to eleven years in schools from East Harlem to Inner London and the suburbs of Washington, DC. Her first book of poetry, *Squeeze: Poems from a Juicy Universe*, examined the universal pleasures of childhood in imaginative free-verse poems. She followed this with *Pumpkin Butterfly: Poems from the Other Side of Nature*, an evocative collection of observations of the natural world across one calendar year that beautifully demonstrates her philosophy that "poems are for noticing."

## WALTER DEAN MYERS                                   *www.walterdeanmyers.net*

You may not know that award-winning author Walter Dean Myers is a collector of antique photographs, which led to his first poetry collections: *Brown Angels: An Album of Pictures and Verse*, *Glorious Angels*, and *Angel to Angel*. More recently, he has collaborated with his illustrator son on the vivid collage-poem picture books *Harlem*, *Blues Journey*, *Jazz*, and *We Are America: A Tribute from the Heart.*

## KENN NESBITT                                              *www.poetry4kids.com*

Kenn Nesbitt may be almost as well known for his extensive, interactive website, Poetry4Kids, as he is for the infectious humor of his poetry. The website includes downloadable poems, podcasts, lessons, contests, games, links, and more. His poetry has been called zany, silly, and sidesplitting, and it includes *Revenge of the Lunch Ladies: The Hilarious Book of School Poetry*, *The Tighty Whitey Spider and More Wacky Animal Poems I Totally Made Up*, and *My Hippo Has the Hiccups and Other Poems I Totally Made Up*, among others.

### NAOMI SHIHAB NYE

Naomi Shihab Nye has a gift for bringing together poets from many paths. She has compiled several distinctive anthologies that include poetry from around the world, such as *This Same Sky: A Collection of Poems from around the World*, *The Tree Is Older Than You Are: A Bilingual Gathering of Poems and Stories from Mexico with Paintings by Mexican Artists*, and *The Space between Our Footsteps: Poems and Paintings from the Middle East*. Her own work is also quite powerful and respectful of children's appetite for both light and serious themes, as in *Come with Me: Poems for a Journey*, *A Maze Me: Poems for Girls*, and *Honeybee*.

### SUSAN PEARSON                                        *www.susanpearson.net*

Susan Pearson compiled her first anthology of bedtime poetry, *The Drowsy Hours*, after twenty years of fiction writing and editing. She loved working with poetry so much that she went on to write her own collection titled *Squeal and Squawk: Barnyard Talk*. New works include *Grimericks* and *Who Swallowed Harold? and Other Poems about Pets*.

### JACK PRELUTSKY                                        *www.jackprelutsky.com*

Jack Prelutsky was honored as the first U.S. Children's Poet Laureate in 2006 and is a prolific writer with many collections of poetry to his credit, including anthologies of many poets' works, such as *The Random House Book of Poetry for Children*, *Read-Aloud Rhymes for the Very Young*, *The Beauty of the Beast*, and *The 20th-Century Children's Poetry Treasury*. Do not miss his comprehensive poem collections, *The New Kid on the Block*, *Something Big Has Been Here*, *A Pizza the Size of the Sun*, *It's Raining Pigs and Noodles*, and *My Dog May Be a Genius*, in addition to his many topical collections, such as *Tyrannosaurus Was a Beast: Dinosaur Poems*, *The Swamps of Sleethe: Poems from beyond the Solar System*, and his guide for young writers, *Pizza, Pigs, and Poetry: How to Write a Poem*.

# In His Own Words

## BY JACK PRELUTSKY

I get letters from kids that say, "Hi, Jack." They don't say, "Mr. Prelutsky," they say, "You must have been writing about my brother," or "How did you know I did this?" I write about what's real to them. When I was a kid, I was subjected to poems about hills and daffodils, which is fine, and there's a place for that, but I was not interested in that sort of thing. I wanted to hear poems about other kids like me and about sports, monsters, dinosaurs, outer space, and weird people—silly things. That's what I write about. I really try to stay in touch with the child I used to be. In all of us are those children that we were, and hopefully remain, in some ways.

It's tough being a kid. People are telling you what to do. Grown-ups are always bossing you around. Life is very earnest and difficult. Bigger kids pick on you. Teachers tell you what to do; you have homework, you have tests. You need a friend to help you see the funny side of all the things that are happening to you. So the humor comes from real experiences. Sometimes I get completely silly and talk about a teacher that's covered with mashed potatoes or something. There's a place for that, too.

Sometimes when I visit the kids and see lights go on in heads, that's a reward. But, it's also that feeling of self-worth, knowing that I'm doing something that makes a difference, that may change the way some kids will grow up. It's getting to meet so many thousands and thousands of people, many of them children, who tell me they love my poems. And it's also a certain feeling knowing that those wonderful nonsensical things that have always run around in my brain actually have some value in the real world! I think I'm very lucky in that I'm able to make a reasonable living doing exactly what I want to do, what I love to do, and don't have to compromise. There are a lot of rewards—there's the reward of walking into almost any library or bookstore in America and seeing my books. Of all these things though, I think it's knowing that you're bringing these values home, and that what you do makes a difference. It can make a difference for a long time; someday somebody not yet born may do something incredible because they read your poems.

*"In His Own Words,"* excerpted from *S. M. Vardell, "An Interview with Poet Jack Prelutsky,"* New Advocate *4, no. 2 (1991): 101–11. Used with permission.*

## If the Moon
*by Jack Prelutsky*

If the moon were a balloon,
We would hardly have to wait
For the moon to disappear . . .
It might suddenly deflate.
If the moon were made of cheese,
As some people used to think,
It would be a dreadful place,
And would definitely stink.
If the moon were fiery hot,
A bright, miniature sun,
All the creatures of this Earth
Would be thoroughly well done.
But the moon is not a sun,
Neither cheese nor great balloon—
We are happy to report
That the moon is just the moon.

**CLASS EXERCISE** Many poems have been written about the moon and what it is like. Use this poem as a prompt to research moon myths and then post a list of "facts" and "myths" about the moon. Is the moon made of cheese? A balloon? Is it fiery hot? Challenge the students to find and share more moon poems, too.

## MICHAEL J. ROSEN                                    *www.fidosopher.com*

Both anthologist and poet, Michael J. Rosen has created a wide range of works, from anthologies to aid the hungry and homeless to lovely haiku collections about animals with *The Cuckoo's Haiku and Other Birding Poems* and *The Hound Dog's Haiku and Other Poems for Dog Lovers*. One recent innovative work, *Running with Trains: A Novel in Poetry and Two Voices*, alternates between two viewpoints, the story of two boys growing up during the turbulent years of the Vietnam War in the 1970s.

## LAURA PURDIE SALAS                                  *www.laurasalas.com*

Laura Purdie Salas has ten poetry collections from Capstone Press that perfectly complement the curriculum with a focus on food, pets, transportation, school, color, space, weather, and more. She uses animal parallels to look at kids and school in *Stampede! Poems to Celebrate the Wild Side of School!* and examines books, reading, and the publishing world in her clever collection *BookSpeak!* Her resource books, *Write Your Own Poetry* and *Picture Yourself Writing Poetry: Using Photos to Inspire Writing* offer young writers guidance in tackling poetry.

## ALICE SCHERTLE

Alice Schertle is both wickedly smart and wryly funny, as you will see in her picture books and collections such as *How Now, Brown Cow?*, poems from a cow's perspective; *A Lucky Thing*, partly about barn life and partly about poetry writing; *Advice for a Frog*, an introduction to exotic and endangered animals; and *Button Up! Wrinkled Rhymes*, from the point of view of children's clothing.

## CAROL DIGGORY SHIELDS

Carol Diggory Shields's poetry collections are full of her views on kids and classrooms. She looks at the funny side of life and learning in works such as *Lunch Money and Other Poems about School* and its sequel, *Almost Late to School and More School Poems*. Two recent collections are ideal for pairing with the school curriculum: *BrainJuice: American History, Fresh Squeezed!* and *BrainJuice: Science, Fresh Squeezed!*

**JOYCE SIDMAN**                                            *www.joycesidman.com*

Joyce Sidman is a Newbery honor author whose beautiful poetry focuses on the natural world. Her ecological trilogy, including *Song of the Water Boatman and Other Pond Poems*, *Butterfly Eyes and Other Secrets of the Meadow*, and *Dark Emperor and Other Poems of the Night*, offers sensitive depictions of animal life in verse. The poems in *This Is Just to Say: Poems of Apology and Forgiveness* have inspired children (and parents) to write their own apologies, and *Red Sings from Treetops: A Year in Colors* brings the seasons to life through all the senses.

**SHEL SILVERSTEIN**                                       *www.shelsilverstein.com*

Surveys of children's preferences as well as statistics on book sales confirm that kids of all ages really respond to the poetry of Shel Silverstein. He wrote about everyday events and childhood experiences, often with an outrageous sense of the absurd. His pen-and-ink cartoon illustrations add another layer of originality and appeal. His most notable collections of poetry are *Where the Sidewalk Ends*, *A Light in the Attic*, *Falling Up*, and *Every Thing On It*, the first two of which are available as audio recordings narrated in Silverstein's own gravelly voice.

---

**PRACTITIONER PERSPECTIVE**

*I am very disappointed that I did not introduce poetry earlier in the year. Now it is so exciting to see the students wanting to go to the library to get poetry books. We do sustained silent reading (SSR) every day after lunch, and my students are so absorbed in their poetry books. Wow! Because they wanted to share poems each day, I made them anthology journals so they could write their favorites and share them later. I have one student who began reading Shel Silverstein's* Where the Sidewalk Ends *about a week ago and reads it only here at school but is already on page 123 out of 164 pages. . . . I learned a good lesson—to introduce poetry in the beginning of the year and use it throughout the whole year.*

Kay Hardy, third-grade teacher
Pasco, Washington

## SILVERSTEIN AND PRELUTSKY POETRY BOOK READ-ALIKES

In survey after survey, we find that many libraries hold multiple copies of Shel Silverstein's poetry collections. His work has been a staple of children's poetry for several decades now. Jack Prelutsky, with his zany humor and musical rhythms, follows in being represented in most library collections. Here are additional poets to recommend when young readers ask for "more like this," with one sample title suggested for each poet. Each of these poets has his or her own unique and distinctive style, of course, but they all offer some of the same qualities in humor, wordplay, topic, or style that young readers appreciate about Silverstein's and Prelutsky's poetry.

Calef Brown, *Flamingos on the Roof*

John Ciardi, *You Read to Me, I'll Read to You*

Kalli Dakos, *Put Your Eyes Up Here and Other School Poems*

Douglas Florian, *Laugh-eteria*

Sara Holbrook, *Weird? (Me, Too!) Let's Be Friends*

Alan Katz, *Poems I Wrote When No One Was Looking*

X. J. Kennedy, *Exploding Gravy: Poems to Make You Laugh*

Karla Kuskin, *Moon, Have You Met My Mother? The Collected Poems of Karla Kuskin*

J. Patrick Lewis, *The Underwear Salesman and Other Jobs for Better or Verse*

David McCord, *Every Time I Climb a Tree*

Judy Sierra, *Gruesome Guide to World Monsters*

Marilyn Singer, *Monster Museum*

Source: Based on Sylvia Vardell, *The Poetry Teacher's Book of Lists* (Seattle, WA: CreateSpace, 2012), 238.

## MARILYN SINGER
*www.marilynsinger.net*

Marilyn Singer's work may be best characterized by its diversity, from the distinctive poetic formats found in the poems for each month in *Turtle in July* to her creation of the "reverso" poem showcased in *Mirror, Mirror*. Her wide-ranging topics include dogs, animals, science, monsters, and nonsense, as seen in *Every Day's a Dog's Day: A Year in Poems*, *Creature Carnival*, and *A Strange Place to Call*

*Home: The World's Most Dangerous Habitats and the Animals That Call Them Home*, among others.

**CHARLES R. SMITH JR.** *www.charlesrsmithjr.com*

Charles R. Smith Jr. uniquely combines poetry (often with a rap rhythm), photography, and the picture-book format to showcase aspects of African American life, culture, and history. His focus on sports and sports figures, in particular, is very appealing to young readers. Look for *Hoop Queens* and *Hoop Kings*—energetic poetry about basketball—or his biographical-poem picture books such as *Twelve Rounds to Glory: The Story of Muhammad Ali* and *Stars in the Shadows: The Negro League All-Star Game of 1934*.

**SONYA SONES** *www.sonyasones.com*

For one of the freshest voices in verse novels, turn to the work of Sonya Sones. Her stories and poems for tweens and older are equally bittersweet and hysterically funny, whether dealing with a family's struggle with mental illness (*Stop Pretending: What Happened When My Big Sister Went Crazy*) or capturing the wild woes of a girl in her search for the perfect boyfriend (*What My Mother Doesn't Know*).

**GARY SOTO** *www.garysoto.com*

Well known for his adult poetry, his young adult (YA) novels, and his picture books, Gary Soto has also penned several outstanding poetry collections for young people, including *Fearless Fernie: Hanging Out with Fernie and Me* and *Worlds Apart: Fernie and Me*, friendship poems that demonstrate his usual sprinkling of Spanish words within English texts. Other notable collections include *Canto familiar*, *A Fire in My Hands*, *Neighborhood Odes*, and *Partly Cloudy: Poems of Love and Longing*.

**JOYCE CAROL THOMAS** *www.joycecarolthomas.com*

Joyce Carol Thomas has penned poetry collections that capture and celebrate African American culture in ways that help all readers acknowledge their roots. Favorites include *Brown Honey in Broomwheat Tea*, *Gingerbread Days*, and *The Blacker the Berry*, all of which are beautifully illustrated by Floyd Cooper.

## JUDITH VIORST

Judith Viorst is probably best known for her groundbreaking picture book *Alexander and the Terrible, Horrible, No Good, Very Bad Day*. With her poetry book *If I Were in Charge of the World and Other Worries: Poems for Children and Their Parents*, she tackles many poignant and hilarious moments of childhood, often with list poems that don't rhyme—a form that children enjoy, much to the surprise of many adults. Check out *Sad Underwear and Other Complications: More Poems for Children and Their Parents*, too.

## APRIL HALPRIN WAYLAND                    *www.aprilwayland.com*

For a blending of art and poetry, look for April Wayland's verse novel *Girl Coming in for a Landing*, illustrated by Elaine Clayton. This is a wonderful work for preteen readers, who can relate to the "poetry is my underwear" emotions and experiences that Wayland depicts.

## CAROLE BOSTON WEATHERFORD                  *http://cbweatherford.com*

Carole Boston Weatherford has been a poet since the first grade and has published an impressive range of poetry books ever since. Along the way, her work has garnered multiple kudos and awards for her powerful stories from African American history, such as *Birmingham, 1963; Becoming Billie Holiday;* and *Remember the Bridge: Poems of a People*, which one reviewer called a "museum of speaking images."

## NANCY WILLARD

Nancy Willard's *A Visit to William Blake's Inn: Poems for Innocent and Experienced Travelers*, an homage to earlier classic works for children, was the first book of poetry to be presented a Newbery Award. Willard's many works of poetry are filled with large doses of magic and wonder.

## ALLAN WOLF                           *www.allanwolf.com*

Allan Wolf is a poet and performer, with hundreds of poems committed to memory. He worked with Poetry Alive!, a national touring company that presents theatrical poetry shows, and was an early organizer of poetry slams. His first poetry book for young people, *The Blood-Hungry Spleen and Other Poems about*

*Our Parts*, is a hilarious look at the human body. In contrast, his novels in verse, *New Found Land: Lewis and Clark's Voyage of Discovery* and *The Watch That Ends the Night: Voices from the Titanic*, are powerful, historical works. Readers in the middle and upper grades will also enjoy his insightful and clever guide, *Immersed in Verse: An Informative, Slightly Irreverent, and Totally Tremendous Guide to Living the Poet's Life*.

### JANET WONG
*www.janetwong.com*

In her poetry collections Janet S. Wong, the child of a Chinese immigrant father and a Korean immigrant mother, blends cultural details with universal feelings. Her works include *A Suitcase of Seaweed and Other Poems*, *Good Luck Gold and Other Poems*, *Night Garden: Poems from the World of Dreams*, *Knock on Wood: Poems about Superstitions*, and *Twist: Yoga Poems*. She's also an innovator in the publishing of the first original poetry e-books, with *Poetry Tag Time*, *P*TAG*, and *Gift Tag* (all coedited with Vardell), as well as *Once upon a Tiger: New Beginnings for Endangered Animals* and *Declaration of Interdependence: Poems for an Election Year*.

### VALERIE WORTH

Valerie Worth was the winner of the ninth NCTE Award for Excellence in Poetry for Children in 1991. Her poems are vivid observations of the quiet existence of everyday objects. Worth's careful attention to rhythm and sound and the striking images and metaphors in her succinct, free-verse poems make for engaging reading. For one collection that includes all ninety-nine of her original small poems and others, look for *All the Small Poems and Fourteen More*.

### JANE YOLEN
*www.janeyolen.com*

Jane Yolen is another example of an author who is well known for writing hundreds of wonderful children's books in other genres. However, she also has many superb poetry collections that are ideal for matching with the study of nature or history, such as *Birds of a Feather* and *Bug Off! Creepy Crawly Poems*, as well as excellent collaborations with other poets, including *Here's a Little Poem: A Very First Book of Poetry* (with Andrew Fusek Peters) and *Take Two! A Celebration of Twins* (with J. Patrick Lewis). Younger audiences especially enjoy her dinosaur poem series, which begins with *How Do Dinosaurs Say Good Night?*

**TRACIE VAUGHN ZIMMER** *www.tracievaughnzimmer.com*

Tracie Vaughn Zimmer is a teacher and writer whose poetry ranges from thematic collections to novels in verse. She received the Schneider Family Book Award for *Reaching for Sun*, and she captures a child's voice with clarity as the protagonist copes with family troubles, isolation, and cerebral palsy. In her picture-book collection *Steady Hands: Poems about Work*, Zimmer cleverly examines a collage of careers, and in *Cousins of Clouds: Elephant Poems* she employs a variety of poetic forms to describe the unique attributes of elephants along with their place in the animal world and in world cultures.

---

### POET PROFILE

## Some Thoughts on Poetry, Sit-Ups, and Pain

### BY JANET WONG

Some people think about poetry the way I think about doing sit-ups: it's good for me, it will strengthen my core, it won't take more than a few minutes a day to be effective—but what a pain! The exercise buffs among you would say (of sit-ups): yes, but the trouble is worth it. No pain, no gain. One minute a day, and you will feel stronger! Two minutes a day, and you will stand straighter! Five minutes, and you will live a fuller life!

I say: and so, too, with poetry.

Results, in a minute a day? Maybe not with lazy sit-ups, easy ones, the kind you do with your legs stretched out flat and your arms pumping your body up. This would be like a minute a day of silly verse, which would be fun and get your blood going and maybe even inspire you to want to do more—but which, unfortunately, would not result in the truly special benefits that come as a result of discomfort and strain. Gain, in poetry and in sit-ups, comes when there is tension, when we are pushed to confront our weakest, flabbiest, grunting, groaning, ugliest human selves. And the tension need not come from dissecting a poem or discussing it (though I would hope that most serious poems would inspire some discussion). Just reading a poem is good enough, reading it aloud. For example:

# Coin Drive

*by Janet Wong*

There's a coin drive going on at our school
for children hurt by the hurricane.
Teacher says, "Handful of dimes is fine.
But only give if you want to share."
Momma says, "Those people should have known.
Should have done more than they did to get out."
Poppa says, "Look how those people stole.
Criminals. Animals, them. Their kind."

I saw the pictures, too, myself.

People with nothing, no cars, for sure.
Swollen old ladies could barely walk.
Crazy boys with stolen guns,
but also daddies grabbing bread.

I saw the pictures, too, myself.

So many bodies floating, dead.
Waiting, water creeping up,
up past neck, past mouth, past eyes.
How long did they wait for help?

I feel proud for the fifty cents
I put today in the coin drive jar.
I feel proud that I can say:
I saw the pictures for myself.

Reading that poem aloud took me sixty-five seconds.

If that poem made you feel any pain or compassion or pride or shame or anger, think about it: a minute a day might be all it takes for you to get serious results from poetry.

I wrote "Coin Drive" a week past Hurricane Katrina as a way to make sense of the disaster, as an expression of confusion and sorrow and anger, and in hope of making someone else see the way I do. What this poem offers, in my view, is an invitation to question, to wonder, to examine our own feelings and ideas about this disaster or other disasters we see in the news.

Some people will say that children are too young to have to think about such things. Perhaps we should shelter them. We should, if only we could. The fact is, though, that most families are not that careful. The TV is on, and so the children have seen scary looting and shooting; the magazines in the supermarket have shown dead, bloated bodies, planting nightmarish images in our children's minds. Because our children have been troubled, they now deserve an explanation. They deserve to hear the complicated and unpleasant stories behind the trouble.

Parents should lead these discussions with their children. But so, too, should we, because we know, sadly, that many parents cannot or will not do this job. We know that we are often the best-informed and most compassionate people in a child's daily life. We teachers and librarians, if we care about the kind of world we live in, need to inspire discussions about social and moral responsibility and current events. Poetry can help us do this. Of course, novels and history books and newspapers can do this, too—just the same way competing in triathlons can strengthen your core—but not as quickly or effectively as poetry (and sit-ups).

Read poetry aloud. Surprise your students by pulling your cell phone out of your pocket and sharing a poetry e-book. Post poems on bulletin boards, in toilet stalls. Leave a basket of typewritten pocket poems by the checkout counter. Add poetry to mandatory summer-reading lists, or hide poetry in the general categories of your reading lists, in the hopes that someone might stumble on them there. Put poetry books out on the tops of shelves so they are easy to find. And don't shy away from the difficult, serious stuff. Poetry can prod our children to grapple with important and painful issues so that they can learn to question, think, understand, and see things for themselves.

A final thought: after one of those challenging, exhausting, exhilarating discussions of poetry and life, throw in twenty sit-ups for fun.

**CLASS EXERCISE** "Coin Drive" is a serious poem that an adult should probably read aloud to children first. Then, when the children are ready to participate, individual volunteers can read the lines designated for Teacher, Momma, Poppa, and the child narrator. The group as a whole can join in on the repeated line "I saw the pictures, too, myself" and on the end line, which is a slight variation of the repeated line. Afterward, children may want to discuss the feelings and images the poem evokes and participate in their own coin drive for a local cause.

---

## Poet Websites and Biographical Resources

Most poets have personal websites with information about themselves, their work, and their availability for public appearances. Of course, websites and URLs change regularly, so be sure to double-check any address provided in this book. Every effort has been made to verify all addresses and to share the most stable sites. Some poets' websites are even rich resources for children, with advice and activities built in. Kristine O'Connell George's website, for example, is regularly recognized as an American Library Association best website for families

**PRACTITIONER PERSPECTIVE**

*Langston Hughes is one of my all-time favorite poets, and I use his "Dreams" poem often in class. First I read the poem aloud to students. Then I tell them I'm going to read it again, and I want them to close their eyes and see what picture the poem creates in their minds. After I have read the poem the second time, students sketch their pictures. Many of them draw broken-winged birds or fields of snow, but others will draw someone in bed dreaming or someone that looks distraught because their dream doesn't come true. I use this as a way to introduce imagery. I've found that this theme of dreams and lost dreams can be used throughout the year with many of our novels, so we refer back to this poem often.*

Emily Felker, fourth-grade teacher
McCall Elementary School, Aledo, Texas

and kids. Other poets, such as Nikki Grimes, Sonya Sones, Joyce Sidman, Jack Prelutsky, and Janet Wong, host lively websites with tips, techniques, and more.

Many publishers regularly feature interviews with poets on their websites. For example, see the Random House "Librarians at Random" page at www .randomhouse.com/teachers or the HarperCollins Children's Publishing website at www.harpercollinschildrens.com/Kids. The Academy of American Poets also offers a massive website with a comprehensive directory of American poets, including some poets writing for children. Check out www.poets.org. Look for *Poetry People: A Practical Guide to Children's Poets* (Vardell 2007) for entries on more than sixty children's poets that feature brief biographical information, selected poetry books and poems they've authored, awards won, related websites, links with other poets and poetry, and suggestions for activities. Volumes 1 and 2 of *Speaking with Poets*, edited by Jeff Copeland (1993, 1995), are excellent print resources that include personal interviews and photos of nearly fifty contemporary poets writing for young people. Lee Bennett Hopkins's oft-cited books *Pass the Poetry, Please!* (1986) and *Pauses: Autobiographical Reflections of 101 Creators of Children's Books* (1995) offer biographical sketches of and autobiographical essays by many favorite poets. And some poets have authored autobiographical narrative works that provide interesting background for reading their poetry.

### Biographies, Autobiographies, and Memoirs of Poets: A Selected List

Monica Brown, *Pablo Neruda*
Jen Bryant, *A River of Words: The Story of William Carlos Williams*
Robert Burleigh, *Langston's Train Ride*
Bonnie Christensen, *Woody Guthrie: Poet of the People*
Floyd Cooper, *Coming Home: From the Life of Langston Hughes*
Douglas Florian, *See for Your Self*
Matthew Gollub, *Cool Melons—Turn to Frogs! The Life and Poems of Issa*
David Harrison, *Connecting Dots: Poems of My Journey*
Lee Bennett Hopkins, *The Writing Bug*
———, *Been to Yesterdays: Poems of a Life*
Judith Pinkerton Josephson, *Nikki Giovanni: Poet of the People*
Barbara Kerley, *Walt Whitman: Words for America*
Kathryn Lasky, *A Voice of Her Own: The Story of Phillis Wheatley, Slave Poet*

J. Patrick Lewis, *Boshblobberbosh: Runcible Poems for Edward Lear*

George Ella Lyon, *Where I'm From: Where Poems Come From*

Kam Mak, *My Chinatown: One Year in Poems*

Milton Meltzer, *Langston Hughes: A Biography*

———, *Carl Sandburg: A Biography*

———, *Walt Whitman: A Biography*

———, *Emily Dickinson: A Biography*

Penelope Niven, *Carl Sandburg: Adventures of a Poet*

Willie Perdomo, *Visiting Langston*

Catherine Reef, *Walt Whitman*

———, *Paul Laurence Dunbar: Portrait of a Poet*

Pam Muñoz Ryan, *The Dreamer*

Amy Strong, *Lee Bennett Hopkins: A Children's Poet*

Jeanette Winter, *Emily Dickinson's Letters to the World*

Janet S. Wong, *Before It Wriggles Away*

Jane Yolen, *My Uncle Emily*

Chin Yu, *Little Green: Growing Up during the Chinese Cultural Revolution*

## Promoting Poets

Once you have expanded your poetry collection to offer a variety of popular poets, it is important that you showcase those poets as well. "After all, the way Prelutsky and Silverstein became household words to many readers was through promotion by teachers and librarians" (Wilson and Kutiper 1994, 277). Just having the books on the shelves is not enough. All the usual methods are helpful, such as shelf and tabletop displays, bookmarks and brochures, and posters and other visuals, including virtual promotion. (Chapter 4 shares more ideas.) However, promoting the poets themselves is worthwhile, too. Designate an area for a featured poet and gather a collection of his or her books to display. Many poets have their own websites, so you can find a few nuggets of biographical information, quotations, photos, and booklists to display to personalize the poet and her or his work. In fact, children themselves can help create such a display, reading and reviewing the books of their favorite poets and looking up interesting information. If you have the background and web space, you might even consider rotating your featured author presentations on your library website, blog, or Facebook page, with direct links to the poet's website.

If your budget allows, hosting a visiting poet is a very powerful way to promote poetry for children. There is nothing quite equal to hearing poems read by the poet her- or himself. Meeting the poet reminds children (of all ages) that poets are people and that poems come from all kinds of personal experiences and emotions. Although this can be an expensive enterprise (costing from a few hundred to a few thousand dollars), it can provide powerful connections and memories for all who participate. Information about hosting a poet can generally be found on a poet's website or through his or her publishing company. If schools and libraries work together to share expenses and coordinate the appearance, this can be even more doable. Also, using current media tools, many poets will also participate in more affordable virtual visits via Skype, FaceTime, and so on. So often we are eager to host authors at book festivals and other occasions, but how often do we consider poets and poetry for special events?

## Conclusion

Keeping up with poetry publishing is much like keeping up with any part of the library collection: it requires some purposeful effort. You can rely on the usual review sources as selection guides, of course, but it also can be helpful to know about major awards and authors who are standards in the field of poetry for children. As mentioned earlier, the foremost awards for poetry writing for children are the following:

- Children's Poet Laureate
- NCTE Award for Excellence in Poetry for Children
- Lee Bennett Hopkins Promising Poet Award
- Lee Bennett Hopkins Award for Children's Poetry
- Claudia Lewis Award
- Lion and the Unicorn Award

Whatever the resources we rely on, it is also important to become familiar with the names of the poets who have children at the heart of their writing. Once we know their names and become familiar with some of their works, we can continue to seek out new titles likely to become gems in our collections. Adding the latest Douglas Florian book, for example, will become just as important as acquiring the latest Rick Riordan novel for young people. Among the poets to be familiar with are

- classic poets
- anthologists
- poets from many cultures
- the major poets profiled earlier in this chapter

Knowing the major poets and awards helps make poetry a priority and helps us feel more confident in selecting and sharing quality works with children. In addition, websites and biographical resources can help us personalize our promotion of poets and poetry. Once we incorporate poetry makers into our literary repertoire, we are one step closer to making poetry an automatic part of our thinking and sharing.

> *Poetry and Hums aren't things which you get,*
> *they're things which get you. And all you can do*
> *is to go where they can find you.*

> —A. A. Milne, *The House at Pooh Corner* (1928)

3

# What Poetry Do Children Enjoy?

*Only the rarest kind of best in anything*
*can be good enough for the young.*
—Walter de la Mare, Poet

HOW DO WE KNOW WHICH POETRY BOOKS TO CHOOSE? IN this chapter, we look at the different ways in which poetry for young people is being published today. We identify the traditional types as well as the more creative formats available and list many sample titles for each. We look at other poetry resources, too, such as websites, magazines, and audiobooks. And we consider studies of children's poetry preferences as well as selection and evaluation guidelines to help you decide what to look for as you develop a varied and balanced poetry collection.

Poetry for young people can have many different faces, from familiar folk rhymes to sophisticated verse novels, from songs and fingerplays to standard anthologies, from traditional Mother Goose rhymes to poem picture books. Having taught sixth graders, I know that the appeal of humorous poetry is very powerful. I believe that it is a good place to begin as we gradually lead children to deeper, richer, more abstract poetry.

Did you know that generally speaking in the field of children's literature, fewer poetry books are published than books in any other genre? Poetry books go out of print more quickly, too. Thus, as you learn about the different kinds of poetry books that are published and what to look for in selecting quality poetry, be aggressive about adding those gems to your collection before they go out of print. Indeed, consider purchasing multiple copies, because popular poetry books seem to disappear off the shelves. Would one copy of *Where the Sidewalk Ends* be adequate for your library? Hardly. Statistics indicate that it is one of the best-circulating titles of any genre. And as we learn new ways of promoting and sharing poetry for children, we will hope to create the same level of interest in new and up-and-coming poets and poetry books. Since only a handful of poetry is published for children each year (some fifty titles, depending on how you define the genre), acquisition is relatively simple once you make poetry a priority.

## Kinds of Poetry Books

What kinds of poetry books are available for children and young adults? Most experts recognize four general categories of poetry books for children:

1. General anthologies
2. Topical or thematic collections
3. Compilations of works by individual poets
4. Single-poem picture books

### General Anthologies

General anthologies include many different kinds of poems by many different poets. Collections like these are usually very global, but they may be organized by subtheme or subcategory (such as the seasons, emotions, or childhood experiences). This kind of poetry collection has probably been around the longest of all and is a practical source for a variety of poems by many different poets. Indeed, inclusion in anthologies is probably the easiest way for new poets to get their work published and their names known. Anthologies also provide an easy way to gather poems that are in the public domain.

In days gone by, anthologies tended to be comprehensive and lengthy, often two hundred to three hundred pages long, but newer anthologies are usually shorter and often richly illustrated. They are still probably accessed most often by adults who share them with children rather than by child readers themselves.

And they can be a helpful beginning point for librarians or teachers who want one place to start for selecting a variety of quality poems. One of the most popular collections continues to be *The Random House Book of Poetry for Children,* compiled by poet Jack Prelutsky and illustrated by Arnold Lobel. It is a good example of the poem variety and friendly format that characterize many contemporary anthologies.

## Ten Anthologies Not to Be Missed

1. Julie Andrews and Emma Walton Hamilton, eds., *Julie Andrews' Collection of Poems, Songs, and Lullabies*
2. Bernice Cullinan and Deborah Wooten, eds., *Another Jar of Tiny Stars: Poems by NCTE Award-Winning Poets*
3. Lee Bennett Hopkins, ed., *Days to Celebrate: A Full Year of Poetry, People, Holidays, History, Fascinating Facts, and More*
4. Paul Janeczko, ed., *Seeing the Blue Between: Advice and Inspiration for Young Poets*
5. Bobbi Katz, ed., *Pocket Poems*
6. X. J. Kennedy and Dorothy Kennedy, eds., *Knock at a Star: A Child's Introduction to Poetry*
7. Bill Martin Jr. and Michael Sampson, eds., *The Bill Martin Jr. Big Book of Poetry*
8. Naomi Shihab Nye, ed., *This Same Sky: A Collection of Poems from around the World*
9. Elise Paschen and Dominique Raccah, eds., *Poetry Speaks to Children*
10. Jack Prelutsky, ed., *The Random House Book of Poetry for Children*

### *Topical or Thematic Collections*

The specialized anthology is becoming a very popular form with publishers and with teachers and librarians who enjoy using thematic collections to supplement the curriculum or connect with specific topics. These are collections gathered around a single topic, such as animals, holidays, or family, or a single theme, such as comfort, love, or peace. They still include poems by a variety of poets, so they provide a good introduction to a variety of poetic styles and voices, all of which are selected to provide different perspectives on the unifying theme or subject.

Topical collections offer a more concentrated exposure to poems on a single topic, thus appealing to a reader's prior interest in a topic, like dogs, or providing an introduction to a topic unfamiliar to readers, such as outer space. These slimmer, specialized collections are usually more visually inviting and are very popular among both adults and children. For one lovely example, look for this smaller anthology of poems about books, reading, and libraries titled *I Am the Book*, selected by Lee Bennett Hopkins, a good example of a contemporary anthology with a variety of distinguished poets in a slim, unillustrated volume. Since all the poems are similar in subject but are written by different poets, this is an excellent example of a topical collection. *The Poetry Teacher's Book of Lists* (Vardell 2012) provides guidance in finding poetry books gathered around dozens of themes and topics, including twenty seasonal and holiday themes (such as Halloween, Hanukkah, Earth Day, and Mother's Day), as well as many teachable topics (such as family, friendship, humor, and coping) and curricular units (such as animals, dinosaurs, food, sports, and trees).

## Ten Topical or Thematic Collections Not to Be Missed

1. Barbara Brenner, ed., *The Earth Is Painted Green: A Garden of Poems about Our Planet*
2. Catherine Clinton, ed., *A Poem of Her Own: Voices of American Women Yesterday and Today*
3. Nikki Giovanni, ed., *Hip Hop Speaks to Children*
4. Jan Greenberg, ed., *Heart to Heart: New Poems Inspired by Twentieth-Century American Art*
5. Georgia Heard, ed., *This Place I Know: Poems of Comfort*
6. Mary Ann Hoberman and Linda Winston, eds., *The Tree That Time Built: A Celebration of Nature, Science, and Imagination*
7. Lee Bennett Hopkins, ed., *Hand in Hand: An American History through Poetry*
8. J. Patrick Lewis, ed., *The National Geographic Book of Animal Poetry*
9. Pat Mora, ed., *Love to Mamá: A Tribute to Mothers*
10. Jack Prelutsky, ed., *The Beauty of the Beast: Poems from the Animal Kingdom*

## *Compilations of Works by Individual Poets*

At some point, most poets like to publish collections featuring only their own work. And of course, such works offer the best way to get a feeling for a poet's unique voice and style. These collections may also have a topical connection, such as animals or holidays or sports, but one person, the featured poet, has authored all the poems.

Single-poet collections are also very popular with both children and adults after they have had some introduction to the writer of a collection. *A Light in the Attic*, for example, is one of the most circulated books of children's poetry ever because there are now several generations of Shel Silverstein fans. Readers seek out the four anthologies of Silverstein's poetry year after year. If you are not familiar with poets like John Ciardi or J. Patrick Lewis, however, you may not pick up a book of their poetry. Unless the book's topic, cover art, or interior illustrations intrigue you, you may not realize that both Ciardi and Lewis, for example, are as clever and humorous as Silverstein. As with all readers' advisory work, of course, this is where the savvy librarian can really make a difference, guiding children (and adults) to collections by poets who may become new favorites.

A list of ten individual poet compilations is harder to assemble, because the titles depend very much on which poets a reader likes. But here are ten books by individual poets that recently appeared among the best-selling titles of children's poetry.

## Ten Individual Poet Compilations Not to Be Missed

1. John Ciardi, *You Read to Me, I'll Read to You*
2. Paul Fleischman, *Joyful Noise: Poems for Two Voices*
3. Douglas Florian, *Omnibeasts*
4. Eloise Greenfield, *Honey, I Love and Other Love Poems*
5. Mary Ann Hoberman, *The Llama Who Had No Pajama: 100 Favorite Poems*
6. Langston Hughes, *The Dreamkeeper and Other Poems*
7. J. Patrick Lewis, *Countdown to Summer: A Poem for Every Day of the School Year*
8. Jack Prelutsky, *The New Kid on the Block*
9. Shel Silverstein, *A Light in the Attic*
10. Judith Viorst, *If I Were in Charge of the World and Other Worries: Poems for Children and Their Parents*

Obviously, there are many more compilations of works by individual poets worth sharing with children. Just as with fiction, when young readers discover an interest in the works of a certain poet, they like to read more books by him or her. So, if young readers or listeners enjoy the art and clever descriptive poems in Douglas Florian's *Insectlopedia*, for example, they will very likely respond to his *Zoo's Who*, *Dinothesaurus*, and *Unbeelievables*, among others. Indeed, once you become familiar with specific poets, you may want to watch for their new publications from year to year. The slim volumes of poetry by individual poets may be the rarest treasures of all, produced in small quantities with great care and culled from a multitude of poems to share the very best with children.

---
**POET PROFILE**
---

## Sharing Poetry Out Loud and Soft

### BY DOUGLAS FLORIAN

Poetry, more so than prose, is usually meant to be read out loud. It begs to be recited to an audience that can laugh, cry, gasp, or groan. It has an immediacy and intensity that so often connect people, and especially children, together. Because each line, phrase, word, or semicolon is so precise and considered, it can illuminate and educate in a most entertaining and emotional way.

Whether through a recording or live, to hear a poet recite a poem adds a whole new dimension to the static letters sitting on a page. With voice the poet can scream or whisper, whine or bewitch, howl or cajole. While prose is by nature prosaic and long winded, poetry is compact and commanding. The listener must be attuned to every word and nuance or risk missing miles of meaning. A poet's voice can s t r e t c h words out or pack them together, fall or rise in tone.

No monotone works here, but rather a moving, meandering, and progressing experience as the very sounds of words can amaze. A coyote can become a howling coyooooote, and shhhhhhhhheep can lull us to sleep better than mere sheep. Words may bounce off one another and echo with alliteration, as in *lizard laze* or *chameleon comedian*.

How can poets impart their intentions to the reader? We have our ways. We use italics to slow things down and emphasize words. Bold type or underlining can signal loudness and force. Line breaks tell where to pause: stanzas or even empty space signify a longer pause. Type fonts and sizes can convey mood or manner. A long dash alerts the reader that some surprise is wending its way, so—get ready!

One who recites poetry can be an actor playing different roles, with different voices, accents, intonations, and emotions, all in the course of one poem. Reciting a poem is "re-sighting" a poem, making it more clear and exciting. Reading a poem aloud makes it come alive and springs it off the page, gives birth to it, nurtures it, and lets it stand on its own two (or even four) feet. A spoken poem is harder to ignore. It's out there in the air, tangible, delectable, not merely intellectual. It enters us through our ears, leaving our eyes free to imagine and dream of all that the poem hints at.

A poem reading can be intimate, close, and cozy, with ten children sitting near the reader, without stage or microphone. It can be communal and commanding, with an audience of hundreds listening to words booming from a powerful sound system in an auditorium. Or it can be both personal and wide ranging, as when poetry is read out loud on the radio or in a recording.

When poetry is recited before people, their response becomes part of the poem. This is especially true with children, with their great spontaneity. Their laughter or tears, their gasps or titters, their groans or moans, and even their

**PRACTITIONER PERSPECTIVE**

*I tried my hand at teaching the kids in my classroom how to write concrete poems. We read* Splish Splash *by Joan Bransfield Graham first, of course. The kids fell in love with the poetry and were thrilled at the idea of writing their own poems. I must say, I was quite amazed. The book uses water as a basis for the poems, so we decided to use "school" as our foundation. My kids wrote about the monkey bars, apples for the teacher, the nurse, and even the trash can! The kids created artistic backgrounds for their poems, and I hung them up for open house. [The] parents were in awe! The poetry was really a hit! It never ceases to amaze me as to what kids can do.*

Monika Walker, first-grade teacher
Plano, Texas

silence all play into the performance, enriching it and amending it, enhancing or detracting from it. Good responses embolden readers, and bad ones enfeeble them. Poets, like comedians, need a good crowd to connect with. Laughter is contagious and humor is infectious. Grief in a poem can be sensed in the silence of the audience, and the audience can signal understanding and recognition by their nods and smiles. A poem read aloud can draw in the difficult child, capture the disruptive child, and grant gifts to the gifted child. Attention spans lengthen and moods swing in positive ways in response to poetry performances. Rhyme and rhythm lend themselves to children most naturally. Alliteration and repetition are intrinsically pleasing and satisfying to a child's ear. A group of poets reciting their own work can create an even more powerful experience. Varieties of forms and voices can have wide-ranging and cumulative effects as the lyrical mixes with the comical, the terse with the florid, and the emotional with the intellectual.

In short, reading poetry aloud connects us and collects us, heals us and reveals us, unites us and delights us in the wonder of words and all they can convey.

## A Poem Can Sing
*by Douglas Florian*

A poem can sing
A poem can sting
A poem can shout
Or leap about
A poem can yell
Or sink or swell
A poem can talk
Or take a walk
A poem can wail
A poem can sail
A poem can wing
A poem can sing

*© 2012 by Douglas Florian. Used with permission.*

**CLASS EXERCISE** With its strong rhythm and rhyme, "A Poem Can Sing" lends itself to being read aloud. Try having two groups of children read alternating lines in call-and-response style. For variety, add motions and gestures that correspond with the words. Pause briefly at the end of each line for the pantomime, or put it all together with a small group of mimes acting out the strong verbs while the rest of the children, in two groups, alternate reading pairs of lines out loud.

---

### Single-Poem Picture Books

Another interesting kind of poetry book is the publication of an individual poem, often a classic work, spread out line by line across the pages of a standard thirty-two-page picture book. These single-poem picture books offer the benefit of extensive illustrations to help readers understand and interpret, or even reinterpret, each line of a poem. Robert Frost's "Stopping by Woods on a Snowy Evening," illustrated by Susan Jeffers, is one of my favorite poem picture books. The literal portrayal of the snowy path is refreshing for any reader who has been forced to analyze the poem's deeper meaning. "The Owl and the Pussycat," by Edward Lear, has been illustrated in picture-book format by several artists, including James Marshall and Jan Brett, and Diane Siebert has taken many of the poems she published in magazines and turned them into breathtaking poem picture books. Siebert's *Heartland, Mojave, Train Song, Cave,* and others are illustrated by a variety of artists and are perfect supplements to a school social studies curriculum.

Poem picture books are not to be confused with poetic or rhyming picture books, such as Dr. Seuss books, with their strong rhythms and frequent rhymes. In a poem picture book, the poem can stand alone—without the book format or the illustrations. In the usual picture book, text and illustrations work together to convey a story. In a poem picture book, the illustrations provide one vision of the poem's meaning. This can help introduce young readers to longer, narrative poems or classic works, as in the Visions in Poetry series. Poem picture books can also be helpful for visually oriented older students who may be familiar with a classic poem but may not find it moving or meaningful until they see it richly illustrated. Such books can also provide a springboard for students to experiment with their own artistic expression of a poem's meaning for them. They can create personal poem picture books for their favorite poems.

One note—these books are often not cataloged or shelved in the usual 811 poetry section. More often they are viewed and handled as picture books and are placed in the E or Easy (or Everyone) section. This is fine if the books are circulating and finding an audience, but if not, it may be worth promoting them specifically as poetry or poem picture books in various creative ways, such as by including them in poetry bibliographies and booklists, linking them with other poetry anthologies, and so forth.

**Ten Single-Poem Picture Books Not to Be Missed**

1. Robert Frost, *Stopping by Woods on a Snowy Evening*, illustrated by Susan Jeffers
2. Edward Lear, *His Shoes Were Far Too Tight*, illustrated by Calef Brown
3. Myra Cohn Livingston, *Calendar*, illustrated by Will Hillenbrand
4. Henry Wadsworth Longfellow, *The Midnight Ride of Paul Revere*, illustrated by Christopher Bing
5. Walter Dean Myers, *Harlem: A Poem*, illustrated by Christopher Myers
6. Edgar Allan Poe, *The Raven*, illustrated by Ryan Price
7. Alice Schertle, *We*, illustrated by Kenneth Addison
8. Diane Siebert, *Cave*, illustrated by Wayne McLoughlin
9. Robert Louis Stevenson, *Block City*, illustrated by Daniel Kirk
10. Ernest Lawrence Thayer, *Casey at the Bat*, illustrated by Christopher Bing

Poem picture books lend themselves particularly well to creative follow-up activities. For example:

Read the poem first without illustrations. Then, on the second reading, show the illustrations and discuss the differences in the experiences, such as how the poem looks, how it makes readers feel, and how the illustrator visualized each line.

Compare multiple picture-book versions of the same poem (e.g., several different illustrators' interpretations of "The Owl and the Pussycat" or "The Night before Christmas" or "Casey at the Bat").

Invite kids to create a homemade book of original illustrations to accompany a favorite poem or the lyrics of a favorite song, working individually, with a partner, or in a small group.

Also, remember to be open to children's different interpretations of the same poem and to encourage their reinterpretations of old favorites.

## Poetic Picture Storybooks

Even simple narrative picture books can be poetic in their use of language. Generally speaking, the text for a picture book is only a page or two of writing, about fifteen hundred words. If you separate the words from the illustrations (especially for older readers), you can get a closer look at the artistry of the writer—the choice of words, the arrangement of lines, the structure of the story. Typing out the text of a favorite picture book can help you see the beauty in the story, the poetry in the language. Some picture-book texts will seem instantly poetic; others may be more expository in nature. Some are deliberately written in rhyme but do not stand alone as poetry. They depend on the combination of text and illustration for their power. It can be a worthwhile exercise for all those who are looking closely at poetry, poetry writing, and poetry in general to consider the variety of picture books that incorporate rhyme and rhythm in their language:

- rhyming picture storybooks (à la Dr. Seuss)
- predictable books (such as *Brown Bear, Brown Bear, What Do You See?*, by Bill Martin Jr.)
- easy-to-read books (controlled-vocabulary readers)
- alphabet books
- counting books

I would not generally consider such works poetry books because their focus is on using rhyme as a vehicle. However, whenever rhyme or poetic language is present, it is an opportunity for children to notice and comment on the words and sounds they hear and read. It is an opportunity to invite children to join in the oral reading. It is an opportunity to link picture books with poems. It is an opportunity to look for poems that piggyback on the story experience. Picture storybooks that contain poetic language make the point that poetry, rhyme, and verse are all around us.

### MARILYN SINGER

## For Me
*by Marilyn Singer*

Telephone call,
Not for me.
Package in the hall,
Not for me.
Card from Bombay,
Not for me.
Letter from L.A.,
Not for me.
New magazine,
Not for me.
Answering machine,
Not for me.
Mama's home—
Come and see.
She found a poem,
Just for me.

Everyone sees things differently. Everyone feels the same emotions. That contradiction tells us part of what poetry is about—the combination of fresh ways of viewing the world with feelings we all share.

In that regard, children's poetry is no different from poetry for adults—good poetry, that is. It surprises us with fresh images and genuine emotions. Of course, the way these are presented differs—and that is something I discovered when I set out to write poems for younger kids. Each word still has to count, but the words are generally simpler, and their pattern is more direct. The rhythms tend to be stronger and the feelings closer to the surface.

Does that clarity and simplicity make such poems easier to write? Nope. To create "young poems," I found that I have to become young. This isn't a matter of getting inside a child's brain but of summoning up my own young mind while using my grown-up craft to fashion my thoughts and feelings into poetry. How do I manage to see and feel like a child? Beats me! But I'm sure glad I can.

I wrote "For Me" when I was in that young mind-set; it's part of a group of diverse pieces about nature, play, emotional states, and so forth. I recall quite well that left-out feeling when all the phone calls, letters, packages, postcards were for my mom, dad, sister, grandmother (or husband, neighbor, or house-guest!). A friend of mine suggested that I like to buy things on eBay because that way I'll always get presents in the mail. He's got me pegged.

I remember, too, the times my mom would read poems to me—and my dad would sing songs—and how special that made me feel. To me, those gifts were more precious than material ones because they shaped my lifelong love of words, music, reading—and they can do the same for kids today.

Teachers and librarians can also convey those gifts. One way to do so is to read poetry aloud to students with enthusiasm. Poetry is meant to be read aloud. And as you read it, it's important to let your own feelings shine through. When I was a high school teacher, I wept every time I read Dylan Thomas's "Fern Hill" aloud to my classes. I couldn't help it. And I had to get beyond embarrassment to explore why the poem affected me so strongly. That led to important and honest discussions about which poems moved my students and why, and about the power of poetry to soothe, stir, sadden, or delight.

Another fun thing to do in the classroom is to have several kids read the same poem with emphases on different sentences or sections. How many ways can one poem be read? A duet or group reading can also elucidate the tension between individual perception and common emotion.

Above all, children are not the only ones who should play with poetry. Adults should, too. Keep your mind open to the wonder of words and the world around you. Come to think of it, that's how we grown-ups can manage to keep our child mind alive—and how we can appreciate (and sometimes create) those special poems for each of us to treasure.

**CLASS EXERCISE** After reading "For Me" aloud once by yourself, invite children to read the line "Not for me" in unison while you read the other lines. For extra support, create a sign with "Not for me" on it and hold it up to cue students to speak.

## Variations of Poetry Book Formats

Although there may be four major types of poetry books (anthologies, topical collections, individual compilations, and poem picture books), one can find poetry in several other variations of those formats. For example:

- collections of a single poetic form (e.g., haiku, concrete poetry)
- verse novels (generally for young adults)
- song lyrics published in book form
- Mother Goose and nursery rhymes
- folk rhymes
- poetry by children
- e-books and poetry apps

### Collections Based on Poetic Forms

In recent years, we have seen the publication of many poetry books that feature one specific form of poetry, such as concrete, or shape, poetry, haiku, and riddle poems. These can be a fun way to introduce the role of form in poetry or simply to add variety to the usual poem diet. Many poets incorporate a concrete poem, riddle poem, or haiku or two in their poetry books. Paul B. Janeczko, for example, explores poetry forms for each letter of the alphabet in *Poetry from A to Z: A Guide for Young Writers,* and he provides a visual introduction to poetic forms for younger children with the assistance of Chris Raschka's illustrations in *A Kick in the Head: An Everyday Guide to Poetic Forms.*

Janeczko and Raschka paired up previously to create *A Poke in the I: A Collection of Concrete Poems,* an inviting introduction to concrete poetry. Many collections of concrete, or shape, poetry are available. Children typically enjoy concrete poetry and take pleasure in the poet's creative use of the physical shape of the poem to convey meaning. It is a poetic form they like imitating and experimenting with. Betsy Franco captures the antics of both dogs and cats in her concrete poetry collections, *A Dazzling Display of Dogs* and *A Curious Collection of Cats*, as does Joyce Sidman in *Meow Ruff: A Story in Concrete Poetry*. Joan Bransfield Graham's books *Flicker Flash* and *Splish Splash* are clever and colorful examples. J. Patrick Lewis's book *Doodle Dandies: Poems That Take Shape* and Heidi Roemer's *Come to My Party* are both appealing books of concrete poetry, too. For a slightly more offbeat collection of concrete poems ideal for the preteen reader, check out *Technically, It's Not My Fault: Concrete Poems* and *Blue Lipstick: Concrete Poems*, both by John Grandits.

Poems in riddle format can also be very appealing to children and offer opportunities for both problem solving and poetry enjoyment. J. Patrick Lewis has several riddle-poem collections, including *Riddle-icious, Riddle-lightful, Arithme-Tickle, Scien-trickery: Riddles in Science,* and *Spot the Plot! A Riddle Book of Book Riddles.* Charles Ghigna created *Riddle Rhymes*, Rebecca Dotlich authored *When Riddles Come Rumbling*, and Stephanie Calmenson produced *Kindergarten Kids: Riddles, Rebuses, Wiggles, Giggles, and More!*—all full of guessing-game rhymes for very young children. Brian Swann offers riddle rhymes from African traditions in *The House with No Door* and from Native American traditions in *Touching the Distance.*

Haiku is an ancient Japanese form of poetry that has been a staple of many library collections. The short, unrhymed nature poems are available in several different collections suitable for children. Two unique picture books that use only haiku poems to tell the story are *Guyku: A Year of Haiku for Boys*, by Bob Raczka, and *Won Ton: A Cat Tale Told in Haiku*, by Lee Wardlaw. Matthew Gollub blends the classic haiku poetry of the famed Japanese poet Issa with biographical narrative in the picture book *Cool Melons—Turn to Frogs! The Life and Poems of Issa.* Pat Mora describes the interesting plants that came from all across the Americas with haiku poems and prose paragraphs in *Yum! Mmmm! ¡Qué rico! Americas' Sproutings,* and Jane Yolen uses nature photographs to complement her nature haiku poetry in *Least Things: Poems about Small Natures.* Jack Prelutsky's collection of animal haiku is illustrated by Ted Rand in *If Not for the Cat*. Michael J. Rosen offers haiku about dogs and birds in *The Hound Dog's Haiku and Other Poems for Dog Lovers* and *The Cuckoo's Haiku and Other Birding Poems*. And for a completely different approach suitable for older children, look for the urban haiku and zany haiku in *Stone Bench in an Empty Park*, edited by Paul B. Janeczko, or *Wing Nuts: Screwy Haiku*, by Janeczko and Lewis.

**Ten Collections That Feature Haiku Poetry**
1. Sid Farrar, *The Year Comes Round: Haiku through the Seasons*
2. J. Patrick Lewis and Paul B. Janeczko, *Wing Nuts: Screwy Haiku*
3. Ryan Mecum, *Zombie Haiku*
4. Pat Mora, *Yum! Mmmm! ¡Qué rico! Americas' Sproutings*
5. Jack Prelutsky, *If Not for the Cat: Haiku*
6. Bob Raczka, *Guyku: A Year of Haiku for Boys*
7. Michael J. Rosen, *The Cuckoo's Haiku and Other Birding Poems*
8. Michael J. Rosen, *The Hound Dog's Haiku and Other Poems for Dog Lovers*
9. Lee Wardlaw, *Won Ton: A Cat Tale Told in Haiku*
10. Jane Yolen, *Least Things: Poems about Small Natures*

## Verse Novels

A relatively new poetic form with roots in ancient epic poetry, the verse novel, or novel in verse, is growing in popularity, particularly with middle school readers. Indeed, the majority of verse novels currently available are probably best suited to young adults. However, there are several examples that children ages nine or ten years and up may enjoy, such as *Amber Was Brave, Essie Was Smart*, by Vera Williams, and *Minn and Jake* and *Minn and Jake's Almost Terrible Summer*, by Janet Wong. The Newbery Award–winning novelists Karen Hesse and Sharon Creech have also authored several interesting novels in verse, including Hesse's Newbery winner *Out of the Dust*, as well as *Witness* and *Aleutian Sparrow*, and Creech's *Love That Dog*, *Hate That Cat*, and *Heartbeat*. Other poets who have created novels in verse well suited to the intermediate grades include Andrea Cheng, Helen Frost, Nikki Grimes, Eileen Spinelli, and Tracie Vaughn Zimmer. The best verse novels are built on poems that are often lovely stand-alone works of art. A narrative unfolds poem by poem, frequently with multiple points of view and in colloquial language. This format is wooing many middle-grade children both to poetry and to reading in general—a promising trend.

## Ten Novels in Verse for the Intermediate Grades
1. Andrea Cheng, *Where the Steps Were*
2. Sharon Creech, *Love That Dog*
3. Helen Frost, *Diamond Willow*
4. Steven Herrick, *Naked Bunyip Dancing*
5. Karen Hesse, *Out of the Dust*
6. Thanhha Lai, *Inside Out and Back Again*
7. Eileen Spinelli, *Where I Live*
8. Robert Paul Weston, *Zorgamazoo*
9. Janet Wong, *Minn and Jake*
10. Tracie Vaughn Zimmer, *Reaching for Sun*

### *Songs in Book Form*

Studying song lyrics can be a backdoor approach to inviting readers into the world of poetry. Because children's interest in music seems to increase in the teen years, older kids may be more familiar with the words to the top songs on the radio than they are with the poetry of Shakespeare or even Shel Silverstein. Writing down song lyrics (or finding them on CD liners or the Web) can help young people look closely at the use of word choice, phrasing, repetition, and figurative language in a poetic format that they might find more relevant. Then we can take the next step by matching songs with poems and examining the similarities and differences between the two forms. (A note of caution: you may have to set some ground rules about what kinds of song lyrics are acceptable in a school or library environment.)

Sharing songs in picture-book form may help younger children see the poetry in the familiar tunes and lyrics they have grown up with. For example, Bruce McMillan's photo illustrations for *Mary Had a Little Lamb* feature a modern, African American Mary in yellow overalls. Patriotic songs that children learn in school may become more understandable through the illustrations in books such as *O Beautiful for Spacious Skies*, illustrated by Wayne Thiebaud, or *America the Beautiful*, illustrated by Wendell Minor. Songs they learned at summer camp are noted in *Camp Granada: Sing-Along Camp Songs*, by Frané Lessac, and songs often learned at preschool can be found in *A Treasury of Children's Songs: Forty Favorites to Sing and Play*, compiled by Dan Fox. If you are comfortable introducing Bible songs and spirituals, share *All Night, All Day: A Child's First Book of African-American Spirituals*, collected and beautifully illustrated by Ashley Bryan. And look to the cultural traditions of your community for more examples of songs strong in rhyme and rhythm, such as Lulu Delacre's *Arrorró, mi niño: Latino Lullabies and Gentle Games*, José-Luis Orozco's *Fiestas: A Year of Latin American Songs of Celebration*, and *Hush, Baby, Hush! Lullabies from around the World*, compiled by Kathy Henderson. The rhythm and repetition of songs echo the elements found in many poems.

### Mother Goose

Over the years, I have found that many children have missed the traditional exposure to Mother Goose rhymes and may know very few of them. That is not just sad; it is a handicap—many works of adult literature that children may encounter in the future make constant reference to Mother Goose rhymes and characters (e.g., *All the King's Men*, by Robert Penn Warren). Even with older children, it can be fun to share Mother Goose rhymes and the history behind them. Consider using *The Annotated Mother Goose*, by William and Ceil Baring-Gould, which is full of the stories behind the rhymes. For example, did you know that "Old King Cole" refers to an actual British King, a brave and popular man, whose daughter was a skilled musician, not just his "fiddlers three"? Or consider the graphic-novel-style *Nursery Rhyme Comics: 50 Timeless Rhymes from*

---

**PRACTITIONER PERSPECTIVE**

*I was very surprised to realize how much poetry I am already using. Every week I start storytime with a poem (an action rhyme), do two to three poems during the session (in the form of fingerplays or flannels), and end with a poem as well (a song that we dance to). At home, I sing songs and read Mother Goose and other books to my eight-month-old. And I have read several poem novels, especially those by Mel Glenn. It is amazing what one will find when putting on poetry-tinted glasses!*

Sarah Dornback, children's librarian
Farmers Branch Manske Library, Farmers Branch, Texas

*50 Celebrated Cartoonists*, which offers fresh, visual interpretations of familiar verses.

There are probably hundreds of book versions of Mother Goose nursery rhymes, and many families undoubtedly have their favorites. New versions illustrated by Rosemary Wells are very popular. They include *My Very First Mother Goose* and *Here Comes Mother Goose*, both based on verses collected by children's folklore expert Iona Opie. Many individual rhymes from these collections have also been reproduced as board books for toddlers. Tomie dePaola's illustrations enliven a collection of more than two hundred rhymes (also collected by Peter and Iona Opie) in *Tomie dePaola's Mother Goose*. For a fresh, contemporary look, share Nina Crews's *Neighborhood Mother Goose* or *Neighborhood Sing-Along*, with lively illustrations that include photographs of children in urban settings. And for a humorous twist, consider Lisa Wheeler's *Spinster Goose: Twisted Rhymes for Naughty Children*. For an ecological spin, look for *The Green Mother Goose: Saving the World One Rhyme at a Time*, edited by Jan Peck and David Davis.

Fingerplays and rhymes with motions and movement are also staples of many children's early introductions to poetry. Although the focus of this book is school-age children, five to twelve years old, participatory rhymes may also engage older children, particularly when you have multiage groups or a book-buddies program that pairs older children with younger ones. Many wonderful collections are available, such as *This Little Piggy: Lap Songs, Finger Plays, Clapping Games, and Pantomime Rhymes* (with CD), compiled by Jane Yolen, and Michael Foreman's *Playtime Rhymes*. And of course, children from non-English-speaking backgrounds also grow up with nursery rhymes, so seek such rhymes out whenever they are available to you in book form. Consider, for example, Alma Flor Ada and F. Isabel Campoy's *¡Pío peep! Traditional Spanish Nursery Rhymes*. For children who missed Mother Goose in their preschool years, are new to nursery rhymes in English, or simply want to revisit nursery rhymes for the pleasure of the sounds and rhythms (and the memories of early childhood!), various versions of Mother Goose rhymes are well worth having in any reputable poetry collection.

### Folk Poetry

Many children—and adults—don't realize that the silly songs, rollicking rhymes, and nonsense games we learn in early childhood are indeed a form of literature. Folk poetry is the poetry that you do not even realize is poetry. Playground rhymes like "Cinderella Dressed in Yellow" have no known author and yet are familiar to many generations of children. These rhyming verses can also be included in our poetry collections. Books of riddles, chants, tongue twisters, jump-rope rhymes, fingerplays, hand-clapping games, autograph sayings, and more often contain poetry and verse. What's more, children are often intrigued to find in print the verses they have heard and known only orally and only outside of school—at home and at play. Alvin Schwartz's collection of uniquely American verse *And the Green Grass Grew All Around* is one of my favorites and has many wonderful examples that children will enjoy. You may be surprised, for instance, to discover that there are second and third verses to poems that you knew only one verse of as a child. For additional examples, look for Iona Opie and Peter Opie's classic *I Saw Esau: The Schoolchild's Pocket Book* or Virginia Tashjian's *Juba This and Juba That*. Authors and collaborators Joanna Cole and Stephanie Calmenson have also created several collections of folk poetry worth knowing about, such as *Yours Till Banana Splits: 201 Autograph Rhymes*. And Judy Sierra has gathered a gem with *Schoolyard Rhymes: Kids' Own Rhymes for Rope Skipping, Hand Clapping, Ball Bouncing, and Just Plain Fun*. Several comprehensive collections of folk poetry are available and very appealing to young audiences of all ages. This medium helps validate children's experiences, link oral and written modes of expression, and invite active and even physical participation (Vardell and Jacko 2005). Children can collect other examples on audio- or videotape and explore neighborhood, cultural, and linguistic variations (Vardell, Hadaway, and Young 2002). They can translate their English favorites into other languages represented in their community. Older children may enjoy exploring the historical roots of childhood folklore or writing down new and unfamiliar examples.

### Poetry by Children

It can also be very meaningful to share poem collections that include works authored by children. Several poets who have worked in schools, in libraries, and with other youth projects have gathered and edited collections of poetry written by children of all ages. Collections such as *Salting the Ocean*, edited by Naomi Shihab Nye, or *Ten-Second Rainshowers: Poems by Young People* and *Soft Hay*

*Will Catch You: Poems by Young People*, both edited by Sandford Lyne, are beautiful books full of unsentimental and authentic young voices. Teacher Timothy McLaughlin gathered Native voices in *Walking on Earth and Touching the Sky: Poetry and Prose by Lakota Youth at Red Cloud Indian School*, and children from around the world contributed to *Come and Play: Children of Our World Having Fun*, edited by Ayana Lowe, and *River of Words*, edited by Pamela Michael. And for a more humorous look at poetry writing, consider Australian author Gary Crew's mock journal *Troy Thompson's Excellent Peotry* [sic] *Book*, which looks like a collection of very personal poems in a child's own handwriting. For children who aspire to be writers or who may find personal poetry writing a helpful release, these books are an invitation to see themselves as writers, to see children as capable of poetic expression, too.

## E-Books and Poetry Apps

New technologies are presenting new ways to capture, produce, and share poetry with young people. Publishers are offering e-book versions of print poetry books for young people, and app or "application" adaptations are coming along, too. These offer new opportunities to enjoy, manipulate, and interact with poems. Few of these first-generation e-books of poetry, however, are maximizing the electronic medium. They are designed for the page rather than the screen. But that is evolving quickly. The PoetryTagTime series of e-books of poetry (*PoetryTagTime, P\*TAG, Gift Tag*), for example, was developed specifically for the Kindle, iPad, and Nook, with strategic book design and page turns. We even coined the word *kindleku* to describe the shortened form of poem that fit the Kindle screen. In addition, some teachers and librarians are capitalizing on the ease of e-book production to publish their own e-books of poetry that showcase the work of children, as did Ken Slesarik with *Poetry Rocks 2012*, part culminating poetry project and part school fund-raiser. Finally, the use of poetry in creating an app (for iPads and iPhones) is another intriguing poetry development, with several based on material for children but few focused on poetry by recognized, contemporary poets. Our current options include the following:

iF Poems (Clickworks, 2011), which allows you to read, listen to, record, and share your favorite poems from a collection of more than two hundred classic (largely British) poems narrated by actors Helena Bonham Carter and Bill Nighy and searchable by author, theme, first line, or category such as "if you are facing grief" or "if you need courage." The poems are designated for three age groups: newborn to six years, seven to twelve years, and thirteen and older; the app also includes extra resources, such as a dictionary of poetic terms and mini-biographies of all the poets.

*The Grim Granary: Poems for Kids Big and Small* (Tusitala Books, 2011), a collection of darkly humorous illustrated poems with audio renditions of each poem available in three languages. "Over 100 pages of verse and accompanying quirky hand-drawn illustrations. Hilarious readings by various narrators with an option to disable audio" (www.tusitalabooks.com/book-apps/the-grim-granary-poems-for-big-and-little-kids).

*Twinkle, Twinkle, Little Star: The Experience* (FlyingWord, 2011), the classic poem featuring the illustrations of Michael Hague, with enhanced art for tablet devices to tilt and turn images in 3-D, pop bubbles, and cause characters to swing from the moon; accessible in nine languages.

These two poetry apps for grown-ups also offer engaging poetry experiences for able readers:

*Poem Flow,* a poem-of-the-day application in which everyone receives the same poem on the same day, creating an "instant, invisible community of simultaneous readers." The poems are classics (for adults), and when turned in your hand, "each poem dissolves in a gentle reading animation" (www.poemflow.com/about).

*POETRY,* the Poetry Foundation's free "mobile poetry library," offers a searchable collection of classic adult poems. "Give your phone a shake to discover new poems to fit any mood" (www.poetryfoundation.org/mobile).

These are just some of the latest tools and technologies that are available for connecting children with poetry with more innovative ways certainly on the horizon. As you immerse children in enjoying poetry, they'll have the knowledge base for envisioning future poetry possibilities themselves.

## Poem Selection Tools

Need help in finding poetry? Choosing the right poem is much like choosing the right storybook or novel: the more poetry books you know, the easier it is to find just the right one. So immersing yourself in the best new poets and poetry books is a good first step. It can also be helpful to maintain your own log, list, blog, or database of favorite poems or poetry books as you read. In this way you can start with a handful of favorites to share and refer to your list over and over again. You can pair poems with other favorite books and activities and continually look for new poems to build your repertoire.

For finding particular poems, there are a variety of resources to try. Several are now available as electronic databases by subscription, which makes searching even easier. A good tool specific to poetry for children is the *Index to Poetry for Children and Young People,* a title, subject, poet, and first-line index to poetry in collections for children and young people, previously published in installments by H. W. Wilson. In total, this reference tool indexes more than 82,700 poems from more than 1,050 collections published through 1997. This resource is now available electronically through H. W. Wilson's Biography Reference Bank Database, a subscription database.

The Columbia Granger's World of Poetry (www.columbiagrangers.org) subscription database includes thousands of poems accessible via the Web, searchable by title, poet, subject, first line, and last line. Granger's has been a definitive source in English for locating poems in anthologies on library shelves since 1904. Although the site is primarily a resource for adult poetry, there are many children's poets represented, including Shel Silverstein, Jack Prelutsky, Arnold Adoff, Janet Wong, and Pat Mora, among others. By and large, this site does not include the actual text of the poems (which are still copyrighted), but it is a helpful poem information locator resource. The Granger Index Reprint series is also helpful and includes many print resources, such as *Poems That Every Child Should Know: A Selection of the Best Poems of All Times for Young People,* among others.

Poem Finder is another web-based subscription service that indexes more than six hundred thousand poems and more than fifty thousand full-text poems and references collected from anthologies, periodicals, and single-author works. Some author biographies, pictures, and explanations of poetry are also available. Poem Finder is a subset of Litfinder, a Thomson/Gale resource, and even includes the "Kids' Korner," with access to poetry in appealing categories for children, such as "Fun and Games," "Animals," and "Family."

An additional electronic database is PoemHunter.com, a resource currently containing 77,956 poems from 9,061 poets as well as songs, lyrics, quotations and even free poetry e-books. This site includes Judith Viorst, Naomi Shihab Nye, Shel Silverstein, and Jack Prelutsky (among their top five hundred poets, no less), but few other contemporary poets who write primarily for children. Nonetheless, the site is free and easy to navigate.

These are great tools to become familiar with. Canvassing colleagues and other poetry lovers (via electronic discussion list) can also turn up poem recommendations. Sometimes you find the perfect poem by serendipity—simply by browsing through relevant anthologies and thematic collections. This is where developing your own personal anthology, log, or database can also come in handy. But having poem-selection tools available can also assist you in expanding your poetry choices.

**PRACTITIONER PERSPECTIVE**

*I finally checked out Shel Silverstein's audiobook version of* A Light in the Attic. *He is an absolute pleasure to listen to! I am amazed at his ability to read each poem with unique expression, and I enjoyed hearing the poems one after the other. He varies the pace of the poems and the volume of his voice to give each reading personality. The background music or sounds bring the poetry to life even more. I am so excited that I ordered this for my new library collection because I know the kids will enjoy it just as much as I did. My favorite reading was of the poem "Squishy Touch," like the Midas touch, except that in this case everything touched turns to Jell-O, not gold. Silverstein brought this poem to life in a way that I never could. He had great sound effects for things turning into squishy Jell-O. Who knew one person could make that many slurpy, squishy noises! (Kids would love to try this as a group reading after hearing Silverstein's version.) I certainly hope that recorded poetry will gain the popularity it deserves, because hearing an author read her or his own poems provides a different perspective for children to enjoy.*

Charry Lackey, librarian
Castle Hills Elementary School, Lewisville, Texas

## Poetry on the Web

As we look for new places for poetry to pop up, you can be sure that the Internet will be among them. The websites below make available actual poems, often accompanied by audio recordings of the poems or biographical information about the poet. Some include teaching activities; some even welcome child participation. Each site also offers links to additional poetry resources on the Web.

### ACADEMY OF AMERICAN POETS                    *www.poets.org*

This site offers poet biographies, sample poems, audio archives, National Poetry Month celebrations, an entire "For Educator's" area, and even a "Poems for Teens" link.

### POETRY FOUNDATION                 *www.poetryfoundation.org/children*

The Poetry Foundation offers a mass of resources regarding adult poetry, as well as a dedicated area for "Children's Poetry" that features information about the Children's Poet Laureate designated by the foundation, children's poem videos, articles about children's poetry, and several hundred classic and contemporary poems for children searchable and organized by topic. In addition, the "Programs and Initiatives" area includes the national Poetry Out Loud competition for high school students.

### POET'S CORNER                       *www.theotherpages.org/poems*

This site includes the full text of several thousand poems published in some form or other before 1923 in the United States and thus in the public domain. The site includes a helpful author, title, subject, and first-line index for searching for poems, too. Many classic poems for children are available here.

### POETRY 180                         *www.loc.gov/poetry/180*

Billy Collins, a former U.S. poet laureate, helped create this site with the goal of making it easy for high school students to hear or read a poem on each of the 180 days of the school year. He suggests reading one poem over the public address system daily, at the end of the day's announcements. Many contemporary poems are provided and may be appropriate for middle-grade children.

## POETRY DAILY                                       *www.poems.com*

This site offers a wonderful way to enjoy a new poem every day, although the poems are not specifically for children. It is a helpful professional source of poetry that you can tap into on a regular basis to feed your own poetic muse.

## GIGGLE POETRY                                    *www.gigglepoetry.com*

This kid-friendly website offers poems to read, with new ones posted regularly, as well as opportunities for interaction. Kids can rate the poems, enter poetry-writing contests, explore fun pages for poetry reading, and the like. There are also resource activities for adults who share poetry with children.

## LIBRARY OF CONGRESS POETRY
## AND LITERATURE CENTER                         *www.loc.gov/poetry*

This site may interest older children who are interested in learning about the poet laureates of the United States, national prizes in poetry, and special poetry events, and in checking out webcasts and podcasts, as well as listening to the archive of recordings of more than two thousand adult poets reading their own work.

### PRACTITIONER PERSPECTIVE

*After I read* My People *by Langston Hughes, with photographs by Charles R. Smith Jr., I went looking for all of the other books written or illustrated by Charles R. Smith Jr. that were available in our library. We have nearly all of them, some in the elementary school library and some in the middle school, including* I Am America. *This book is an interesting one to have in an American school overseas because so many of our students have American passports but have been living in other countries all their lives (like my own children). They are America, too! Sometimes kids like ours really struggle with identity issues and pause for quite some time when people ask where they are from.* I Am America *might help our third-culture kids like this realize that they fit right in because of their diversity!*

Carol Neeland, middle school information technology teacher
Wassenaar, The Netherlands

## Poetry in Magazines

Many magazines and serials that are published for children regularly feature poems. In fact, magazines are often the first medium in which many new poets get their work published. The poems in magazines are often new and not yet available in books, so they can be fresh and fun to seek out and share. Several literary magazines, such as *Cricket*, *Spider*, and *Ladybug*, include poetry by leading contemporary children's poets in every issue. Nature, science, and entertainment magazines also include poetry regularly. See, for example, *Ranger Rick*, *Your Big Backyard*, *ChickaDEE*, *Odyssey*, and *Highlights for Children*. Children who are avid subscribers may enjoy sharing poems from their favorite magazines.

## Audio Poetry

In an ideal world, we would have access to all children's poems read aloud by the poets who wrote them. Hearing poems read aloud by their authors is a terrific experience. As technology improves, it may get easier to record, publish, and access audio files of poetry. Meanwhile, we have access to much poetry for children in CD or audiobook form. Two major publishers of audiobooks for young people, Listening Library and Recorded Books, offer several choices, such as the work of Jack Prelutsky, Margarita Engle, and Karen Hesse (via Listening Library), and Calef Brown, Sharon Creech, Kalli Dakos, Helen Frost, Nikki Grimes, J. Patrick Lewis, Joyce Sidman, and Carole Boston Weatherford (via Recorded Books). Sourcebooks offers packaged poetry along with CDs in Nikki Giovanni's anthology, *Hip Hop Speaks to Children*; *My Hippo Has the Hiccups and Other Poems I Totally Made Up*, by Kenn Nesbitt; *The Tree That Time Built: A Celebration of Nature, Science, and Imagination*, edited by Mary Ann Hoberman and Linda Winston; and *Poetry Speaks to Children* and *Poetry Speaks: Who I Am*, both compiled by Elise Paschen and Dominique Raccah.

Publishers such as HarperCollins (Harper Children's Audio) and Scholastic (including Weston Woods) often publish audiobook versions of print books they produce, such as the big Shel Silverstein collections. The Caedmon Records imprint, now a part of HarperAudio, has a long history of issuing excellent recordings of poetry, including classic works by the likes of A. A. Milne. Audio Bookshelf offers Paul Fleischman's Newbery Award–winning poetry book *Joyful Noise* as well as works by Ashley Bryan. Live Oak Media's audio poetry includes award-winning selections by Walter Dean Myers, Marilyn Singer, Javaka Step-toe, and Vera Williams. Also look for the many, many audiobook collections of Mother Goose nursery rhymes and of poetry by classic poets of the past, such as the Voice of the Poet series.

It is also possible to use the Internet to access some audio files of poetry read aloud. For example, Audible (www.audible.com), a major provider of audio-books via downloadable files, offers more and more children's poetry books, such as *Joyful Noise*. Other poetry-related websites, such as the Academy of American Poets, include audio files among their links. The website PoetryMagazine .com is also rich in audio. Of particular note is this site's emphasis on providing audio recordings of many leading poets reading their own works aloud as well as interviews with and speeches by many different poets. The site does not include children's poets, but it is an inspiring example.

More and more children's poets are using their personal websites to provide audio recordings of themselves reading their own poetry, including Joyce Sid-man, Nikki Grimes, and Janet Wong, among others. Kristine O'Connell George, for example, reads more than a dozen of her poems in her "Poetry Aloud" link at www.kristinegeorge.com, accessible via simple free software such as RealAudio or Windows Media Player. If equipment and access are available, such audio experiences can be powerful components in children's exposure to poetry. Audio recordings help children hear the sounds of the words, the rhythm of the lines, and the expression of the reader in ways that make poetry come alive. And although you yourself can provide some insights by reading a poem aloud, doing so does not compare to the unique and memorable experience of hearing a poem read by its author. It is worth the extra effort to seek out such recordings because they are the next best thing to personal visits from the poets.

## Children's Poetry Preferences

As we gather poetry books and seek out poems we think children will enjoy, it helps to know a little about what previous studies have found about children's poetry choices. In several studies of young people's responses to poetry (Terry 1974; Fisher and Natarella 1982; Kutiper and Wilson 1993), there were fairly consistent results. Their findings include the following:

- Narrative poems that tell a story are the most popular form of poetry.
- Free verse and haiku are the least popular forms of poetry.
- Students prefer poems with strong sound patterns, rhyme, and rhythm.
- Children prefer humorous poetry, poetry about familiar experiences, and animal poetry.
- Younger students prefer contemporary poems.

Although these are helpful guidelines for selecting poems, they are not absolutes. Children enjoy many forms of poetry, including free verse and haiku, in general. There is also no guarantee that every humorous narrative poem about animals will be a hit with every group of children. Also, most studies in the past were based on a limited exposure to poetry over a brief period of time. Thus, we can hope that as children gain greater contact with more poetry, their appetite for poetry will grow in diverse directions. For example, I might rely on the studies' findings in my initial selection of poems to share with a new group of children, but as I get to know the children better and deepen my own knowledge of poetry, I feel more confident as I cast about for the right poems to share.

Poet Georgia Heard encourages us to remember what it feels like to be a child, to bear in mind the importance of liking poetry, and to introduce the joy of poetry. She encourages natural talk and integrating the sharing of poetry into the daily routine. We should train children's ears and start with poems that guarantee success because they are easy to comprehend. Her advice for beginners includes respecting the mood of the poem, reading slowly, reading the poem multiple times, and displaying the text of the poem. She urges students to make their own anthologies of favorite poems and to study individual poets and their works in depth. Her perspective as a poet and her experiences as a poet in residence working with children in the schools are especially insightful. Although it is helpful to be familiar with studies of children's preferences and development, we can also make a difference for children by sharing our own parallel journeys with poetry with them.

## Evaluating Poetry

How do we evaluate poetry? Poetry is clearly different from prose in its form and structure. But it has poetic elements that give it additional distinctiveness:

rhythm, sound, language, imagery, and emotion. As you read poems, you can probably say whether you like them or not. Saying why you like them can be more challenging. For example, see if you can pinpoint how a poet is using language that makes the poem special or distinctive. Is it a unique use of figurative language, such as similes and metaphors? Or is it distinctive sound qualities, such as alliteration or onomatopoeia? Naming such elements is not an essential part of sharing poetry with children, although kids often notice them even when they do not know the terminology. Instead, familiarity with poetic elements can help us understand what is hooking us as readers and listeners. And we can look for more! Does the humor in the poem come from the poem's subject? From clever wordplay or puns? Sensory images can also be a powerful draw. Through their powerful use of language, poets can help us see, smell, hear, taste, and even feel that we can touch things. We often rely on poetic elements to guide us in discussing the genre. Which seem most prominent? How does the poet use particular poetic elements to special effect?

Sometimes the best we can do is describe the poetry:

- What is it? Humorous? Abstract? Familiar? Fresh?
- How does it work? Through rhyming? Free verse? Shape?
- Is the use of language distinctive? Which words stick with you?
- Can you visualize the image or feel the experience? Why?

Do not forget to look at a poetry book as a whole, too. Are the poems appropriate for young people? Is there a balance and variety of poems? Is the book well organized and designed? Do the illustrations complement or overpower the poems? Does the book make you want to read more poems by its poet (or anthologist)? Consider the following guidelines, based on questions developed by Goforth (1998), which might provide assistance in evaluating individual poetry books:

**Language**—determine the quality of the poetry by considering questions such as the following:
- Does the poetry have the potential to evoke sensory images?
- Does the poetry have a cadence, a beat, a definite rhythm?

- If the poetry is written in a rhyming format, are the rhymes natural?
- Are the sounds of the poetry appealing?
- Does the poet use language in unique, impressive ways to succinctly present ideas, descriptions, and emotions?
- Does the poet present fresh, imaginative ideas and feeling?

**Organization**—Consider the overall organization of a book by asking questions such as the following:

- Which poets are represented? Are they generally familiar or unfamiliar to young readers?
- How current are the poem selections? Does that make a difference?
- How are the poems grouped or organized? Is the overall length of the collection appropriate? Of each section?
- Is there evidence of different styles and modes of expression across the collection?
- Do the poems stimulate a variety of thoughts and emotions?
- Is background information on the poets or poems provided?
- Is there a table of contents? Subject index? First-line index? Are they helpful?

**Layout**—Review the layout of the book by considering questions such as the following:

- Are the poems arranged according to a particular theme?
- Are appropriate illustrations or visuals used to enhance and supplement the poetry?
- Are the poems and illustrations arranged in a suitable visual design?
- Is there a distinctive use of spacing, line breaks, and poem formatting?

**Appeal**—In matching poems and children appropriately, these questions might also help:

- Does the poet use poetic types and forms that are naturally appealing to young people and retain their attention?
- Are familiar childhood experiences or interesting topics presented in the poem?

- Does the poem extend and enrich a person's insight or knowledge?
- Will the poem's language be understood by the audience, yet expand their linguistic abilities?
- Does the poem stimulate the emotions and imagination of the intended audience?

The preceding questions can help us look critically at the poetry books we encounter. They can help us break down the process to look at a book's language, organization, layout, and appeal to children. But ultimately, some trial and error is involved, too. Perhaps more than any other genre, poetry knows no age level or bias. Although poems may appear short and simple on the surface, they may be deceptively complex. And although long narrative poems may seem off-putting to young readers, they can still be engaging when read aloud. So much depends on what we enjoy and how enthusiastically we share it. And the more poetry we know and the more ways we share it, the more likely we are to experience success. So, build the poetry collection, read regularly and widely, and expand your repertoire of poems for reading aloud and performing. That is the recipe for guiding children toward pleasure in poetry.

## Conclusion

It seems there is a renaissance in publishing poetry for young people, with more choices available than ever. Gone are the days of the three-hundred-page anthology presented in small print with no pictures. Poetry books today are short and focused, often richly illustrated. They are visually inviting, and they contain works by more new poets than ever before: poets of color, poets from around the world, and even children and young people publishing their own poetry. Look on your bookshelves. Are any of the foregoing kinds of poetry on your shelves? Are you surprised by how much poetry you may already be using? From now on you will be wearing "poetry-tinted" glasses and looking for poetry all around you.

As much as I enjoy the poetry of Shel Silverstein and Jack Prelutsky and appreciate how much they have done to make poetry popular with children, I think you can see why I feel it is so important to become familiar with many poets and seek out many different kinds of poetry. This variety is so much more meaningful—and bound to capture even more children. Just as with fiction, we need to seek out a range of realism, fantasy, history, mystery, and other genres to lure as many different readers as possible. The more variety we share, the more likely we are to reach more prospective poetry lovers.

As we expand the poetry holdings in our library collections, there are many different kinds of poetry books we can add. The usual categories apply, of course:

- general anthologies
- topical or thematic collections
- individual poet compilations
- single-poem picture books

But there are also many other kinds of poetry books that interest and delight children, from Mother Goose to verse novels. In addition, one can find poems on the Web, in magazines, and in audio formats to expand children's exposure to poetry. Finally, there are helpful guidelines and questions to ask as we assess the quality of the poetry books we encounter. Bottom line: the breadth of poetry available today makes it easier than ever to find poems that children will enjoy again and again.

*Poetry teaches us the power of a few words.*

—Ralph Waldo Emerson, writer

4

# How Do You Promote Poetry?

*Genuine poetry can communicate before it is understood.*
—T. S. Eliot, poet

OW DO WE PROMOTE POETRY EFFECTIVELY? IN THIS CHAP-
ter, we focus on what to do with poetry once you've found
it. We look at the physical place of poetry in the library, how
to feature poetry books in unique ways, how to use displays
and materials to promote poetry, and how to connect poetry
in a variety of formats through an array of preexisting activities. In addition, we consider how to connect poetry with other genres and
across the school curriculum.

## The Poetry Shelf

Think about what books you have in the children's and young adult area of your
library: fiction, a great and never-ending variety; nonfiction, about a multitude
of subjects; and poetry. These are the primary genres we recognize in literature.
We hope that children will experience all three as they evolve as readers, and we
recognize that each reader will have individual favorites. But how likely are children to discover the poetry books in your collection? Obviously, poetry will be a
smaller subset of the total library collection than fiction or nonfiction, but that
does not mean that it has to be tucked away on the lowest shelf in the farthest

( 105 )

region. Are the poetry books as easy to find as the fiction and nonfiction? Are they in a child-friendly location and easily reachable? Is the area well labeled and can it be quickly identified? Do poetry posters and book displays invite children to browse through poetry even if they are not immediately seeking it out? Are some poetry books displayed face out? Is there room on the poetry shelves for expansion? Are the poetry books on the shelf current? Are the poetry award winners represented and highlighted? Are there multiple copies of the most current and popular titles? If there is a separate area for teen or young adult poetry, is that also clearly accessible? If we are serious about helping children discover poetry and then return to it again and again, we need to make this gem of the library obvious, easily reachable, and even unavoidable.

## Creating a Poetry-Rich Environment

Creating an environment that values poetry depends partly on the physical arrangement of space and materials and partly on the emotional climate established by the library staff. Once the poetry books on the shelf are accessible and inviting, the next step is to create a space for sharing poems. Obviously, a designated area for storytime can serve for poetry sharing, too. But it can also be helpful to have a portable microphone for children who want to read aloud (children often read poetry with very soft voices, even when they are otherwise loud!), and projection equipment can be useful if you want to provide enlarged versions of poem texts so that children can participate in oral or choral reading and poem performance activities.

It can also be fun to involve kids in exploring the poetry environment by presenting a poetry scavenger hunt. Such an activity can be especially productive at the beginning of a year or to kick off a poetry study program. Create a simple grid or list of different kinds of poetry books you would like participants to discover—books beyond the ones they may readily know. Children can work individually or with a partner to locate specific poetry books and browse through them. You can even provide sticky notes that kids can use to mark poems to share, if they desire. This exercise will familiarize participants with the variety of poetry resources available and may lead them to further browsing and reading of poetry. A related activity is a poetry "treasure hunt" in which you challenge students to find poetry books that contain different poem elements, such as rhyme, alliteration, and the like.

**POETRY SCAVENGER HUNT**

Students can work in pairs or small groups to see who can find the most items first. Perhaps they'll want to share a newfound favorite poem, too.

- Find a book of rhyming poetry.
- Find a book containing nonrhyming poetry (free verse).
- Find a book of bilingual poetry.
- Find a book of concrete or shape poetry or haiku.
- Find a book of poetry published before 2000 (not Mother Goose).
- Find a collection of Mother Goose poetry.
- Find a poem picture book (containing a single poem).
- Find a book of poetry by an African American poet.
- Find a book of poetry by Jack Prelutsky or Shel Silverstein.
- Find a thematic collection of poetry (linked by subject, like Halloween poems).

**TREASURE HUNT FOR POEM PARTS**

Challenge kids to work with a poetry buddy to search for the following poetic parts in one single poetry book. By the end, they may also have found a fun poem to share, too.

- Find a line of poetry that mentions an animal or color.
- Find a line of poetry that mentions the name of a person or place.
- Find two lines of poetry that rhyme.
- Find three pairs of rhyming words.
- Find a line of poetry with alliteration (repeated first letter).
- Find a line of poetry that is four words long.
- Find a line of poetry that has ten syllables or more.
- Find the title (or page number) of the shortest poem in the collection.
- Find the title of the last poem in the collection.
- Find the first line of the first poem in the collection.

Source: Based on Sheree Fitch and Larry Swartz, *The Poetry Experience: Choosing and Using Poetry in the Classroom* (Markham, ON: Pembroke, 2008), 16.

Our own modeling is another essential ingredient in creating a poetry-priority environment. I am always tickled pink to learn how others choose to connect kids and poetry. One teacher in Maine has had lots of success infusing poetry throughout the school, including in the cafeteria, with a giant pickle jar full of poems that are randomly chosen for read-aloud breaks at lunchtime. Public librarians in my own city collaborated to launch a children's poetry festival. A school librarian in west Texas got a grant to host a poet (Pat Mora) for a week throughout her entire school district.

Have we found poetry that we enjoy and can recommend with genuine enthusiasm? Have we familiarized ourselves with some children's favorites so that we can promote those? Do we mention poetry choices when general subject requests come up? Do we always include poetry books on our recommended reading lists and bibliographies? Do we incorporate poems into our storytimes and read-alouds? Do we plan special events that focus exclusively on poetry? Wilson and Kutiper (1994, 278) reported that "one elementary school library media specialist noted an increase in poetry circulation after sharing a single poem with students each week as they entered the library." Once we have upgraded our own poetry knowledge, our enthusiastic endorsement can add spice to any literary opportunity. It becomes quite natural to think in terms of poetry when

**PRACTITIONER PERSPECTIVE**

*This school year, I decided to pair Mother Goose rhymes with picture books for my kindergarten lessons since I noticed that most students did not know the rhymes. It has been lots of fun! I've paired "Jack Be Nimble" with* Stop Drop and Roll *by Margery Cuyler during Fire Prevention Week. I've also paired "Hickory Dickory Dock" with* If You Take a Mouse to the Movies *and talked about how differently the two mice acted. I also have a flannelboard of* If You Take a Mouse to the Movies *with enough parts for each student to place on the board. It was very interactive and fun. I make sure to open and close each class period reciting the rhyme. I also give the students a small sheet with the rhyme on it to take home and practice reading with whoever will listen. Students look forward to it each week.*

Carol Kolenet, elementary school librarian
Dingman's Ferry, Pennsylvania

we plan activities, and fitting poems in here and there becomes second nature. And you may find yourself surprised that some children who never responded before open up when you open the door to poetry.

## Occasions to Celebrate Poetry

As we design an environment where enthusiasm for poetry will flourish, we should also consider what Georgia Heard calls poetry rituals. These include a variety of activities that occur on a regular basis, from the simple (monthly posting of poetry quotations) to the more elaborate (creating an annual digital film of children performing favorite poems.) Such activities become poetry traditions and provide a natural way to incorporate poetry into existing routines. They give children something to look forward to and in many cases provide opportunities for children to participate. As Brountas (1995, 42) has said, "Poetry is a lovely gift we give to children that appreciates in value and lasts throughout their lifetime." Below is a list of possible poetry rituals—think about choosing one to add to your current literary routine:

- Place a poster-sized poem (about books, libraries, or reading, for example) at the entrance to the children's area; rotate posters each month.
- Start and end each gathering with a poem. For example, always use the same poem to gather children together, but end each session with a different poem that connects with the story, lesson, or activity.
- Finish each day or week with a poem tied to current or historical events of the day or week. Share holiday poems from varied perspectives to celebrate special holidays.
- Invite children to perform their own poem readings on the last Friday of the month (or on another set day).
- Read aloud a personally relevant poem for each child's birthday (e.g., a birthday poem or a favorite of the birthday child). Invite families to donate a new poetry book in honor of the birthday child.
- Have a designated area (physical or virtual) to feature new poetry book acquisitions and to highlight kids' reviews of the books.
- Research poets' biographies and celebrate poets' birthdays by sharing some of their poems.

- Combine poems with food, sharing a poem about food while children enjoy a snack at lunch, snack time, Mother's Day tea, or open house. Choose poems from an e-book (such as *Poetry Tag Time*) and project the poem for all to see during the event or create a slide show of children's poems to project.
- If audio announcements are made on a regular basis, include the oral reading of a poem (by a child volunteer) either daily or weekly.
- If radio or cable television time is available, include a poem about books, reading, or libraries to begin or end a segment.

## CELEBRATING POETS' BIRTHDAYS

### January
2  Jean Little
5  Monica Gunning
6  Carl Sandburg
7  Minfong Ho
18 A. A. Milne
19 Pat Mora

### February
1  Langston Hughes
2  Judith Viorst
11 Jane Yolen
20 Kenn Nesbitt
21 Francisco X. Alarcón
26 Allan Wolf

### March
1  Alan Katz
4  Craig Crist-Evans
12 Naomi Shihab Nye
13 David Harrison
17 Lilian Moore; Ralph Fletcher
18 Douglas Florian
26 Robert Frost

### April
7  Alice Schertle
12 Gary Soto
13 Lee Bennett Hopkins
20 April Halprin Wayland
22 William Jay Smith
28 Barbara Juster Esbensen

### May
2  Bobbi Katz
5  J. Patrick Lewis
6  Kristine O'Connell George; José-Luis Orozco
8  Constance Levy
12 Edward Lear
17 Eloise Greenfield
25 Joyce Carol Thomas

### June
1  Bruce Lansky
7  Nikki Giovanni
8  Judy Sierra
16 Kalli Dakos
24 John Ciardi
26 Nancy Willard

If you are truly ambitious, try sharing a different poem each day of the year. There are a few resources available to assist with this gigantic effort, including older anthologies and some calendars and websites. But most of these rely, out of necessity, on classic poems in the public domain. If possible, seek out lively, contemporary poems that correspond with events and happenings of relevance to the children you serve. One excellent resource is Lee Bennett Hopkins's book *Days to Celebrate: A Full Year of Poetry, People, Holidays, History, Fascinating Facts, and More.*

## July

10 Rebecca Kai Dotlich;
   Patricia Hubbell
13 Anna Grossnickle Hines
16 Arnold Adoff
17 Karla Kuskin
19 Eve Merriam
27 Paul B. Janeczko

## August

12 Mary Ann Hoberman;
   Walter Dean Myers
15 Betsy Franco
17 Myra Cohn Livingston
19 Ogden Nash
21 X. J. Kennedy
29 Karen Hesse
31 Dennis Lee

## September

5 Paul Fleischman
8 Jack Prelutsky
9 Aileen Fisher
15 Sara Holbrook
25 Harry Behn; Shel Silverstein
30 Janet S. Wong

## October

3 Marilyn Singer
20 Nikki Grimes
27 Lillian Morrison
29 Valerie Worth
31 Joan Bransfield Graham

## November

13 Robert Louis Stevenson
15 David McCord
22 Brod Bagert

## December

1 Carol Diggory Shields
5 Christina Rossetti
10 Emily Dickinson
13 Georgia Heard
21 Susan Pearson
27 Juan Felipe Herrera

Source: Based on Lee Bennett Hopkins, *Pass the Poetry, Please!*, 3rd ed. (New York: HarperCollins, 1998), 225–27.

## National Poetry Month

Probably the biggest celebration of poetry occurs during April, now designated as National Poetry Month across the United States. There are a variety of ways to make poetry special in April. Do not wait until April, however, to share good poems with children. April is simply a good time to reach out to parents, families, caregivers, and the community at large to share what you have been discovering all year long: poetry is wonderful! Then consider how you want to participate in the next nationwide celebration of poetry. And for an autumn poetry occasion, consider celebrating Black Poetry Week every year during the third week of October. Showcase the work of classic African American poets such as Langston Hughes, Gwendolyn Brooks, Ashley Bryan, Nikki Giovanni, Eloise Greenfield, Nikki Grimes, Patricia McKissack, Carole Boston Weatherford, and Walter Dean Myers, or the emerging talents of Charles R. Smith Jr., Curtis Crisler, Hope Anita Smith, and Jaime Adoff.

Any of the poetry rituals suggested here could be initiated to celebrate National Poetry Month—if they are not already in place. But even more ambitious events are possible with a little bit of creativity and organization. Potato Hill Poetry, a wonderful web resource, suggests many unusual and innovative options at www.potatohill.com/npm.html. It is ideal if you can involve colleagues and kids in orchestrating these special celebrations.

### Ways to Celebrate National Poetry Month

- Start each day with a poem read aloud by a different guest reader: thirty poems for thirty days.
- Set up a coffeehouse-style poetry reading in your classroom or library. Don't forget the refreshments!
- Contact local banks and businesses to ask them to consider displaying student poetry on their walls.
- Write poems on postcards or letters and mail them to friends and neighbors.
- Contact radio stations about hosting a live, on-air poetry reading at the school, the library, or the radio station.
- Record a poem on your answering machine at home or school or as a cell phone message.

- Make a National Poetry Month time capsule. Students can submit favorite poems or their own original writing. Put the works in the time capsule and seal it ceremoniously, not to be opened until National Poetry Month next year.
- Send a poem to your state or local representative or other government official.
- Make National Poetry Month buttons. Inscribe them with haiku, short poems, or favorite lines of poetry. Wear the buttons the whole month of April.
- Become pen pals with another classroom or student group, locally or nationally, and pass favorite and original poems back and forth throughout the month. Make a book of your correspondence.
- Plan a poetry reading for a senior center, hospital, or local business.
- Experiment with developing a poetry blog or other web resource where students can share favorite poems or respond to posted poems.

## Poetry Displays

We all know that a good visual display generates interest in library materials. When was the last time that poetry for children was the priority in your display? Highlighting new poetry books, low-circulating poetry-book gems, books by featured poets, or children's favorite poetry books will make poetry for children more visible in the library. You can use traditional shelf, tabletop, and show-case book displays or other creative approaches, physical and virtual. Poet Janet Wong talks fondly of her poetry suitcase filled with objects that correlate with some of her poems. These physical objects (a shoe, a pomegranate) can easily be displayed to add interest to the corresponding poems. Favorite poems can be made into poem posters (please follow fair-use practice) and displayed on doors, in hallways, at entrances, and elsewhere. One enterprising teacher displays poems on the wall over the pencil sharpener or the water fountain, where children often have to stand and wait (and can read idly). Poet Georgia Heard encourages children in the schools to create a living anthology. She says, "Instead of collecting poems we love and putting them in a book, we'll make an anthology out of the walls and spaces around the school. It will be our jobs to make sure poetry is all around the building so that other students and teachers can have a chance to read some poetry" (1999, 23). This is very similar to the initiative launched by the Poetry Society of America, the Poetry in Motion project, which put poems in public transportation systems around the country. Sit on the subway in New York and you are likely to find poems and poem excerpts to read among all the ads and graffiti.

New or favorite poems can also be displayed via mobiles and other three-dimensional displays. One librarian created a "poet tree" by using rolled-up brown paper to create the tree trunk and branches and inviting children to write their favorite poems on green paper cut into leaf shapes that were then attached to the tree limbs—the more leaves and poems, the better. If you have access to a hallway, you might consider creating a "hall of poets" that features children's favorite or own original poems, the writing of local poets, the work of favorite or featured poets, or a combination of these. If you want to go the extra mile, create simple mats to go around each poem or frame them in inexpensive picture frames for added impact. And if you want a poetry mascot, consider using Danitra Brown (in the poetry of Nikki Grimes) or Everett Anderson (in the poem picture books of Lucille Clifton) or Fearless Fernie (in the poetry of Gary Soto). These characters appear in multiple poetry collections and thus suggest a variety of themes to explore. Other distinctive personalities emerge from children's poetry as well, such as Mother Goose characters, Anna Banana or Miss Mary Mack, the Owl and the Pussycat, and Casey (at the bat).

Finally, if you have access to a school or library blog, website, or Facebook page, consider adding a poetry presence to that display. Poetry quotations can easily be featured on a rotating basis. If more space is available, showcase children's original poems (with their permission), information about new poetry book acquisitions, lists of children's favorite poems or poetry books, or a featured poet of local or national stature. Once again, children themselves can assist you with taking your poetry display efforts online. They often have very creative ideas and the technology skills to translate them into reality!

## Poetry Promotion Materials

Along with creating displays, we know that promotional materials are helpful in communicating with patrons of all ages. We regularly produce or purchase timely bookmarks, booklists, book giveaways, and other materials. How often have we considered featuring poetry in those promotional efforts? Ready-made, commer-

## POEMS ABOUT LIBRARIES

To celebrate National Library Week or use as an open invitation to the library at any time, you can share, read, or display any of the following poems about libraries:

Kalli Dakos, "When the Librarian Reads to Us," in *Put Your Eyes Up Here and Other School Poems*

Kristine O'Connell George, "School Librarian," in *Swimming Upstream: Middle School Poems*

Eloise Greenfield, "At the Library," from *The Friendly Four*

Nikki Grimes, "At the Library," in *It's Raining Laughter*, and "42nd Street Library," from *Jazmin's Notebook*

Monica Gunning, "The Library," from *America, My New Home*

J. Patrick Lewis, "Necessary Gardens," in *Please Bury Me in the Library*; "#174 The Librarian," "#116 Library Fine," and "#89 New York Public Library," from *Countdown to Summer: A Poem for Every Day of the School Year*; and "Librarian," from *The Underwear Salesman and Other Jobs for Better or Verse*

Beverly McLoughland, "Surprise," in *Good Books, Good Times!*, compiled by Lee Bennett Hopkins

Jane Medina, "The Library Card," in *My Name Is Jorge on Both Sides of the River: Poems*

Eve Merriam, "Reach for a Book," in *Book Poems: Poems from National Children's Book Week, 1959–1998*, edited by Mary Perrotta Rich

Naomi Shihab Nye, "Because of Libraries We Can Say These Things," in *Fuel*; and "The List," from *A Maze Me: Poems for Girls*

Jack Prelutsky, "It's Library Time," from *What a Day It Was at School!*

Shel Silverstein, "Overdues," from *A Light in the Attic*

Gary Soto, "Ode to My Library," in *Neighborhood Odes*

Valerie Worth, "Library," in *All the Small Poems and Fourteen More*

Tracie Vaughn Zimmer, "Librarian," from *Steady Hands: Poems about Work* cially produced poetry bookmarks, posters, and the like are available for purchase from multiple sources, including ALA, DEMCO, and Upstart. But many libraries like to create their own innovative and current materials. Of course, that is a wonderful idea and enables one to target a specific audience in more meaningful ways.

One warning, however: copyright laws regarding reprinting of poems are very strict. It is not legal to reproduce a published poem for mass distribution without obtaining permission from the publishing company and the poet (and often paying permission fees). Although this can be frustrating, we need to remember how few poetry books are published each year and thus how little poets earn in contrast with the J. K. Rowlings in the field of literature. It is acceptable to cite poem titles, poets' names, poetry-book titles, poetry website URLs, and the like. Unless poems are in the public domain, however, we are not being poetry advocates if we reproduce them without permission. Poems are in the public domain if seventy-five years have passed since the poet's death, assuming that the poet is the copyright holder. If this is the case, you can use the poem in any way you choose. That is why the classic poems are so often used and reused. Otherwise, I recommend contacting the publisher of the poems you intend to use and asking for permission to feature the poems in your promotional efforts. If your purpose is short-term and nonprofit, you can often get permission. If you do, be sure to include the appropriate credit line in your print materials. If you do not, please respect that poet's right to safeguard her or his artistic creation. Other alternatives are to create your own original verse, to use quotes or slogans, and to recruit local poets to write for you (they still deserve compensation but are usually less expensive or willing to volunteer their poems), or invite children to share their original work (and secure permission from them and their families). Developing original poetry promotion materials can be challenging, but if we focus on getting patrons to "think poetry" as a first step, then we can lead them to the actual poems and poetry books on the library shelves.

## When to Share Poetry

Too often, poems are tacked on as an afterthought. We share them occasionally because we think we should. Sometimes we don't even have time to get to poetry. But poetry should be infused throughout our interactions with children. One teacher, Tonya Rodriguez, tried a project that she called Three Minutes a Day Can Make a Difference. It was her contention that she could share a poem

## TEN TIPS FOR PRESENTING POETRY TO YOUNG PEOPLE

1. Be yourself. You needn't and shouldn't show reverence for poetry by means of an artificially dignified atmosphere.

2. Energy is the key—but it shouldn't be forced. It can be quiet energy.

3. A brisk pace is good and energizing, as long as you're willing to be flexible and slow down when the situation needs it.

4. In some ways, you can be less "in charge." Much of the learning in poetry comes from the inside out. Decide thoughtfully what you're going to do, then go for it. Relax and have fun. Freely intersperse humor and seriousness.

5. It's probably best not to push your beliefs about the beauties of poetry but to let them emerge through examples and practice.

6. Don't overexplain and do avoid abstractions.

7. Read poetry aloud with energy, expressiveness, and rhythm (this can be the variable rhythm of everyday speech). For example, read or tell the Greek myths as if they happened this morning.

8. Make a conscious choice as to whether to read with pauses at the ends of lines (which tends to emphasize the breath, the connection of poetry to the body) or not (which can emphasize the flow of sound and ideas).

9. It's helpful to admit your own errors, blank-outs, and ignorance. This helps create openness and acceptance.

10. Be open to children's visions—they really have them.

Source: Based on Jack Collom and Sheryl Noethe, *Poetry Everywhere: Teaching Poetry Writing in School and in the Community* (New York: Teachers and Writers Collaborative, 2005), 5–7.

effectively and even invite the children to participate or respond to it in just three minutes. So for about a month, she took three minutes a day to do just that. Within a week, children were reminding her when she had forgotten their three-minute poetry break. By the end of the month, they were asking to hear favorite poems over again. Three minutes a day had made a difference. It had shown these students that poetry is enjoyable, even memorable.

Caroline Feller Bauer takes a similar approach with her book *The Poetry Break* (1995). She proposes a wandering poetry presenter who drops in to share a poem with classes throughout the school throughout the day. Her book is an excellent resource for creative ways to present poetry. The poetry break is an outstanding way to infuse poems throughout a school or library program. Whether a poem is used for beginning the day, starting off the hour, making the transition to lunch or a break, or wrapping things up, the idea of breaking for poetry is very practical since it can be accomplished in just a few minutes. Of course, that does not mean that a more in-depth study of poetry is not a good idea. It is. But for the average teacher, librarian, day-care provider, or parent, sharing a three-minute poem break is a good way to begin.

Poetry sharing should probably begin with an intentional plan to incorporate one new strategy into your existing routine. However, once you experience success—and children's enthusiastic responses—you will begin to look for other ways to include poetry, perhaps via poetry rituals or celebrations, or just by being ready for serendipity and the teachable moment. The more poetry you know, the more poetry you try with kids, and the more poetry kids encounter, the more opportunities will present themselves.

## Maximizing Alternative Media

As we consider various ways to present and promote poetry, it can be helpful to consider alternative media as well. Adding variety to our presentation methods provides a leaven that both adults and children enjoy. In particular, remember that many poems are available in audio form, often read by the poet her- or himself. That is a powerful experience and worth sharing. Many examples of poetry in audio form, in magazines, and on the Web are detailed in chapter 3.

If you're looking for fresh ways to approach poetry with young people, you might consider multimedia methods for experiencing the visual and aural qualities of poetry. Using popular Internet sites, CDs, digital tools, and a variety of software, you can lead kids in exploring the imagery, emotion, and language of poetry in ways that are creative, playful, and multisensory. For example, websites like SoundCloud (http://soundcloud.com) make it easier than ever to record and upload "homemade" audio yourself.

Look to the Internet for many examples of poetry in various visual formats. You can find video vignettes of young people reading poetry aloud, including their own original poetry, as well as teachers presenting a variety of poetry lessons. There are class projects on Shel Silverstein's life or poetry, and a "Poem PowerPoint" of Naomi Shihab Nye's poetry, just to name a few. In some cases, kids create unique avatars or alternative personas to share their responses to poetry, complete with rap soundtrack. Nearly everyone enjoys searching YouTube for fun, but it can also be a great site for poetry resources. The site A Poem from Us (http://apoemfromus.com) offers anyone the opportunity to share a video of him- or herself reading a poem and even makes the poems accessible through a custom QR code.

Another trend is the video booktalk or digital book trailer. A few poetry examples include *Chess Rumble*, by G. Neri and Jesse Joshua Watson; *The Death of Jayson Porter*, by Jaime Adoff; and *Girl Coming in for a Landing*, by April Halprin Wayland. Some are created by the poet, some by the publisher, and some by fans—a project possibility for kids, teachers, and librarians. You can also find live action and animated, amateur adult- and student-created video interpretations of poems such as "Today Is Very Boring" and "Homework, Oh Homework" by Jack Prelutsky or "Crocodile's Toothache" and "Whatif" by Shel Silverstein. Some video poems use the audio track of the poet's reading, and others use the voices of children performing the poem. The whole series "Billy Collins Animated Poetry" offers creative interpretations of Collins's poetry, which, in turn, prompted video responses from fans—also posted for the public.

Now teachers and librarians can promote books and poetry reading by creating "homemade" book trailers. Author Pamela Lowell shared her "Five Easy Steps to Making a Great Book Trailer" in *VOYA* (February 2010), including (1) study examples, (2) tell a story, (3) use royalty-free images and music, (4) choose the right movie-making tool, and (5) preview and launch. Sample other book trailers at sites such as YouTube, Watch the Book (www.watchthebook.com), Book Trailers (http://booktrailers.ning.com), Book Trailers for All (http://book trailersforall.com), or Book Trailers (www.book-trailers.net). The variety is tremendous, but most are very short (one minute long) and incorporate book covers and bibliographic information, especially the book's title and author's name, as well as images, music, sound effects, and voice-over commentary.

Easy-to-use movie-making software includes Windows Movie Maker (for PCs), iMovie (for Macs), and Animoto (http://animoto.com), for example. Free images can be found at Flickr (www.flickr.com), FreeFoto.com, and Creative Commons (http://creativecommons.org), and music selections and sound effects are available at Partners in Rhyme (www.partnersinrhyme.com), Brainy Betty (www.brainybetty.com), and Open Music Archive (www.openmusicarchive.org). Those are the basics.

But what I find especially interesting is the application of this new approach to the promotion of poetry, in particular. Brevity, imagery, musicality, voice—these are all powerful characteristics that poetry offers in abundance. A well-made trailer can serve to capitalize on these qualities and can become almost poetic itself with the artful combining of words, images, and sound. We can create these for high-tech booktalking to motivate reading of poetry, or students can

**PRACTITIONER PERSPECTIVE**

*When I taught sixth-grade English, we did the required kinds of poetry and the lessons we were supposed to do, but then we decided to do something fun. I told the students that we were going to transform the room into a 1950s beatnik coffeehouse. They looked at me as if I had three heads, so I showed them a clip from the movie* Funny Face, *with Fred Astaire and Audrey Hepburn, and they were fascinated. The kids wrote their own poetry—any kind they wanted, on any subject they wanted. They brought pillows from home, and we all dressed in black. My student teacher and I brought hot chocolate (in place of coffee) and cups. We got a spotlight from the Drama Department, moved all the furniture next to the walls, and turned out the lights. I put a stool at the front of the room and announced that the kids could volunteer or not. When someone got up to recite, we snapped our fingers and said, "Oh, yeah, baby, I feel your vibes!" and "Go, man, go!" and turned the spotlight on them. We drummed on the floor and clicked for applause as we exclaimed, "Oh, that is so deep, man!" The readers laughed at us, and we laughed with them. Eventually, everybody participated. Someone on my team got the principal to come down to the room, and she thought it was a blast. The kids had a great time, learned a little cultural history, wrote some very nice poetry, and ended up thinking poetry was fun!*

Bonnie Boyd McCormick, librarian
Crownover Middle School, Denton, Texas

create their own trailers as responses to their favorite poetry books—which will, in turn, inspire other kids to want to read those books. (This is also an excellent vehicle for reinforcing copyright awareness in selecting text, images, sounds, and music.) Poetry books are the perfect source material for digital video treatment because they are particularly evocative in their use of images, language, and even sound.

## Conducting Spoken-Word Events

In "Poetry at the Crossroads of America," Sam White wrote about his experiences while standing on the sidewalk in front of the MTV studios at Broadway and Forty-Fifth Street in New York City and reading ten of his favorite poems to passersby: "I suspected reading a poem in Times Square would be like throwing an ice cube into a forest fire. I didn't know what place poetry—to my mind the quietest art form—would have." But it worked. People stopped. People listened. People doubled back to get a copy of the homemade anthology White had created. He says:

> I believe they stopped at first because these are odd words to hear seemingly out of nowhere, but they took an anthology or stayed to hear the poem read because it's poetry . . . and it made them feel human. Stopping in the middle of the busiest intersection in the country to listen to a poem is a radical act in a hyperactive age. . . . You need only slow and listen. (www.pw.org/mag/0301/newswhite.htm)

This is an impressive example of the power of the spoken word as an art form. It is an experience children of all ages respond to—the immediacy of storytelling along with the music of language. For most children ages five to twelve, however, it is not generally a performance experience they initiate, at least as soloists. In chapter 5, we present a variety of techniques for involving children in spoken-word performance, but we take a gentle approach that asks kids to participate in groups of various sizes. It usually requires a bit of maturity, confidence, and experience to prepare poetry for formal, public performance, although there are amazing exceptions, of course. Spoken-word events, poetry slams, open-mic readings, and the like usually target an adult or young adult audience.

For elementary school children, I prefer to emphasize choral reading, reader's theater, poetry jams, poetry café readings, puppets and poetry, and so on, à la Sara Holbrook's approach in *Wham! It's a Poetry Jam: Discovering Performance Poetry* (2011). Such spoken-word events allow children to participate with the support of a partner or group and help them gain confidence as they share poetry with an audience. For example, try a "Poetry Tag" poetry jam and invite one volunteer to choose a favorite poem to share. Then another child can choose a word or image from the first poem and find another poem connected to that topic or word or image to share. Other children continue the connection with additional poems. For example, Rose Rauter's "Peach" might connect to Constance Levy's "Moon Peach" or Eve Merriam's "Sunset" with one poem connected to the next. This creates a synergy of poetry sharing that is fast paced and inviting. Children look at poems in more open-ended ways, seeking connections and ready to share them in an almost gamelike fashion. For examples look at my "Everyday Poetry" column in *Book Links* (Vardell 2011) or the PoetryTagTime e-books of poetry I compiled with Janet Wong, featuring many of the best poets writing today in a chain of connected poems, including *PoetryTagTime* and *P\*TAG*. Each poet explains the connection and the inspiration for her or his poem.

Invite guests to read poetry aloud, particularly professional actors in your area who can offer a polished delivery of poetry and/or bilingual members of your community who can read poems both in English and in other languages. For younger children, try using puppets to share poems aloud. One children's librarian enjoys creating her own finger puppets out of felt to use with the poem "My Shadow," by Robert Louis Stevenson, for example. She made a person-shaped finger puppet using a die cut and felt and then made an identical black one to represent the shadow. The kindergarteners found it fascinating. Another librarian involved all the sixth graders on her campus in conducting a Poet's Day as a culminating activity for their unit on poetry. Each student selected a favorite poem and then researched the poet. Each decided how to perform his or her poem, whether to memorize the poem, whether to use props, and so forth. On the actual day, the kids were scattered all over the building. They stood frozen until touched and then performed their poems and shared some quick biographical information about the poets. The rest of the school loved hearing the poems that the sixth graders performed.

Another teacher formed a poetry troupe and worked with volunteers to perform their favorite poems at school and library events (such as open houses and parent-teacher association meetings). And one other colleague allowed her older students to select some of their favorite poems to perform for younger students. They chose to come in costumes and use props. Some worked in pairs; all were successful. And with older students, verse novels can often be adapted for reader's theater performance, with excerpts being shared by multiple voices reading different parts. See chapter 3 for examples of verse novels appropriate for nine- to twelve-year-olds.

All children should have the opportunity to enjoy poetry as an event, to see the power of spoken-word performance. Volunteers who are eager for the limelight can even work with a coach or mentor to prepare readings and performances for a public audience. We should support their efforts, suggest creative alternatives, provide comfortable venues for practice, and never pressure children who prefer to follow rather than lead.

**POET PROFILE**

## In His Own Words

### LEE BENNETT HOPKINS

The main reason I compile theme-oriented collections of poetry such as Marvelous Math is because I am an elementary school teacher. I compile the kinds of poetry books I wish I had had while I was teaching. And why not combine poetry with mathematics? Why not combine poetry with every area of the curriculum? My philosophy is that poetry must be shared every day in every way possible.

Sometimes the subject I am working on sparks me to write a verse of my own, one that I might never have thought about doing before.

I love the sky, particularly at night. Wherever I am I look out the window at the sky's vastness, its mystery, thinking how the moon and stars are above me yet also above people miles and miles away.

The sky and math seem to go together. Taking terms like *decimal points, fractions, percentages, multiply,* and *finite* seemed a natural link to create a metaphor between mathematics and the wonders of sky. The sky is indeed "mathematic filled," isn't it?

Find time to share poetry with children. Enhance storytimes by combining a poem with a picture book. For example, when sharing a classic such as *The Snowy Day*, by Ezra Jack Keats, finish the session with Gwendolyn Brooks's "Cynthia in the Snow," from her must-have volume *Bronzeville Boys and Girls*. Within a few minutes children will hear the text of a Caldecott Award–winning volume and also hear words by a Pulitzer Prize–winning poet.

Give children poetry. It is one of the best gifts you can give them—a gift to last a lifetime.

## Sky
*by Lee Bennett Hopkins*

Decimal point
meteors
streak
through the night—

Fractions
of moonbeams
gleam
white-bright—

Percentages
of stars
seem
to multiply—

in the finite
dramatic
mathematic-filled
sky.

"Sky," by Lee Bennett Hopkins, copyright © 1997 by Lee Bennett Hopkins, from *Marvelous Math: A Book of Poems*, published by Simon and Schuster, 1997, is used by permission of Curtis Brown, Ltd.

**CLASS EXERCISE** After reading "Sky" out loud once, turn out the lights and invite the children to read it with you by flashlight in four groups, one group per stanza.

## Featuring the Poets

A final feature of an environment that encourages a love of poetry is the celebration and study of the poets themselves. From featuring a poet of the month to hosting a visiting poet, there are many ways to showcase the people behind the poems we love. Highlighting a variety of poets on a rotating basis will provide more depth of exposure to their poems and poetry writing. Start with the award-winning poets and other contemporary poets whose works children enjoy (see chapter 2). And look for poets who may live and work in your immediate vicinity.

Collect the poet's works and make them available. Create a bulletin board, poster, or display featuring the poet. Include a photo, a printout of his or her website home page, and a few fun facts about his or her life. Read the poet's works aloud often. Look up biographical information about the poet and share it with children. Look for poet-related autobiographies, video and audio interviews, and websites to share. Investigate setting up an online chat with or even a guest appearance by a poet. Be sure to prepare the children beforehand with extensive reading. If funds allow, see about setting up a poet-in-residence program, inviting a poet to work with children on an ongoing basis for a short period of time.

You will also find speeches and readings by and interviews with poets such as Billy Collins, Pat Mora, Nikki Grimes, and Naomi Shihab Nye—and an *American Idol*–style introduction of J. Patrick Lewis—on YouTube. Some poets even feature video clips on their personal websites. Michael Rosen, for example, has forty-nine videos of himself reciting poems from an out-of-print book. Renée M. LaTulippe's website, No Water River (www.nowaterriver.com), offers video

## BLOGS ABOUT POETRY FOR YOUNG PEOPLE

There are a surprising number of blogs that feature poetry for young people on a regular basis offering timely, chatty, and varied information with several blogs written by the poets themselves. In addition, many bloggers participate in the regular "Poetry Friday" celebration in the "kidlitosphere," posting a poem or poetry-related items on Fridays. Here are some of the best blogs that consistently feature poetry for children and young adults:

*Alphabet Soup,* by Jama Rattigan, http://jamarattigan.livejournal.com

*Bookjoy,* by Pat Mora, http://sharebookjoy.blogspot.com

*Chicken Spaghetti,* by Susan Thomsen, www.chickenspaghetti.typepad.com

David L. Harrison's blog, http://davidlharrison.wordpress.com

*The Drift Record,* by Julie Larios, http://julielarios.blogspot.com

*Father Goose,* by Charles Ghigna, http://charlesghigna.blogspot.com

*Florian Café,* by Douglas Florian, http://floriancafe.blogspot.com

*GottaBook,* by Greg Pincus, http://gottabook.blogspot.com

*The Miss Rumphius Effect,* by Tricia Stohr-Hunt, http://missrumphius
effect.blogspot.com

clips of children's poets reading from their work along with extensive teaching connections. Some poets are open to participating in virtual visits via online chatting or webcams, too.

We often feature popular fiction writers with displays and booktalks in our daily work. But have we considered giving poets this same publicity? Creating time and space for featured poets helps introduce their work and encourage children to read more poetry. In addition, it can be inspiring for your would-be poets to see that there are successful adults who have made poetry writing their career.

## Pairing Poetry

One way to begin incorporating poetry is to inject poems into the genres and disciplines that are already a part of your schedule. If you regularly read a picture book out loud, try following up with a poem that has a similar subject or

*Nikki Sounds Off,* by Nikki Grimes, www.nikkigrimes.com/blog

*The Poem Farm,* by Amy Ludwig VanDerwater, http://poemfarm.blogspot.com

*Poetry for Children,* by Sylvia Vardell, www.poetryforchildren.blogspot.com

*Poetry at Play,* by Poetry Advocates for Children and YA, http://poetryat play.org

*Polkabats and Octopus Slacks,* by Calef Brown, http://polkabats.blogspot.com

*Read Write Believe,* by Sara Lewis Holmes, www.saralewisholmes.blogspot.com

*Wild Rose Reader,* by Elaine Magliaro, http://wildrosereader.blogspot.com

*Wordswimmer,* by Bruce Black, http://wordswimmer.blogspot.com

*Writing and Ruminating,* by Kelly Fineman, http://kellyrfineman.livejournal .com

*Writing the World for Kids,* by Laura Purdie Salas, http://laurasalas.livejournal .com

*A Wrung Sponge,* by Andromeda Jazmon, http://awrungsponge.blogspot.com

*A Year of Reading,* by Franki Sibberson and Mary Lee Hahn, http://reading year.blogspot.com

theme. If you enjoy reading aloud excerpts or installments of novels, try sharing a related poem to set the stage. If you regularly field questions about classic poems, suggest contemporary poems as bridges to understanding the older works. If you regularly provide support for science or social studies units, try connecting thematic poetry collections with those topics. No matter what we are already doing, poetry can help supplement, support, and enrich it.

Start with a story or book you share often and look for a matching poem. But do not be surprised if you start to work in the opposite direction, falling in love with a poem and seeking out a novel or picture book to pair it with. For example, share Judith Viorst's now-classic picture book *Alexander and the Terrible, Horrible, No Good, Very Bad Day* and follow it with Karla Kuskin's poem listing the same kind of bad-day woes, "I Woke Up This Morning," in *Moon, Have You Met My Mother? The Collected Poems of Karla Kuskin.* If you introduce novels to

## SUGGESTED PAIRINGS OF FICTION AND POEMS

| Novel | Poem |
| --- | --- |
| Lane Smith, *Grandpa Green* | Nikki Grimes, "Duet," in *Stepping Out with Grandma Mac* |
| Brian Selznick, *The Invention of Hugo Cabret* | Amy Ludwig VanDerwater, "Two Puzzling," in *Incredible Inventions*, edited by Lee Bennett Hopkins |
| Maurice Sendak, *Where the Wild Things Are* | Douglas Florian, "A Monster's Day," in *Monster Motel* |
| Kevin Henkes, *Kitten's First Full Moon* | Karla Kuskin, "Moon, Have You Met My Mother?" in *Moon, Have You Met My Mother? The Collected Poems of Karla Kuskin* |
| Judith Viorst, *Alexander and the Terrible, Horrible, No Good, Very Bad Day* | Karla Kuskin, "I Woke Up This Morning," in *Moon, Have You Met My Mother? The Collected Poems of Karla Kuskin* |
| Judy Blume, *Superfudge* | Judith Viorst, "I Love Love Love My Brand-New Baby Sister," in *Sad Underwear and Other Complications: More Poems for Children and Their Parents* |
| Christopher Paul Curtis, *Bud, Not Buddy* | Sara Holbrook, "Blueprints?" in *Am I Naturally This Crazy?* |
| Lois Lowry, *Number the Stars* | "Birdsong," in *I Never Saw Another Butterfly: Children's Drawings and Poems from Terezin Concentration Camp, 1942–1944*, edited by Hana Volavkova |
| Linda Sue Park, *A Single Shard* | Langston Hughes, "Dreams," in *The Dreamkeeper and Other Poems* |
| Louis Sachar, *Holes* | Eloise Greenfield, "Education," in *Nathaniel Talking* |

young readers in booktalks or through reading aloud in installments, consider sharing a poem to whet their appetites for the story that follows. For example, Langston Hughes's famous poem "Dreams" can help introduce Linda Sue Park's Newbery Award–winning *A Single Shard,* and Eloise Greenfield's poem "Education," from *Nathaniel Talking,* can set the stage for Louis Sachar's Newbery Award–winning book *Holes.* And, of course, there are many different ways to match a poem with a work of fiction. You may choose a poem that is similar in subject or suggests the same emotions or feelings. And once you make such connections, do not be surprised if children come to you with poems they feel match stories they are reading or books you are sharing. Making connections can be contagious.

Pairing one poem with another can also be an enjoyable activity. In fact, once you find two poems that seem similar, you will often find yourself hunting for more and more and more similar poems, until you build your own topical collection. Of course, any two poems on the same subject can be matched, compared, and discussed. And poems can be about the same topic but reflect very different points of view, style, or tone. For example, one might be humorous and the other serious. Or you can select two poems that are similar in form—two ballads or two haiku—and talk about the choices each poet made in creating her or his poem just that way. You do not have to be an English teacher with a master's degree to guide this experience. When you share poems on a regular basis and are open to children's individual comments and responses, you may be surprised at what kids notice. Their spontaneous observations are the first steps in literary analysis. They may not always notice what you notice or what you think they should notice, but they notice plenty and will share that with you, if you are receptive.

As you experiment with pairing poems, it can be helpful to have a handy list of contemporary poems that parallel some of the classic poems kids may encounter in school or in more formal poetry experiences. Sometimes a contemporary poem can offer a bridge to understanding an older, classic poem. Or for students who are already familiar with the classic poems, pairing those poems with contemporary poems can provide a basis for comparison and discussion. Encourage children who particularly enjoy this exercise to seek additional poems to pair with classics and to share them. It may also be worthwhile to collaborate

## SUGGESTED PAIRINGS OF CLASSIC POEMS
## AND CONTEMPORARY POEMS

| Classic Poem | Contemporary Poem |
| --- | --- |
| William Blake, "The Tyger" | Clare Bevan, "Tell Me, Tiger," in *All the Wild Wonders: Poems of Our Earth*, edited by Wendy Cooling |
| Robert Frost, "Stopping by Woods" | Douglas Florian, "Winter Night," in *Winter Eyes* |
| Langston Hughes, "Dreams" | Chanelle Douville, "Still I Dream," in *Walking on Earth and Touching the Sky: Poetry and Prose by Lakota Youth at Red Cloud Indian School*, edited by Timothy McLaughlin |
| Henry Wadsworth Longfellow, "Paul Revere's Ride" | Bobbi Katz, "A Conversation on the Edge of War," in *We the People* |
| Edna St. Vincent Millay, "Afternoon on a Hill" | Felice Holman, "Who Am I?" in *The Tree That Time Built: A Celebration of Nature, Science, and Imagination*, edited by Mary Ann Hoberman and Linda Winston |
| Ogden Nash, "The Tale of Custard the Dragon" | Shel Silverstein, "Sarah Cynthia Sylvia Stout Would Not Take the Garbage Out," in *Where the Sidewalk Ends* |
| Laura E. Richards, "Eletelephony" | Calef Brown, "Kansas City Octopus," in *Polkabats and Octopus Slacks* |
| Carl Sandburg, "Fog" | Valerie Worth, "Frost," in *All the Small Poems and Fourteen More* |
| Robert Louis Stevenson, "My Shadow" | Joan Bransfield Graham, "Light," in *Flicker Flash* |
| Ernest Thayer, "Casey at the Bat" | Charles R. Smith Jr., "The Amazing Jason Williams," in *Hoop Kings* |

with young adult librarians or high school teachers, who may use classic poetry more often.

Pairing nonfiction and poetry may seem to be an unlikely partnership at first, but these two different genres can complement each other by showing children how writers approach the same topic in very different and distinctive ways. In addition, children will see that they can learn a lot of information from both a poem and a work of nonfiction. Poetry has an advantage over nonfiction in that it typically consists of many fewer words. Poems can be read and reread in very little time. Each rereading can be approached in a slightly different way; for example, through choral reading or poetry performance. Poems can also serve to initiate a topic or to enrich and extend it. Their length is less intimidating to children who may be overwhelmed by longer prose and streams of new vocabulary. Although poetry may also present new words and concepts, its shorter appearance provides a motivating advantage. Poems and nonfiction books can be linked by topic to provide multiple perspectives on the same topic. Look for poetry anthologies organized by subject matter when possible, since they help make the content connection obvious (full publication information for the suggested books that follow can be found in appendix C).

**PRACTITIONER PERSPECTIVE**

*My daughters at four and five years old lost their great-grandfather, with whom they had blown and caught bubbles while listening to him recite poetry to them. They wanted to relate to him even though he had died, so I suggested they write their favorite poem that he had recited to them. We placed each poem in a helium balloon and they released them after the funeral. That was the beginning of their balloon-poem ritual. At five other funerals they have continued this ritual for other great-grandparents, then for holidays, and just because. I helped them construct the words at ages four and five, but now I watch them work for days to create their perfect poem with the ideal message. They share these poems before releasing only if they desire. Now, in high school, they think nothing of releasing poems and feel that they have done this all of their lives. This has been a ritual that has allowed them to express their inner feelings, reflect, make a connection, and be comforted.*

Karen McKenzie, science lead teacher
Chapel Hill Academy, Fort Worth, Texas

## SUGGESTED PAIRINGS OF NONFICTION BOOKS AND TOPICAL POEM COLLECTIONS

| Nonfiction Book | Topical Poem Collection |
| --- | --- |
| Melissa Sweet, *Balloons over Broadway: The True Story of the Puppeteer of Macy's Parade* | Jack Prelutsky, *It's Thanksgiving!* (Thanksgiving) |
| Kadir Nelson, *Heart and Soul* | Patricia McKissack, *Never Forgotten* (African American history) |
| Susan Campbell Bartoletti, *Hitler Youth: Growing Up in Hitler's Shadow* | Debbie Levy, *The Year of Goodbyes: A True Story of Friendship, Family, and Farewells* (Holocaust) |
| Steve Jenkins, *Actual Size* | Valerie Worth, *Animal Poems* (illustrated by Steve Jenkins) (animals) |
| Peter Sis, *The Tree of Life: Charles Darwin* | Mary Ann Hoberman and Linda Winston, eds., *The Tree That Time Built: A Celebration of Nature, Science, and Imagination* (evolution) |
| Sy Montgomery, *The Tarantula Scientist* | Lee Bennett Hopkins, ed., *Spectacular Science: A Book of Poems* (science) |
| Tanya Lee Stone, *Almost Astronauts: 13 Women Who Dared to Dream* | J. Patrick Lewis, *Vherses: A Celebration of Outstanding Women* (women) |
| Caitlin O'Connell and Donna M. Jackson, *The Elephant Scientist* | Tracie Vaughn Zimmer, *Cousins of Clouds: Elephant Poems* (elephants) |
| Brian Floca, *Moonshot: The Flight of Apollo 11* | Amy Sklansky, *Out of This World: Poems and Facts about Space* (space) |
| James M. Deem, *Bodies from the Ice: Melting Glaciers and the Recovery of the Past* | Jane Yolen, *Once upon Ice and Other Frozen Poems* (ice) |

Poetry's brevity, conceptual focus, and rich vocabulary make it a natural teaching tool for connecting with nonfiction. Like nonfiction, poetry can be informative as well as inspiring. Several additional advantages come with using poetry across the curriculum:

- Poetry is accessible to a wide range of reading abilities.
- The brief format of much poetry taps the essence of a subject.
- Poetry can provide sensory experiences, giving children the sense of touching, feeling, smelling, hearing, and seeing.
- Poetry can make a topic memorable through the use of highly charged words and vivid images.
- Poetry can help children talk about issues that concern them.

---

**POET PROFILE**

---

# In Her Own Words

## NIKKI GRIMES

I can't overestimate the value of poetry performance. I get letters and e-mails from K–12 teachers from all over the country, and from as far away as New Zealand, all commenting on the excitement their students are experiencing as open-mic poetry readings and slams are making their way into the classroom. Kids who were falling asleep are suddenly lit up with enthusiasm. This is one bandwagon we all need to jump on!

The form of poetry performance may differ from elementary school to middle school to high school, variously incorporating call-and-response, oral interpretation, reader's theater, choreographed poetry, and poetry slams. In general, though, performance is a tool in confidence building and in nurturing a love of, and respect for, language. Some of the backstory on Bronx Masquerade demonstrates what I mean.

For several years, I'd had the idea to write a book in which I'd follow a group of high schoolers over the course of a year, exploring their lives in poetry and prose. I'd sketched out the characters and their issues and began writing their monologues and poems. What I didn't have was an overall plot.

Enter Drew Ward, a local poet and high school teacher. Drew was teaching a section on the Harlem Renaissance and wanted his students to meet a living poet from Harlem who'd been influenced by the poets of that era. I obliged with a school visit. What I didn't know was that Drew had started an open-mic series in his classes earlier in that year, and by the time of my visit, a poetry movement was in full sway. Students from other classes frequently got passes to visit his homeroom so that they could observe, and even participate in, these readings.

How did this come about? In teaching students about the Harlem Renaissance with an emphasis on poetry, Drew brought in poetry to read, including his own. The students liked what they heard, and after Drew read one of his pieces, a student raised his hand and said, "I have a poem. Can I read mine?" Drew said yes. Immediately, other hands went up around the room. There were, he discovered, closet poets in each of his classes, and so he scheduled regular readings, eventually setting up a stage, of sorts, in the center of the room. He brought in spotlights and a video camera to document it all, and the budding poets were off and running. Those readings are still going on, and they inspired the plot of *Bronx Masquerade*.

I sometimes run into that first crop of kids on the street in my community, and they're still talking about that experience, four years later. They express how much they learned about themselves and one another, how their preconceived notions of other races and other cultures disintegrated. Within that experience, they formed a sense of community that none of them thought possible. All that from a series of poetry readings!

Looking for a way to get your students' attention? This is one way to do it.

## April Ala Carte
*by Nikki Grimes*

The long afternoon walk
whet my appetite.
I greedily scooped
two dollops of cloud
from the sky

*(continued)*

drizzled them
with sunshine
and silently
said grace

*© 2012 by Nikki Grimes. Used with permission.*

**CLASS EXERCISE** After sharing "April Ala Carte," encourage the kids to consider what their recipe for a perfect April afternoon might be. Which ingredients would they include? Clouds? Sunshine? And what might their quantities be? A teaspoon? A pinch? Work together to create a collective poem with the students' own ingredients and measurements.

## Poetry across the Curriculum

Enterprising teachers and librarians will find that poetry lends itself to integration across the curriculum, in areas such as language arts, science, mathematics, and social studies. If you offer instructional support on a regular basis, there are several ways that poems can enhance current teaching and learning in every subject area. Poetry breaks across the curriculum can serve to

- jump-start or introduce a lesson or topic
- present examples of terminology or concepts
- offer a transition between activities
- supply a stretching (poetry) break
- provide closure
- extend a topic further

Three rich resources full of strategies for connecting poetry with the major curricular areas (math, science, and social studies) are Barbara Chatton's book *Using Poetry across the Curriculum* (2010); poet Sara Holbrook's *Practical Poetry: A Nonstandard Approach to Meeting Content-Area Standards* (2005); and Bernice Cullinan, Marilyn Scala, and Virginia Schroder's collaboration *Three Voices: An Invitation to Poetry across the Curriculum* (1995). My own book *The Poetry Teacher's Book of Lists* (Vardell, 2012) provides 155 bibliographies, tips, and strategies for selecting and sharing poetry across the curriculum, including lists of poetry about animals, baseball, birds, cats, colors, dinosaurs, dogs, food, gardens and gardening, insects and bugs, mathematics, science, space and the planets, sports, time, trees, U.S. history, war and peace, weather, world history, and much more. (For more information, visit http://poetryteachersbookoflists.blogspot.com.)

However, in her work *Give Them Poetry: A Guide for Sharing Poetry with Children K–8*, Glenna Sloan issues "a word of caution in the matter of 'using' poetry in the service of other areas of study: Poetry should be allowed to develop literacy on its own" (2003, 16). There are many possibilities for linking poetry with subject matter, but do not forget to stop and enjoy the poems for their own sake, too.

## Poems for Reading and Language Arts Study

Once you start gathering a small collection of poems related to social studies, science, or math, you may be surprised to discover how many poems you can find. But remember that poetry study deserves a place in the reading and language arts curriculum, too. We have seen how poems can be matched with novels, picture books, and nonfiction books. Poems can even serve to gently reinforce mini-lessons on grammar and parts of speech. And of course poems can serve as a subject of study all their own. A unit devoted exclusively to poetry can focus on

- one favorite poem (e.g., Longfellow's classic poem "Paul Revere's Ride")
- a thematic collection of poems (e.g., poems about school)
- a poetic formula (e.g., concrete poems)
- a stylistic device (e.g., personification)
- one poet (e.g., Joyce Sidman)

This crystallized focus of poetry can aid children as they use their word knowledge to make sense of new content. A poem's context can help the reader or listener incorporate new vocabulary. Poetry also contains elements of predictability, such as rhyme, rhythm, and repetition, which make reading easier. When children read a poem, hear a poem read aloud, and participate in a choral reading of a poem, they have had multiple modes of reinforcement for meaningful language learning.

With the new Common Core standards that include a strand on developing poetry knowledge, more focus is being brought to the genre. More and more teachers and librarians are integrating poetry into their pedagogical practices using a variety of lessons and approaches. Paul B. Janeczko provides guidance in his book *Reading Poetry in the Middle Grades: 20 Poems and Activities That Meet the Common Core Standards and Cultivate a Passion for Poetry*. Another example, *The Poetry Friday Anthology*, offers a poem a week for the whole school year for kindergarten through fifth grade (and another edition for middle school), with activities tied to curriculum objectives and Common Core standards. Pausing to share a poem—and reinforce a language skill—on Poetry Friday is an easy way to infuse poetry into current practice.

## POETRY ABOUT SCHOOL: A THEMATIC COLLECTION

Children particularly enjoy poetry about school since they spend most of their daily lives there. The ups and downs of classroom life make fine grist for both humorous and serious poetry. Share the following books of poems as a school year begins, for special school events, and even with homeschooling families.

Brod Bagert, *School Fever*

Kalli Dakos, *Put Your Eyes Up Here and Other School Poems*

Betsy Franco, *Messing around the Monkey Bars and Other School Poems for Two Voices*

Helen Frost, *Spinning through the Universe: A Novel in Poems from Room 214*

David L. Harrison, *Somebody Catch My Homework*

Lee Bennett Hopkins, ed., *School Supplies: A Book of Poems*

Dorothy M. Kennedy, ed., *I Thought I'd Take My Rat to School: Poems for September to June*

Jack Prelutsky, ed., *There's No Place Like School*

Laura Purdie Salas, *Stampede! Poems to Celebrate the Wild Side of School!*

Carol Diggory Shields, *Almost Late to School and More School Poems*

## *Poetry and the Social Studies*

We have long recognized the value of children's literature for teaching social studies with the annual publication of "Notable Children's Trade Books in the Field of Social Studies," sponsored by the National Council for the Social Studies. The annual "Notables" list typically includes four to five books of poetry each year. A variety of poetry forms and formats have been included over the years, from haiku to poetry written by children, anthologies, reenvisioned classics, biographical poetry, and novels in verse. Several poets frequently create poetry works relevant to the social studies, including Marilyn Nelson, Margarita Engle, Jen Bryant, Carmen T. Bernier-Grand, Linda Oatman High, Nikki Grimes, Carole Boston Weatherford, and J. Patrick Lewis.

Pile up the poetry books, bring together teachers and librarians, or challenge the children with a social studies–themed poetry scavenger hunt. Many examples of social studies–related poems can be found in various anthologies and poetry books. Those poems can be used to introduce the topic of a lesson, to supplement the content, or to extend the themes studied. Such poetry nuggets can give children a hook for incorporating new information. When integrated into traditional social studies lessons, they also provide motivation and variety. Many works lend themselves to a dramatic read-aloud reader's theater style, with kids taking on different roles or characters (particularly with the novels in verse). Others would be powerful in combination with a nonfiction work on the same topic, to examine how information is integrated into poetic forms. Still others incorporate art and illustrations from primary sources alongside the imagery of the poetry, helping young people visualize other times and places.

## Ten Poetry Collections for Social Studies Not to Be Missed

1. Lee Bennett Hopkins, ed., *My America: A Poetry Atlas of the United States*
2. Lee Bennett Hopkins, ed., *America at War*
3. J. Patrick Lewis, *Monumental Verses*
4. Milton Meltzer, ed., *Hour of Freedom: American History in Poetry*
5. Nora Panzer, ed., *Celebrate America in Poetry and Art*
6. Neil Philip, ed., *Singing America: Poems That Define a Nation*
7. Laura Amy Schlitz, *Good Masters! Sweet Ladies! Voices from a Medieval Village*

8. Diane Siebert, *Tour America: A Journey through Poems and Art*
9. Hana Volavkova, ed., *I Never Saw Another Butterfly: Children's Drawings and Poems from Terezin Concentration Camp, 1942–1944*
10. Carole Boston Weatherford, *Remember the Bridge: Poems of a People*

## *Poetry and Science*

The list "Notable Children's Trade Books in the Field of Science" appears every spring in the journal *Science and Children* and often includes one or two books of poetry on the list each year. It reminds us that all kinds of books have a great deal of potential for supporting science learning. Poetry, in particular, offers the special language, imagery, and conciseness that helps introduce or reinforce important science concepts. A brief consideration of a handful of poetry books

### PRACTITIONER PERSPECTIVE

*I teach zoo school in the summer. I usually work with the third and fourth graders for a week to teach them about the different animals found in the zoo and then take them on tours. When we spent an entire day on snakes last week I decided to include Shel Silverstein's poem "Boa Constrictor" and see what movement the kids could incorporate into it. I got all the kids on the floor for the lesson and spent about ten minutes talking about the boa and the characteristics the snake has. We discussed how snakes can unhinge their jaws and swallow their prey whole. Then I got out the Silverstein book and the kids got very excited: "I have that book!" "My teacher read that to us!" and so on. I told the kids to listen to the poem once with their eyes closed. They all had smiles on their faces. Then we spread out and I read it again as they acted it out with whatever movements they wanted. It was very funny watching them, and I barely made it through the poem without laughing. The best thing was that some of them had memorized the poem, and they quoted it along with me. After we finished, they begged me to read some more and were even willing to trade their zoo visit for a chance to hear more poems! I told them we could do some more later, and they made sure I kept my promise.*

Lindsey Mendrop, librarian
Weatherford Ninth-Grade Center, Weatherford, Texas

will quickly reveal many poems that connect with the sciences and several poets who regularly create poetry books with science-rich content, like Joyce Sidman, Marilyn Singer, Avis Harley, Jane Yolen, and Douglas Florian. In fact, there are many thematic poetry collections devoted to science-related subjects, such as animals, weather, seasons, space, dinosaurs, and geography, to name a few. Share science poetry titles in combination with a nonfiction work on the same topic, to examine how information is presented in prose or poetry. Or consider how the book's illustrations (whether as paintings, prints, or photographs) offer details alongside the poetry. Encourage children to think like a poet and a scientist in carefully observing the world around them using all their senses, maintaining an avid curiosity about how things work, and gathering "big words" and key vocabulary in their reading and their writing.

## Ten Poetry Collections for Science Not to Be Missed

1. Barbara Brenner, ed., *The Earth Is Painted Green: A Garden of Poems about Our Planet*
2. Kate Coombs, *Water Sings Blue: Ocean Poems*
3. Douglas Florian, *Omnibeasts*
4. Mary Ann Hoberman and Linda Winston, eds., *The Tree That Time Built: A Celebration of Nature, Science, and Imagination*
5. Lee Bennett Hopkins, ed., *Spectacular Science: A Book of Poems*
6. Jack Prelutsky, ed., *The Beauty of the Beast: Poems from the Animal Kingdom*
7. David M. Schwartz and Yael Schy, *What in the Wild? Mysteries of Nature Concealed . . . and Revealed*
8. Joyce Sidman, *Ubiquitous: Celebrating Nature's Survivors*
9. Amy Sklansky, *Out of This World: Poems and Facts about Space*
10. Jane Yolen, *Once upon Ice and Other Frozen Poems*

### Poetry and Mathematics

Again, in the area of mathematics teaching and learning, poetry has a great deal of potential. Indeed, because much of mathematics deals with numbers, theories, and calculations, the language and imagery of poetry may help children visualize abstract concepts and operations. Hunting for math poems, however, is a bit challenging. A handful of poetry anthologies are devoted exclusively to math topics, but many more math-related poems can be found in general anthologies.

**Ten Poetry Collections for Mathematics Not to Be Missed**

1. Betsy Franco, *Counting Caterpillars and Other Math Poems*
2. Betsy Franco, *Mathematickles!*
3. Lee Bennett Hopkins, ed., *It's About Time*
4. Lee Bennett Hopkins, ed., *Marvelous Math: A Book of Poems*
5. J. Patrick Lewis, *Arithme-Tickle: An Even Number of Odd Riddle-Rhymes*
6. J. Patrick Lewis, *Edgar Allan Poe's Pie: Math Puzzlers in Classic Poems*
7. Richard Michelson, *Ten Times Better*
8. Mary O'Neill, *Take a Number*
9. Nikki Siegen-Smith, *First Morning: Poems about Time*
10. Jane Yolen, *Count Me a Rhyme: Animal Poems by the Numbers*

Interdisciplinary or thematic teaching is one popular way to bring the curricular areas together for maximum learning. According to Barbara Chatton (2010), including poetry in thematic units that seek to integrate subject areas offers multiple opportunities for extending instruction:

- Poetry can provide cognitive transfer from concept to concept.
- Poetry deepens comprehension by providing another example of a concept.
- Poetry provides more personal connections.

The more connections we can provide among what children are learning in various areas of study, the deeper their learning will be. If poetry can be that vehicle for connecting books, skills, concepts, and information across the curriculum, we owe it to children to infuse poetry wherever we can.

## Conclusion

Once we are well versed in children's poetry, recognize popular titles, and know major poets, how do we present poetry effectively? We can begin by conducting a quick assessment of our facilities and activities, checking the poetry shelves, and looking at our programming calendars. Are there poetry events and celebrations in the works? What poetry-related visual aids, digital resources, and promotional materials are visible (or in the files)? Is poetry part of future planned displays?

Then, as we incorporate poetry into our routines, we need only three minutes to begin to make a difference. Whether we use poetry breaks or another approach, we can quickly incorporate poems into existing activities. In addition, we can add novelty by incorporating a variety of media alongside the poetry we select. As we build on that base, we can also create spoken-word events that help children enjoy the oral qualities of poetry. One additional way for promoting poetry is to highlight the poets themselves.

Finally, as we inject poetry into our plans, we can pair poetry with other genres, such as fiction and nonfiction, or couple related classic poems and contemporary poems. Or if we consider the school curriculum of language arts, social studies, science, and mathematics, we can find many relevant poems. A quick list to guide a poetry checkup might include the following:

- Check the children's poetry shelves for ease of access and appeal.
- Look for signage that highlights children's poetry.
- Create promotional materials and displays that include children's poetry.
- Plan for National Poetry Month.
- Consider establishing poetry rituals as part of your routine.
- Start sharing children's poetry in as little as three minutes' time.
- Emphasize aural qualities of children's poetry (as in spoken word).
- Feature children's poets in displays, materials, and booktalks.
- Pair children's poetry with picture books, novels, and nonfiction.
- Inject children's poetry into instruction in language arts, social studies, science, and mathematics.

With these building blocks in place, poetry can have a well-established place in any library. What's next? Strategies for sharing poetry and inviting children to read along are helpful in making poems come alive. Once we have invited children into the world of poetry, our next step is to engage their active participation in that world.

> *Instead of building a fence of formality around poetry,*
> *I want to emphasize its accessibility, the sound, rhythm,*
> *humor, the inherent simplicity. Poetry can be as natural and*
> *effective a form of self-expression as singing or shouting.*

—Karla Kuskin, poet

5

# How Do You Present Poetry to Children?

*Poetry always remembers that it was an oral art before it was a written art. It remembers that it was first song.*

—Jorge Luis Borges, poet

HOW DO WE INTRODUCE POEMS TO CHILDREN? WHAT strategies are engaging and effective for young audiences? In this chapter, we consider basic guidelines that can assist adults when they read poems aloud. We look at how to set the stage for children to participate and consider in detail ten key strategies for enabling their active participation. Finally, we examine creative alternatives that add variety to poetry-sharing activities.

## Why Share Poetry Out Loud?

The first step in inviting children into the oral world of poetry is very simply to read poems aloud. Hearing poems read out loud helps children attend both to the sounds of the words and lines and to their meaning. It sets the stage for children's participation in the read-aloud process. It familiarizes them with what the words of the poem should sound like and engages their listening comprehension in making sense of the poem's meaning. In addition, there is an affective benefit in that a reader can communicate to children his or her personal pleasure in poetry, in the sounds of words, in the rhythm of the lines. Also, through our willingness to share poems out loud, we subtly extend an invitation to children to follow our lead in trying on poetry.

Poetry is meant to be read aloud. Meaning is more clearly communicated when a poem is both read and heard. As poet Brod Bagert (1992) has said, exactly as songs are not just sheet music, poetry is not just text. The rhythm or rhyme of poetry can help children begin to get a sense of the sound of artful yet natural language. When children participate in reading aloud, they have the opportunity to develop their own oral fluency. Experimenting with various approaches to reading poetry aloud can help children express themselves and build confidence.

## Guidelines for Oral Reading of Poetry

So how do you begin? As I experimented with sharing poetry with children of different ages, I found specific steps for leading children to become comfortable with performing poetry out loud. I always begin by choosing poems that I enjoy. That may seem obvious, but so often we choose poems that we think we should choose or that we think children may enjoy. Over the years, I have found that it is hard to sell a poem that does not speak to me personally. And there are so many poems available nowadays that it is easier than ever to find poems you connect with. Of course, each person may choose completely different poems. I enjoy sharing humorous poems and find that most children respond readily to humor, but there are many other possibilities, too.

Next, I practice reading the poem aloud to myself a few times to get comfortable with the words, lines, pauses, and rhythm. Poet Eve Merriam advocates reading out loud, even when you are by yourself (www.poetryfoundation.org/bio/

**PRACTITIONER PERSPECTIVE**

*It is interesting that the idea of reading poetry with the right expressions and voice seems new and exciting, but we read prose stories out loud to children in this manner all the time. What is it about poetry that causes us to think we need to read in a different way? I know that not all picture books or even all novels make good read-alouds, but poetry is meant to be heard. It seems, then, that it would not be too difficult to use poetry during read-aloud times. But we just don't think about it much.*

Jackie Chetzron, librarian
Lake Highlands Junior High, Richardson, Texas

eve-merriam). And Chatton (2010) suggests avoiding the tendency to read in a singsong voice and instead paying attention to the line breaks for read-aloud cues.

On his Poetry180 website, former poet laureate Billy Collins writes about reading a poem:

> Reading a poem slowly is the best way to ensure that the poem will be read clearly and understood by its listeners. Learning to read a poem slowly will not just make the poem easier to hear; it will underscore the importance in poetry of each and every word. A poem cannot be read too slowly, and a good way for a reader to set an easy pace is to pause for a few seconds between the title and the poem's first line. . . . Read in a normal, relaxed tone of voice. It is not necessary to give any of these poems a dramatic reading as if from a stage.

I prepare a brief introduction to cue the children to listen to a poem rather than to a story or other genre. For example, I might say, "I have a few poems here I'd like to share with you. They are short and funny and you may have heard them before. If not, you're in for a treat. I'll read the poem out loud and you can follow along." I always read the title of the poem, then the poet's name, then the poem itself. I follow this pattern every time so that listeners become familiar with the routine and learn where the reading begins and ends. As I introduce successive participation activities, it helps to have this routine in place.

Poet and anthologist Lee Bennett Hopkins suggests the following strategies for reading a poem aloud:

> Choose a poem you like that you think the audience will enjoy too. Familiarize yourself with the poem by reading it aloud to yourself several times. Get the feel of the words and rhythm. Mark words and phrases you want to emphasize. Read to the group in a natural style. Follow the rhythm of the poem. Note how the physical appearance of the poem on the page dictates the rhythm and mood. Stop for a moment at times when it pleases you and when it fits with the content and mood of the poem. Use your normal voice, as if describing a daily event. Be sincere. Stay quiet at the end of the reading. (www.rif.org/educators/rifexchange/programdescriptions/QA_show205.mspx)

Cullinan, Scala, and Schroder (1995) recommend that we read a poem at least twice, although children may often ask to hear it even more. Poet and teacher Georgia Heard (1999) says that we should make sure there is a lot of silence around a first reading. Try mentally counting to five if you are initially uncomfortable with the quiet. Give children a few moments to absorb the words and meaning of the poem.

## Using Body Language Effectively

It is also helpful to consider your nonverbal presentation of poetry, including the hand gestures and facial expressions you use. In his article "Act It Out: Making Poetry Come Alive," Bagert (1992) encourages us to become aware of how we can use our faces, voices, and bodies to perform poetry effectively. With modeling and practice, each nonverbal variable can be more consciously manipulated. He recommends the following exercise:

Make a sad face. Droop your eyes, pout your bottom lip, tilt your head to the side and say, "I am not very happy." You will find that voice, body, and timing tend to follow your expression. Now try to defy nature. Make the same sad expression and try to say "I am very happy" in a cheerful voice. You will find that it is very hard to sound happy when your face is sad. Conduct the search for what a poem means and how to perform it by asking a single question: What face should I make when I say these words? Then make the face and say the words. (Bagert 1992, 19)

Be aware of how you can use your face and gestures to enhance your poem delivery. Audiotape or videotape yourself occasionally to assess your delivery. You may be surprised at the difference between how you think you are coming across and how you are actually coming across. Experience with book reading and storytelling is helpful too, of course, but poetry reading is even slower and filled with more pauses than prose reading. Fortunately, children are generally very forgiving and ready to engage in whatever we prepare and share.

## Getting Children Involved

Reading the poem out loud oneself, however, is only the first part of sharing poems with children. Although it can be enjoyable for them to listen repeatedly

### UNDERSTANDING LINE BREAKS AND WHITE SPACE IN POEMS

Poet Georgia Heard (1999) teaches us about line breaks and white space as cues that can enhance our effectiveness when reading poems aloud. In fact, she lists what she calls line-break fundamentals:

- Line breaks are there on purpose to help us pause.
- Line breaks affect a poem's rhythm (short lines are more choppy).
- Each poem line is a unit of meaning.

Heard also talks about the use of white space and the creation of stanzas. She tells us that poets use white space to

- slow a poem down
- encourage the reader to stop and think
- set off the final line and give it more impact
- single out a line

If we study the way a poem is presented on the page, we can use the poet's cues to guide our oral reading.

to an enthusiastic and knowledgeable adult share appealing poems out loud, the idea is to invite children into the pleasures of poetry through participating in the experience more actively. Thus, the rest of this chapter focuses on ways to invite children into the read-aloud performance of poetry. In the past, this was often called choral reading of poetry. This label is fine, but it suggests a chorus style of reading poetry in groups. I have found that there are many ways to involve children in large groups and in small groups, and as single volunteers. Others use the term *poetry performance* for reading poems aloud. This label is also fine, but it often suggests a more formal, polished performance that is based on knowing the poem by heart or poetry created on the spot for an audience. Although some children enjoy poetry so much that memorizing a poem or performing it in front of an audience is a treat, I look for ways to involve kids of all kinds in experiencing poetry in more informal, spontaneous ways. Poet Sara Holbrook reminds us to "show the world that poetry was never meant to simply lie quietly on the page, any more than kids were meant to sit quietly in their seats to read it" (2002, 54).

What about shy children? I have visited many libraries and classrooms of all levels to lead poetry performances and often find that there are a few children who do not participate, even after several visits. And that is perfectly fine. My goal is to invite children into poetry—as far as they want to go. Over time, I generally find that kids warm up and jump in—but not all of them. Even if I were their classroom teacher, I would still not require all children to perform in

## PRACTITIONER PERSPECTIVE

*One fun activity I tried was having students write an ode to their favorite animal or object. We then used modeling clay to sculpt that animal or object. After it dried and was colored, I invited them to write their favorite line from their poem on the body or base of their sculpture. We then had a mini–sculpture garden on display with many accompanying poems. Students who were shy about sharing their poetry in previous weeks were way more eager to share their words in conjunction with a visual art piece. The one that sticks out in my mind was a hilarious ode to a pickle!*

Xelena González, early literacy specialist
San Antonio Public Library, San Antonio, Texas

## POETRY-BREAK POINTERS

- The poetry break can begin with a sign, bell, and/or chime announcing Poetry Break.
- Be sure to give the title and author of the poem.
- If possible, show the book the poem comes from.
- Feel free to reread the poem immediately.
- Be sure to enunciate each word distinctly (and check uncertain pronunciations and meanings beforehand).
- Avoid singsong delivery of rhyming verses.
- Use commas and periods as signals to pause in the read-aloud.
- Read mini-conversations in poems with dramatic voices and vocal changes.
- Glance at the audience occasionally.
- Consider sharing the poem read by the poet, if available on audio.
- Add variety in setting the stage with a flashlight or music.
- Invite a guest presenter to share a poem (including in multiple languages).
- A favorite puppet can present the poem.
- A portable microphone can add to the effect.

To add variety, poem introductions can include

- information about the poet
- information about the topic of the poem
- how you felt when you first read the poem or how it affected you
- why you chose that poem (or for that particular day)
- a prop that fits the poem
- a "this reminds me of" connection to another poem, book, song, and the like

Source: Based on Caroline Feller Bauer, *The Poetry Break: An Annotated Anthology with Ideas for Introducing Children to Poetry* (New York: H. W. Wilson, 1995), and John O'Connor, *Wordplaygrounds: Reading, Writing, and Performing Poetry in the English Classroom* (Urbana, IL: National Council of Teachers of English, 2004), 115.

front of the whole class. There are many other smaller steps they can take to get comfortable expressing themselves orally. I was one of those shy children who are mortified to be required to speak in front of a group. I still have vivid memories of standing up by the teacher's desk in sixth grade to recite a Longfellow poem. Not a fun and happy moment. Yes, it is true that we get more confident with practice and experience, but we should also be able to build that confidence in safe and supportive surroundings. Educator Regie Routman (2000) has found that children proudly read aloud their favorite poems in group environments when they are supported and comfortable.

## Ten Strategies for Sharing Poetry Out Loud

Through research and reading as well as trial and error in classrooms and libraries, I have identified ten general strategies for involving children in reading poems out loud. This is not rocket science. You may have heard of all these or tried them yourself in the past. However, I have ordered them in a way that eases children into participating in comfortable ways, provides the adult leader with a helpful framework, and suggests specific poems for each approach. In addition, the diversity of the approaches adds spice to the practice of reading poetry aloud. Just trying the different strategies and incorporating them into your read-aloud repertoire will add a variety of tools that will come in handy again and again.

The ten strategies I have found most successful are presented in order of general difficulty. They begin with recommending that the adult take the lead, but they gradually invite greater and greater child participation. This helps children get their feet wet at participating in the oral reading of poetry in groups so that they gain confidence and get comfortable with volunteering to read solo lines, poems for two voices, and so forth. As the strategies get more complicated, they take more explaining and preparation, but the results can be very rewarding for everyone involved. The strategies are the following:

1. Modeling: The adult reads the poem aloud.
2. Unison: Everyone reads the poem together at the same time.
3. Refrain: Children join in on a repeated line, stanza, or word.
4. Movement: Children read in unison using motions or gestures.
5. Call-and-response: Two groups read alternating (not simultaneous) lines or stanzas.

6. Groups: Multiple groups read various lines or stanzas.

7. Solos: Individual children read individual lines.

8. Two voices: Two people read two parts, sometimes with simultaneous but different lines.

9. Canon: Two groups read the same poem, with one group delaying its start until the other reaches a predetermined point.

10. Singing: Children sing poems set to familiar tunes.

Once you are familiar with these strategies, you can combine them in a variety of ways. Once children gain some experience, they themselves will often spontaneously suggest performance possibilities. And of course, every poem performance should be celebrated and acknowledged with soft applause (the golf clap), a silent cheer, pats on the back (each person patting herself or himself on the back), or even finger snapping, just as they do at coffeehouse poetry readings.

---

**POET PROFILE**

# In His Own Words

## J. PATRICK LEWIS

Poetry is the singular literary genre that begs to be read out loud, even if you are in a room all by yourself. As I tell children at school visits, you want your ears to have as much fun as your mouth is having. Among its many charms, poetry's sheer musicality is undeniable.

Having said that, I hasten to add that there is the reading of a poem and then there is the droning on. Ask third, fourth, and fifth graders to read poetry in front of the class, and you will not want for volunteers. Yet almost invariably, the young reader does a disservice to the verse. With most child readings, a good poem is made bad; a bad poem is made worse. The child reader buries his or her face in the page, mumbles to the first row of listeners (at best), and reads in a monotone with the rapidity of tracer bullets—da-dum, da-dum, da-dum, da-dum / da-dum, da-dum, da-dum, da-dum. (The final *da-dum* usually falls off—da-*dum*—like the last poor petal on a dead flower.)

Even though the English language is heavily iambic (da-DUM, da-DUM, as in, for example, "Hel-LO, is AN-y-BO-dy THERE?"), reading in a singsongy style is far from natural. If this is not the way people actually speak, then why should it be the way they recite poetry?

But at the end of a mediocre presentation, the child is rewarded with a hearty round of applause from both teacher and class, thereby, unfortunately, confirming in his or her mind that this was a bravura performance.

I don't want to explore here the reasons why poor poetry reading among schoolchildren is the norm. Is it due to the influence of TV? The way children hear poetry that is read to them? Perhaps it's the pernicious view that all poetry must rhyme. Whatever the causes, children can do better, can become accomplished poetry readers and reciters themselves, if they are given the best models, namely teachers and librarians who care deeply about the written word.

One does not have to speak in the stentorian voice of, say, Dylan Thomas, to be a mesmerizing, or simply an effective, poetry reader. The words sing themselves. What would help inordinately, however, is prereading. Teachers or librarians owe it to their young audiences to read with the feeling the poet intended, to read with the right pauses (at the caesuras, to be technical, or at the line breaks, unless they are enjambed), to slow it down and make each word count. And to do this, one must have read the poem, practiced the poem (out loud, all alone), before dispensing such a verbal gift to the young.

Reading deserves the same kind of close attention as writing. Reading in a stumbling, halfhearted way is akin to writing with slipshod spelling and indifference to grammar.

But prereaders are always ready to take their breath away. Pull the emotion out of the poem; let it rest in the palm of your hand. Tell them, "Look. Look at what you have just heard. Then be quiet. Let the words sing."

## An Ant's Life
*by J. Patrick Lewis*

No one has called me "The Insect Express."
The life of an ant is slow-going.
    I haul heavy loads through a universe
    Of primeval forests, for better or worse.
    Yet you'll never hear me, a worker ant, curse:
I'm too busy tugging and towing.

A locust's been caught climbing up an oak tree.
Ant colony troops are ascending.
    Today, I'm assigned to an abdomen glob.
    Tomorrow, I may join the pall bearer mob
    In dragging a stag beetle home. That's my job.
The life of an ant's never-ending.

*© 2012 by J. Patrick Lewis. Used with permission.*

**CLASS EXERCISE** This poem is ideal for performing with pantomime since there are so many possible motions and gestures. Children can move slowly, bend as if carrying a heavy load, then tug, tow, climb, and drag. Create simple antenna for your volunteer mimes with headbands, pipe cleaners, and pom-poms on the end of the pipe cleaners. If you are really ambitious, use a giant-sized prop for the "ants" to carry, such as a large box painted white (as a giant sugar cube) or a large garbage bag filled with stuffing and tied (as an "abdomen glob"). Half the group can read the poem aloud while the other half pantomimes, and then reverse roles and repeat.

### Strategy 1: Modeling

In strategy 1, the adult reads the poem aloud. It is best to begin by choosing poems you enjoy personally and sharing them with expression and enthusiasm (for poems cited throughout this chapter for the ten strategies, see appendix

A). Try to avoid the common tendency to read lines, especially rhyming lines, in a singsong voice. Chatton (2010) recommends studying the line breaks to determine how the poem should be read. Do not rush the lines. Look around the room as you read the poem, if you can. If possible, display the words of the poem on a poster or chalkboard or with an overhead or digital projector. Seeing the words while hearing them provides additional reinforcement for children learning to read or learning English (Hadaway, Vardell, and Young 2002). I always begin by reading every poem aloud. It is an important way to ensure that the vocabulary and pronunciation will not be stumbling blocks for any child. As you choose poems to share with children, begin with those that strike your fancy. Obviously, a fluent adult reader can read any poem aloud. However, because it is hard to manufacture enthusiasm, choose poems you enjoy so that your enjoyment shows in your voice and face. Read the poem aloud slowly and with expression. Be prepared to read it several times—children generally want and need multiple oral readings.

I often choose poems with seasonal relevance. For example, in November I might start with "Our Daily Bread," by Janet Wong. In February, I might read "Valentine's Day," by Marilyn Singer. Each poem offers a slightly different point of view on the familiar celebrations of Thanksgiving and Valentine's Day. If you want to begin with humorous poems on families and housework, try the classic and much-anthologized "Mummy Slept Late and Daddy Fixed Breakfast," by John Ciardi, or "Sarah Cynthia Sylvia Stout Would Not Take the Garbage Out," by Shel Silverstein. Both are longer narrative poems with fun surprise endings. Or for a hilarious tongue twister, read "Allicatter Gatorpillar," the tongue-tangling poem by Calef Brown. Feeling brave? Try free-verse poems, which often surprise children with their lack of rhyme. I have enjoyed sharing an untitled poem by Karla Kuskin that begins with some rhyme—"Three wishes / Three. / The first / A tree"—and then goes on to itemize three wishes for a happy afternoon: a tree, a chair, and a book. For greatest effect, read this poem out loud while seated in a chair near a window with a view of a tree. A perfect companion poem to this one is "Quiet Morning," by Karen B. Winick, with a dog along for a reading morning. Then invite the children to find their own wished-for books or favorite reading spots. "My Needs," by JonArno Lawson, might launch a thoughtful discussion, or try Gary Soto's "Ode to Family Photographs," a wry look at the common experience of taking photos in which people's heads are inadvertently cut off. If you have such a family photo yourself, share it. I did this and the kids really enjoyed seeing a crooked photo of my family—without their heads!

### Strategy 2: Unison

In strategy 2, everyone reads the poem together at the same time. Once I have set the stage for hearing poems out loud, I invite children to join in for unison read-aloud. I choose a shorter poem with a strong rhythm and first read the poem out loud as a model. Even nonreaders can participate in reading aloud when their voices need not carry the whole poem. Of course, you have to provide the words of the poem in some format that is visible to the group. And remind the children of the protocol: you read the title of the poem and the name of the poet, and then the kids join in. One poem that has been irresistible to first through fourth graders is "My Monster," by Douglas Florian, a poem that humorously compares teachers to monsters. Or try the fun two-line poems in Marilyn Singer's *Twosomes,* such as "Porcupines," which compares hugging a porcupine to hugging a cactus, or "The Giraffe," from David Elliott's animal poetry book *In the Wild.* On a more serious note, Langston Hughes's classic poem "Dreams," in eight short, straightforward lines, expresses a powerful message regarding dreaming about the future. Eloise Greenfield's "Education" is a short, potent poem about getting involved in a fight. And on a lighter note, share Karla Kuskin's "I Woke Up This Morning" by beginning with soft voices and gradually getting louder as the poem builds momentum. It is the perfect follow-up to a read-aloud of Judith Viorst's classic picture book *Alexander and the Terrible, Horrible, No Good, Very Bad Day.*

### Strategy 3: Refrain

In strategy 3, invite group participation by encouraging children to join in on a repeated line, stanza, or word. This strategy for choral reading requires that children learn about timing and jump in only when their lines come up. However, they still participate as a whole group, with no pressure to perform individually. As always, you read the poem out loud first. Then in repeated readings, invite the children to join in on a line or refrain that pops up repeatedly in the poem.

This time, you can enable participation by putting the repeated stanza, line, or word on a large strip of paper or a display board or projected on a screen rather than displaying the text for the entire poem. Doing so makes this strategy even easier to carry out with large groups of kids. However, if it is possible to show the whole poem, that is always ideal. Children are even more likely to learn the poem if they can both hear it and see it.

Many poems are particularly effective for the refrain performance strategy. Once you begin gathering poems to read aloud, you may be surprised by just how many have a repeated stanza, line, or word. Probably the most successful such poem I have tried is "Homework! Oh, Homework!" by Jack Prelutsky. This popular lament on the woes of homework touches a responsive chord among children. They enjoy saying the repeated line "Homework! Oh, homework!" with a great deal of anguish. Another poem with a repeated line is "Things," by Eloise Greenfield. In this commentary on the lasting value of poems versus other, more fleeting pleasures, the repeated line "Ain't got it no more" allows the kids to use slang that would usually lead to their being corrected. "Trespass," by Kristine O'Connell George, invites children to say the key word *someone*, a stand-alone line; the lines "Amazing, your face / Amazing" in "Amazing Face," by Rebecca Kai Dotlich, allow kids to open and close the poem; and the title line "Welcome to the night" in the poem by the same name by Joyce Sidman has added drama when read aloud by a chorus of voices. There are so many examples of poems with repeated lines that children enjoy performing. Among them are "Look in a Book," by Ivy O. Eastwick, about the power of reading a book; "If My Hand Didn't Get So Tired," by Kalli Dakos, about the possibilities in writing; and "The Boa," by Douglas Florian, a pithy portrait of the snake.

Once the children get the hang of simple refrains, a more challenging variation involves reading poems with a repeated word that appears in different places. The repeated word may not be at the beginning of a line but rather in the middle or at the end, which motivates children to pay closer attention and to practice the reading more than once. Another Prelutsky poem that is very effective with this strategy is "Louder Than a Clap of Thunder!" in which the repetition of the word *louder* describes the snoring of the narrator's father! The word *louder* begins many, but not all, of the lines of the poem, so alert the children to that variation ahead of time. Two additional examples use repetition in creative depictions of winter. Frank Asch's poem "Sunflakes" imagines snowy traditions in sunny weather with cleverly coined words such as *sunman* and *sunball*. Karla Kuskin's poem "Snow" portrays a more traditional picture of winter's snowy moments. But remember, the repeated word *snow* occurs in various places in the lines of the poem, sometimes as part of a compound word. The read-aloud can be somewhat chaotic at first but is lots of fun.

Another possibility for spontaneous group participation is to find poems that include counting or days of the week. Most children are well versed in counting from one to ten or reciting the days of the week, so when poems incorporate these elements, they invite impromptu involvement. For example, Prelutsky's poem "Countdown" begins "There are ten ghosts in the pantry," which encourages the children to shout out the decreasing numbers, starting with ten. Or in Florian's poem "Weather It," each line begins with a day of the week that the children can anticipate and announce. Such techniques not only simplify participation but also reinforce the learning of basics, especially for younger children or children learning English.

### Strategy 4: Movement

Strategy 4 combines unison reading with appropriate motions or gestures. This is a bit more challenging because it involves listening for cues and integrating physical movement. However, children often have had experiences pantomiming motions to songs like "I'm a Little Teapot" in preschool, so strategy 4's kinesthetic approach incorporates many familiar gestures. Lots of poems include descriptions of movement that are natural for children to act out, such as the explicit movements in "Boa Constrictor," by Shel Silverstein, or "The Bully," by Douglas Florian. Others have a topic or even a rhythm that lends itself to pantomime or movement. Motions can be as simple as alternating standing and sitting, clapping at key intervals, or gesturing with hands. In Rebecca Kai Dotlich's "A Circle of Sun," the words suggest possible movements such as leaping, skipping, and swinging. "Medusa," by Bobbi Katz, invites children to act out a bit of this myth complete with a "head full of snakes." And children can pantomime the two methods of roasting in "Toasting Marshmallows," by Kristine O'Connell George. You might want to perform Prelutsky's poem "I Am Running in a Circle" outdoors so that kids can actually run in a circle. And with the poem "August Heat" (anonymous), children can perform the repeated line "and sit" from their chairs. Try assigning four different groups to sit at different intervals as the line "and sit" is repeated four times. It is also possible to incorporate basic American Sign Language into poetry readings.

### Strategy 5: Call-and-Response

In the fifth strategy, call-and-response, two groups read alternating (not simultaneous) lines or stanzas of a poem. Once children are familiar with poems that are read aloud in parts, try dividing the group in half to practice call-and-response. The best poems for this performance strategy are those with lines that are structured in a back-and-forth way. In "Worker Bees," by Douglas Florian, for example, alternating lines can add emphasis to the complaints of the "sister" worker

---

**PRACTITIONER PERSPECTIVE**

*I used an opportunity to explore poetry performance with my daughter and nieces (age eight, ten, and twelve years) when we were outside after a swim. We used Paul Fleischman's book* Joyful Noise: Poems for Two Voices *and a collection by Lee Bennett Hopkins called* Side by Side: Poems to Read Together. *The poems in* Joyful Noise *are mostly call-and-response, and I introduced these first. I was going to model a poem, but my daughter said, "I can do that," and joined me. Others wanted to try it, too. It really amazed me how they took to Fleischman's book. Given its vocabulary and depth, it is not an easy read, and the format is challenging and unfamiliar, with two columns of alternating lines and some lines in unison. Though the children mentioned that the poems were difficult, they kept going back to try another and another, sometimes starting over to practice the lines, helping each other with difficult words, and commenting on the content: "Oh, that's really sad," or "Butterflies make a chrysalis, but a moth has a cocoon." I was reluctant to try this book with young readers, I admit, and actually decided not to buy another book in the same format because I (mistakenly) thought that the children would not enjoy it. Now I know better. They merely need time to find out about it, play with it, and practice it on their own terms. We just need to bring as many poems to the picnic as we can and let the children decide which ones to sample.*

Jean Collier, librarian
Foster Village Elementary School, North Richland Hills, Texas

bees. In "Copycat," by Sara Holbrook, the lines sound just like two groups of children mimicking each other, each repeating what members of the other group say. It is the perfect poem to read out loud antiphonally. Another great example for two groups is "Clock-Watching," by Carol Diggory Shields, which features the interplay of one child's daydreaming and working through the school day. Shel Silverstein's "The Meehoo with an Exactlywatt," a poem based on the knock-knock-joke formula, is ideal for two groups to read by alternating lines. The same format works for Jack Prelutsky's Thanksgiving poem "I'm Thankful," which, in alternating lines, juxtaposes two points of view on thankfulness. Janet Wong uses spacing to indicate the two parts in her poem "Speak Up." Here many voices could read the left side of the poem, which represents a group of questioning children, while a solo voice (perhaps the adult) responds by reading the right side of the poem, which expresses an immigrant child's point of view. One other poem that reveals cultural bias is "Two Plus Two, or Why Indians Flunk," by Beverly Slapin, which juxtaposes the voice of an ill-informed teacher to the voice of an innocent Native American girl. Finding poems for call-and-response is a bit more challenging because it requires a tension in the back-and-forth of the lines that does not occur in many poems. Nonetheless, this approach provides an inviting way for children to participate in groups and demonstrates the added emphasis that many voices can provide.

### Strategy 6: Groups

If you have tried all the variations in strategy 5, the children are probably eager to try even more challenging choral-reading methods. Strategy 6, using multiple small groups, is the next step in bringing poems to life through oral presentation. Reading in multiple groups puts the focus on fewer children and thus may take more practice. But when children have participated in unison and large-group read-alouds, practicing is not usually a problem. They are usually eager to give it a try. Take "Face It," by Janet Wong, for example. This poem has three stanzas that reflect the writer's musings on her nose, her eyes, and her mouth and how each represents a different part of her identity. Three groups could each read a different stanza, using motions to point to each body part in turn. Four groups will work well for reading aloud "The Season's Campaign," by Joyce Sidman, with each group representing one of the four seasons. Or four groups can each read a stanza about spring in Lee Bennett Hopkins's poem "Spring." Kids will also enjoy "The Question," by Karla Kuskin, a poem that poses multiple answers to the question "What do you want to be when you grow up?" Different groups can each pipe in with a different answer. In Shel Silverstein's poem "Smart," each stanza reveals a bit more about a child's misunderstanding about the value of a dollar bill and various coins. This structure makes it easy for each group to read a different stanza. In "And the Answer Is . . . ?" by Carol Diggory Shields, there are two major stanzas, one reflecting the point of view of a student who is anxious that the teacher might call on him or her and the other presenting the perspective of a student who is eager to be called on. Typically, each group reads a different stanza. Ask for volunteers, or invite children to participate in the groups

## TEN STRATEGIES FOR SHARING POETRY OUT LOUD: IN A NUTSHELL

1. **Modeling:** The adult reads the poem aloud to the class. Choose poems you like and read them slowly but expressively. Show the poem via a projector or on a poster while you read it so the children can follow along with the words.
2. **Unison:** The adult still reads the poem out loud first. But then everyone joins in on repeated reading to read the poem in unison. You can adapt this approach with "echo" reading of some poems, in which children repeat lines after you read each one, echoing your reading.
3. **Refrain:** The adult leads the poem reading, but children participate in a word or phrase or refrain that is reoccurring, much like the classic Greek chorus joining in for repeated lines.
4. **Movement:** Use unison reading or leader reading of a poem with action words and phrases and invite listeners to join in with designated motions or gestures.
5. **Call-and-response:** The whole group is divided into two smaller groups to take turns reading lines in a back-and-forth kind of way.
6. **Groups:** The class or large group is divided into multiple groups for multiple stanzas. This takes some practice with timing but creates a wave effect, with the poem flowing across the room.
7. **Solos:** Individual children volunteer for individual solo lines. *Volunteer* is the key word. Do not put children on the spot. If you continue sharing

according to their seating arrangements. One other quick and effective method is to use a deck of cards. Give each child a card, and use color (red and black) to form two groups or suits (clubs, hearts, diamonds, spades) to form four groups.

### Strategy 7: Solos

Some poems are listlike in their structure and work well for what is sometimes called line-around choral reading, in which individual voices read individual lines. After children have participated in group variations, most are usually eager to volunteer to read a line solo. However, be sure that children are familiar with the poem before they volunteer for individual lines, and allow children to volunteer rather than be called upon. Children who are particularly shy or who

poetry orally every day, eventually nearly everyone will want a turn to shine. Many "list" poems work well in the read-aloud solo-line-reading format.

8. **Two voices:** This is the most complex form of choral reading. It takes a bit of practice but is very powerful. Two individuals volunteer to practice and perform poems for two voices (often with overlapping lines). It can be effective with two groups rather than two individuals, but it does take practice. (Underline the lines that are spoken simultaneously to help cue the children. Be aware that they may be saying different words at the same time.)

9. **Canon:** Reading poems in a canon in two alternating groups with staggered beginnings is one other strategy that involves timing and overlapping lines. It can be a fun challenge, just like singing "Row, Row, Row, Your Boat" in a canon. Poems must have a very regular beat or meter and some repetition. Physically clapping the rhythm of the poem together can also help with reading a poem canon style.

10. **Singing:** Perhaps the silliest form of choral reading is singing poems. It's not especially difficult, but it is irresistible fun and does require a bold adult (or child) to get it started. You simply sing poems by adapting those that have a strong, rhythmic beat to familiar tunes that have the same beat or meter, such as "Mary Had a Little Lamb," "Row, Row, Row Your Boat," "Ninety-Nine Bottles of Pop," "On Top of Old Smoky," and the like.

are struggling with learning English can feel especially vulnerable about mispronouncing words or making mistakes in timing. With practice, the interplay of group voices and individual ones can be very powerful for bringing a poem to life. Try "Whatif?" by Shel Silverstein, with a different voice reading each what-if worry line. Another thoughtful poem is "Where I Live," by Anna Grossnickle Hines, a contemplation of how we create peace. Or try reading Carol Diggory Shields's mock recitation of the Pledge of Allegiance, "Pledge," with individual voices alternating with the whole class. (Be sure to clarify in advance what the correct Pledge of Allegiance should sound like.) Laura Purdie Salas's found poem, "Top Ten Rules for Our Zoo Field Trip," is hilarious read line-by-line by ten volunteers, and Georgia Heard's "Recipe for Writing an Autumn Poem" cleverly combines cooking and poetry. Other poems that incorporate a linear format that lends itself to line-around reading include "April Fool," by Myra Cohn Livingston, a humorous list of April Fools' jokes; "By Myself," by Eloise Greenfield, a listing of personal qualities; or the classic poem "What Is Red?", a series of images of things that are red in color or feeling and one of Mary O'Neill's several color poems.

Most of the preceding examples begin and end with a line or lines that could be led by a narrator, with the intervening lines read aloud one by one by individual volunteers. Begin by reading the entire poem aloud as the leader, then seek volunteer readers and allow them a moment to practice their lines. They may turn to a buddy nearby to read their line aloud softly or to double-check a pronunciation. Then cue the oral reading as usual with the title of the poem followed by the name of the poet. It will be important to provide the text of the poem in a readable format—via a projector, a poster, or a PowerPoint slide.

### Strategy 8: Two Voices

Probably the most difficult form of choral reading is poetry written for two voices, which requires that two people read two parts, sometimes with simultaneous but differing lines. It requires the performers to synchronize their reading and get used to hearing two completely different lines being read at the same time. Paul Fleischman may have written the best-known examples of poems for two voices: the Newbery Award–winning *Joyful Noise,* a collection of poems about insects, and *I Am Phoenix,* a collection of poems about birds. These are excellent beginning points for children in the middle grades. Two of my favorites are "Honeybees" and "Book Lice," both popular with older children and adults. Fleischman has even created what he calls spoken quartets, or poems written for four simultaneous voices, in his book *Big Talk*.

Mary Ann Hoberman's You Read to Me, I'll Read to You series offers stories in poems written for two voices (usually adult and child), and Lee Bennett Hopkins has compiled a poem anthology designed for paired reading in *Side by Side: Poems to Read Together*. School is the topic of Betsy Franco's partner poems in *Messing around the Monkey Bars and Other School Poems for Two Voices*. All provide poetry ready-made for reading aloud in pairs.

Other poems, not necessarily written for two voices, can be adapted for performance by two voices through the arrangement or rearrangement of lines. Some lines can be identified for voice 1 or voice 2, with key lines designated for both voices. Although they take practice, poems for two voices are almost magical when read aloud. One example is "Pianoball," by Joyce Shipley, which juxtaposes a child practicing the piano to a contrasting narration of friends playing baseball outside the window—two perspectives perfect for two voices. Or Marilyn Singer's "reverso" poems in *Mirror, Mirror*—like "In the Hood"—provide two paired poems in two points of view ideal for two children to read aloud. And *Take Two! A Celebration of Twins*, by J. Patrick Lewis and Jane Yolen, contains many selections appropriate for two readers, twins or not.

If you hunt, you can find poems that may not be intended for two voices but may be very effective when delivered that way, particularly bilingual poetry collections with poems that appear in two languages. For example, Jennifer Clement's poem "Árbol de limón / Lemon Tree" appears in both Spanish and English

---

**PRACTITIONER PERSPECTIVE**

*My kids are "writing" poetry using book titles on the spines of books, and we're all loving it! The kids choose two or three books whose titles read like a poem. They're having a great time, and I'm pleasantly surprised at how creative they are. One of the boys used the books* Tough Times *and* Suck It Up *to write his poem. We're stacking the books, tying them with a ribbon, and displaying them on our tables for others to see. It's a fast, fun way to get the kids interested in poetry.*

Debbie Owen, middle school librarian
Frisco, Texas

(translated by Consuelo de Aerenlund) in Naomi Shihab Nye's collection *The Tree Is Older Than You Are*. If you are a Spanish speaker, you can read the poem in Spanish, followed by a reading in English. Or you can ask a Spanish-speaking volunteer from the audience to read the Spanish version. Once the readers have taken turns presenting their versions of the poem, both read their versions simultaneously. Just be sure to encourage the readers to pause at the end of each line and to start the next line together. The effect is quite stunning.

### Strategy 9: Canon

In a canon, two groups read the same poem, but one group delays its start until the other reaches a predetermined point. Reading poems in a canon is one other strategy that involves timing and overlapping lines and can be challenging for children. In addition, not many poems lend themselves to reading in a round. They must have a very regular beat or meter and some repetition. But when you find a suitable poem and try this technique with children, you will find it is fun and challenging, just like singing "Row, Row, Row, Your Boat" in a canon. One example that lends itself to canon reading is the title poem "Can You Dig It?" by Robert Weinstock, with its pileup of hilarious adjectives. Another is Jane Yolen's "Oh Fly," with its staccato rhythm. For variety, try "No," by Judith Viorst, or "I'm Much Too Tired to Play Tonight," by Jack Prelutsky. These usually take practice, but they can be very appealing, like chanting or cheering at a sports event. Asking the children to clap the rhythm of the poem can also help them with reading a poem canon style.

### Strategy 10: Singing

The final strategy for performing poetry is to sing poems by setting them to familiar tunes. This is not a particularly complex method, although it can require extra preparation, and it is irresistibly fun. Alan Katz's books of "silly dilly" songs are prime examples of this song-poem match. I have tried this approach with nearly every age level, and children of all ages love the connection of music and poem. Basically, you match poems and song tunes that contain the same meter in their first lines, often with an equal number of strong stresses. Count the beats in the first line or two of the poem, and then count the beats in the first line or two of the song to see if they match. This strategy seems to be most effective with nonsensical or humorous poems and with tunes that have a strong, rhyth-

## SELECTED TUNES FOR MATCHING WITH POEMS

"Are You Sleeping?" (eight beats in the first line)

"Battle Hymn of the Republic" (fourteen beats)

"Bingo" (eight beats)

"Clementine" (eight beats)

"The Farmer in the Dell" (six beats)

"Home on the Range" (five beats)

"Hot Cross Buns" (six beats)

"If You're Happy and You Know It" (eleven beats)

"I've Been Working on the Railroad" (eight beats)

"London Bridge" (seven beats)

"Mary Had a Little Lamb" (seven beats)

"Ninety-Nine Bottles of Pop" (ten beats)

"Old MacDonald" (seven beats)

"On Top of Old Smoky" (six beats)

"O Tannenbaum" (eight beats)

"Ring around the Rosy" (six beats)

"Row, Row, Row Your Boat" (five beats)

"She'll Be Coming Round the Mountain" (twelve beats)

"Three Blind Mice" (six beats)

"Turkey in the Straw" (five beats)

"Twinkle, Twinkle, Little Star" (seven beats)

"When Johnny Comes Marching Home" (nine beats)

"Yankee Doodle" (seven beats)

mic beat, such as "Row, Row, Row Your Boat" or "Mary Had a Little Lamb." One of the children's all-time favorites has been "School Cafeteria," by Douglas Florian, a hilarious poem about cafeteria food that can be sung to the tune of "Ninety-Nine Bottles of Pop." "Calling All Readers," by Laura Purdie Salas, and "The Dog Ate My Homework," by Sara Holbrook, are both fun poems to sing to the tune of "On Top of Old Smoky." Or try singing "Birthday Lights," by Calef Brown, to the tune of "Twinkle, Twinkle, Little Star" as a birthday-poem treat.

The appeal of music is undeniable, and connecting music with poetry makes the poems especially memorable. Setting poems to music is one of my favorite poem-sharing strategies because kids always love it. And you may be surprised by how many poems have strong-enough rhythm and structure to be effective when sung. Many of Jack Prelutsky's poems, in particular, match song tunes, which may not be surprising given that he was a singer and musician before turning to poetry. Try singing "Allosaurus," his poem describing the ferocious qualities of a dinosaur, to the tune of "Row, Row, Row Your Boat." It is a hilarious juxtaposition of lyrics to tune. Or use the same melody to accompany Judith Viorst's poem "Someday Someone Will Bet That You Can't Name All Fifty States," which leaves one state off the list. See if the children can guess which one.

Matching poems and songs has been a fun trial-and-error exercise for me. I made a list of my favorite childhood song tunes (you may have a very different list), counted the beats in the first lines of each tune, and started hunting for poems with the same number of beats. Then I tried singing the poems myself. Sometimes the beats fit, but the tune just did not match the poem, so I kept looking. Once you introduce this strategy, you may be surprised by how much the children enjoy it and how eager they are to join the search. What good practice this provides for the children's study of poetic meter, which they will encounter later in their school careers.

**POET PROFILE**

## Beyond Self-Expression

### BROD BAGERT

Writing poetry usually begins as an act of self-expression, but too often it ends there. Self-expression is a wonderful thing, but it's only a first step in the development of a poet. It's what Virginia Woolf alluded to in *A Room of One's Own* (1929) when she wrote that "the impulse toward autobiography" being spent, the writer begins "to use writing as an art, not as a method of self-expression."

While this concept is a little tricky to grasp in the context of poetry, it becomes almost self-evident in the context of the novel. Novelists have always written in the voice of characters, a practice that I think accounts in part for the novel's popularity. So the question is, what would happen if poetry took a lesson from the novel? I asked myself that question some years ago, and the answer has driven my work ever since.

As a young poet I loved to hear the sound of my own voice, but after writing five or six hundred self-expressive poems I began to get a little bored with it. So instead of continuing to peer into the inner world of self, I began to look outward to the world of others and discovered a chorus of voices longing for expression. I began to write in those voices, and immediately my poetry began to change. I discovered that writing in the voice of others forced me into a more consistent use of common dramatic elements, things like setting, action, conflict, even dialogue. Here's an example of such a poem:

## A Pioneer Heart
*by Brod Bagert*

I was here,
once upon a time so many years ago.
I lived,
I died,
and my children buried me;
but I am not yet gone,
and if you look for me
you will find me.

You will find me in faded ink
    on the yellow pages of a diary
    or the letters I sent to the home I left behind.

You will find me in the things my fingers touched—
    my Sunday bonnet,
    a patch of quilt from the bed of a child,
    a tattered photograph pressed between the pages of a Bible.

*(continued)*

Yes I was here . . .
>    I shivered beneath a roof of sod
>    on a bed alive with lice
>    through the howling dark of prairie night
>    in the grip of winter ice.
>
>    I removed a bloody ball of lead
>    with the blade of a kitchen knife,
>    and once I labored two long days
>    to give the gift of life.
>
>    I cooked . . . I plowed . . . I mowed . . .
>    I laughed out loud . . . I cried.
>    I loved a man and the life we made,
>    and mourned him when he died.
>
>    Through rain and fire, flood and drought,
>    with hope, desire, fear and doubt,
>    I breathed the very air you breathe . . .
>    walked the ground you walk . . .
>    and died.

But I am not yet gone,
not completely,
and I want you to find me.
I long for you to know
the throbbing power of the pioneer heart
I felt so long ago.
Like the seed I sewed each spring
that heart inside me grew,
a heart whose beat will never die
for it still beats on in you.

*© 2012 by Brod Bagert. Used with permission.*

We tend to think of poems as either rhyming poems or nonrhyming poems. This poem demonstrates how a single poem can move into and out of rhyme and therefore be both a rhyming and a nonrhyming poem at the same time. Making rhymes in the English language is very difficult, so moving into and out of rhyme in the same poem also opens new possibilities for poets writing in English.

So permit me a sweeping overgeneralization: when poets go beyond self-expression and write in a voice other than their own, their poetry becomes more dramatic, which results in better poems, a broader audience for poetry, and eventually more poets in print.

It's perfectly OK to encourage young writers to use poetry as a vehicle for self-expression, but you can also encourage them to reach beyond self-expression to the idea of writing as art. It's not a path for everybody, but the few who reach it will be on their way to writing some very engaging poetry.

**CLASS EXERCISE** Children may want to try writing in the voice of another as Bagert suggests. Invite them to bring old photos from home, or cut out an image from a magazine or newspaper, or select an antique photograph from a web resource such as Shorpy (www.shorpy.com). They can partner with a friend to conduct a mock interview speculating about the story behind the picture then use the eleven-line biopoem formula (detailed in chapter 6) to jump-start or guide the writing process. Display the poem and image together or challenge students to guess which poem accompanies which image if displayed separately.

---

## Combining Strategies

As you experiment with using each of these ten strategies for sharing poems with children, it will quickly become obvious that you can combine and overlap the strategies. For example, many poems have both a repeated line or refrain suited to whole-group participation and a linear list format that invites individual volunteers. For example, "Delicious Wishes," by Douglas Florian, repeats the words "I wish" many times within a series of lines to express multiple wishes. The words "I wish" can be read by the whole group while individual volunteers read individual "wish" lines. The poem "It's a Wonderful World, but They Made a Few Mistakes," by Judith Viorst, begins and ends with the titular line but also contains a variety of individual lines ideal for solo voices.

In some poems, we can juxtapose lines that lend themselves to whole-group reading to stanzas or lines that are suited to small-group reading. For example, the poem "I Rise, I Rise," about a young man's first buffalo hunt, repeats the phrase "I rise, I rise," which the whole group can recite. In between are lines from the buffalo's point of view, which for contrast small groups or pairs of children can read aloud. Another example is "Napoleon," a poem by Miroslav Holub of the Czech Republic, which appears in translation in *This Same Sky: A Collection of Poems from around the World*, selected by Naomi Shihab Nye. This poem describes a classroom moment from the perspectives of a teacher-narrator, the class as a whole, and an individual student named Frankie. Many poems offer similar combinations of whole-group, small-group, individual, and other read-aloud configurations. Often a poem will show you how to perform it if you study the lines and their arrangement on the page. Once you begin inviting children's participation in poem performance, you will find that they themselves will have ideas about how to try a poem this way or that way. Follow their lead!

**PRACTITIONER PERSPECTIVE**

*I have had great success with the middle school students I work with. The key? Just do exactly what you are asking them to do. Want them to wear costumes? Make sure you wear one, too! They have to see you doing it before they will even think about trying it. You have to be passionate and encouraging. Have fun! Let them know it is OK to laugh at yourself. I think kids take themselves too seriously and miss a lot. Want them to read dramatically? Make sure you do the same! Use different voices, make different faces, and use dramatic hand gestures. They will laugh and, you can hope, be tempted to try doing the same thing. You will not get results overnight, but the kids will slowly come around. They have to trust you first, and they will have to watch you perform a few times to understand how cool it really is. Try it all with the middle school kids. They will love you for it!*

Wendy Watson Fox, media specialist
St. John Catholic School, Panama City, Florida

## Seeking Out Audio Poetry

Enthusiastically sharing poems out loud with students for the pleasure of the words, sounds, rhymes, and meaning is our primary responsibility. Steinbergh (1994) recommends having a listening center or audiobook adaptations to highlight oral poetry as well. Poems on tape, along with their corresponding written forms, make excellent additions to the library. They provide further practice in listening and reading; more models of effective reading aloud, pronunciation, and expression; and other samples of writing. Many recordings of poets reading their own poems are available, and there is nothing quite like them. Shel Silverstein's gravelly voice, Jack Prelutsky's outrageous singing, and Ashley Bryan's mellifluous delivery are all amazing examples. And when children become comfortable with reading poetry aloud, they may want to tape-record themselves reading a favorite poem aloud, copy the poem in their best handwriting, illustrate it, and present their poem performance as a gift to a loved one. Such an activity can be a source of pride in addition to providing language practice. Several Internet sites offer audio versions of poems, including new kinds of experimental poetry. Check out the following:

Poets and Writers Inc., www.pw.org: Multimedia area with audio, video, podcasts, and slideshows

PoetryMagazine.com, www.poetrymagazine.com: Audio and video clips of individual poems and poets

Favorite Poem Project, www.favoritepoem.org: Videos of average citizens reading their favorite poems

Poetry Archive, www.poetryarchive.org: Archive of audio recordings of poets reading their work, including a children's poetry area

LibriVox, http://librivox.org: Amateur recordings of literary works in the public domain

## Other Creative Alternatives

Once the invitation to share poems chorally has been extended, children can generate their own creative alternatives or combine some of the strategies above. For instance, Georgia Heard reported that "one first-grade class performed a poem using silent movements, and the rest of the class guessed which poem they were performing" (1999, 13). Barbara Chatton (2010) challenges us to consider adding pantomime, sound effects, and background music to our read-alouds and inviting children to translate their favorite poems from English into their first language or American Sign Language. Caroline Feller Bauer (1995) encourages us to experiment with using special effects, varying voice volume and pitch, adding sound effects, or reading poems to carefully selected music. Children may want to adapt their favorite poems to rap, chants, or yells, and then accompany them with puppets, props, gestures, or clapping. Poet Sara Holbrook, in her book *Wham! It's a Poetry Jam: Discovering Performance Poetry*, provides helpful guidelines for staging poems in a variety of ways, including hosting contests and competitions.

Alma Flor Ada and her coauthors of the poetry program *A Chorus of Cultures: Developing Literacy through Multicultural Poetry* suggest that "physical involvement puts children at ease and encourages listening comprehension" and that "representing the actions of a poem, the feelings in the poem, allowing even for silent participation, especially for children acquiring English," is essential to language learning (1993, 32). Invite the children to create their own poetry performance techniques. Acting out a poem enables children to better understand the poem's meaning, its events or scenes, and the sounds and rhythm of its language. However, the emphasis of a poetry performance should be on the process of discovering a poem's meaning, not on executing a polished product, so props and costumes should be minimal.

## Creative Alternatives for Performing Poetry

- Employ props and physical objects referenced in the poem.
- Try puppetry for poem character voices.
- Find or create simple masks to suggest poem personae.
- Fold paper into origami shapes related to the poem.
- Draw a simple picture (à la Pictionary) while reading the poem.
- Cook, mix, or bake along with the poem reading, like a cooking show.
- Perform the poem using signing (American Sign Language).
- Choose poems with monologues or dialogues for solo and duet performances.

- Try role-playing (with hats or simple costumes) to convey the character in a poem that has a strong persona or point of view.
- Select excerpts from a novel in verse to perform with multiple narrators in reader's theater style.
- Act out movements or emotions in the poem through pantomime.
- Use simple movements like a hop or bounce for poems with a regular rhythm.
- Create simple sound effects as the background for a poem reading.
- Add a musical soundtrack as the background for a poem performance.
- Orchestrate a "flash mob" reading of a favorite poem.

As a traveling company of professional actors who present "verse as theater," the organization Poetry Alive! (http://poetryalive.com) shows us how poems can be shared in lively, personal ways. They suggest a sequence that consists of adult reading of poems, guiding children in choosing poems, establishing poetry teams, scripting the chosen poem into a kind of play, scoring the motion and emotion of the poem with gesture or pantomime, and then performing the poem. When Poetry Alive! members perform a poem, they have memorized it. They give performance points for having a confident stance, facing the audience, using an outside voice, filling the space, and using big gestures. They even insist on taking a bow! Oral reading demonstrates for children the ways to use the voice to express thoughts, feelings, and moods. Thus, it is important to establish a respectful sense of audience for poetry performances. Poetry performance can help teach children to listen attentively, respectfully, and responsively. Some children may discover a real affinity for expressing themselves through poetry performance. This may even lead to establishing a poetry troupe and having students perform poems at other libraries or on the morning announcements at school or during poetry month. You will find *Forget-Me-Nots: Poems to Learn by Heart,* compiled by Mary Ann Hoberman, an invaluable resource, as well as the Poetry Out Loud competition resources for tweens preparing for high school. Some children may want to investigate participating in University Interscholastic League or other organized events that hold competitive recitations of poetry. If you're really feeling ambitious and the performance bug has caught on, consider orchestrating a flash mob to perform a poem as a group in a public venue.

This requires coordination and practice, but it could be a fun and memorable moment. Be sure to film it to enjoy again and again.

As poet Brod Bagert (1992, 23) says about encouraging children's involvement in poetry, we can "awaken inside them the power of their own presence, and breathe life into young spirits." As the poets themselves have said, poetry is meant to be heard and savored person to person. Emily Dickinson wrote in her poem No. 89:

> A word is dead
> When it is said,
> Some say.
> I say it just
> Begins to live
> That day.

## Conclusion

As we move into sharing poetry out loud with kids, we need to make sure that we will be comfortable and confident in taking the lead. That includes, for example, getting comfortable with quiet moments, understanding how to interpret line breaks, using appropriate facial expressions, and planning effective introductions. And we can experiment with ten different strategies that involve children in the oral reading of poetry. To review, make yourself a checklist of poetry performance strategies and challenge yourself to try each one—eventually!

- Begin with the leader reading aloud and modeling.
- Read poetry aloud in unison.
- Invite group participation with repeated refrains.
- Use movement with poems.
- Organize call-and-response read-alouds.
- Use multiple groups.
- Lead line-around and solo line readings.
- Orchestrate poems for two voices.

- Lead two groups in reading a poem as a canon.
- Set poems to familiar tunes and sing them.

And as you become comfortable with these approaches, try creative alternatives and combinations, including sign language, puppetry, and the like.

*Poetry begins in delight and ends in wisdom.*

—Robert Frost, poet

6

# What Happens after You Share the Poem?

*Poetry comes nearer to vital truth than history.*
—Plato, philosopher

HAT HAPPENS AFTER YOU SHARE POETRY WITH CHILdren? What kinds of questions are appropriate to ask? How do you lead a discussion gently? In this chapter, we consider how to encourage children's responses to poetry through drama, music, art, and other activities. We also briefly examine how best to nurture budding poets and how to share children's responses in meaningful ways.

## Asking Questions

When we read aloud a poem to children, we are often hesitant about what to do next. We need to give a few moments for the poem to sink in, but the silence sometimes seems uncomfortable. And we would like to know what kids are thinking. Did they enjoy the poem? Understand it? Want to hear it again? How do we ask them without being too pushy or ruining the magic of the moment? Following up on a poetry reading is not a lockstep process: Read poem, ask questions, done. It is more intuitive, following the lead of the children, the poem, the moment. And this becomes clearer and more natural the more often you share poems with children. Nonetheless, there are a few guidelines that can help establish some basics.

In her work in the schools, Amy McClure (1990) found that the children seemed unsure of what was expected and were more concerned about offering correct answers than exploring alternative possibilities. How do we avoid this trap, this conditioning from our own past? Here are question prompts that invite young people to think about the poem in relation to their own life experiences. Choose only two or three questions at most to guide discussion, and vary which questions you use regularly. Consider letting students choose which questions they want to tackle once the question prompts are familiar:

- What does the poet say to you in this poem? Why do you think the poet said that?
- Does this poem remind you of anything you know about?
- How are the people in this poem like people you know? Or not like people you know?
- Would you like to go to the place described in this poem? Why or why not?
- Did the things in this poem ever happen to you? Where or when?
- What things are there in this poem to see? Have you seen them before? Where?
- Is this poem honest or true? Do you believe what it says? Why or why not?
- What things happen in this poem that you would like to happen to you? Or not happen to you?
- What do you think made the poet write this poem?
- Are there any words or lines that you think are interesting? Why?

These discussion questions are based on Patrick Groff's "poetry talk" questions in David Booth's and Bill Moore's *Poems Please! Sharing Poetry with Children*, Amy McClure's facilitating questions in *Sunrises and Songs: Reading and Writing Poetry in an Elementary Classroom*, and Aaren Perry's "Poetry Critique Guide Sheet" in *Poetry across the Curriculum: An Action Guide for Elementary Teachers*.

Pulitzer Prize winner Jorie Graham (2005) explores the value of poetry in the education of our children in a thought-provoking essay in which she comments:

When you give a child poems (remembering, once the silence closes back over the end of the poem, not to ask "what does this mean?" but rather, "what did you feel?" or "what did you see?"), you are opening up different parts of his or her reading apparatus than fiction or drama or journalism open up. (http://64.77.108.137/poetry_thinks.htm)

Our questions need to be as open ended as possible, and we need to be open to all kinds of responses from children. They may not give us the answers we expect to hear, but their answers will help us understand how they see the poem and perhaps help us see the poem itself in new ways.

Colleague June Harris wrote about sharing poetry with her students:

What I learned . . . is that when we give students a "translation" of a poem, they stop thinking about it. They take our word, give those words back to us, and don't bother thinking or discussing any more. I've found it much more effective to let *them* come up with ideas, only correcting or intervening when they make inferences *not* supported by the words in the poem. As long as they can support their statements, I've found it more worthwhile to let them do the interpreting. (Personal communication, fall 2006)

We can follow up our questions by probing gently to help children articulate their reasons for their responses—often a challenge for young children. It is an interactive dynamic that involves a give-and-take, not a "guess what the grown-up is thinking" game.

Georgia Heard says:

To read and understand the meaning of a poem takes patience. . . . Reading a difficult poem challenges us to read in a different way. We must learn to read a poem multiple times, and even then keep returning to it. It's a very different kind of reading than what most of our world demands—quick, easy sound bites to get us through the day. (1999, 44)

Some poems are immediately accessible, but others need more time to grow on us. Do not be surprised if children refer to a poem days or weeks after you shared it.

As Booth and Moore recommend in their book *Poems Please! Sharing Poetry with Children*:

> We must seek our children's views, listen to their interpretations, treat them with respect and seriousness, interact with them in consultation and conferences, allow conversation and informal discussion, and encourage the explorations of their own experiences in relation to the poems. We must not make them afraid to say the wrong thing, but enable them to voice their own ideas. . . . Open-ended, divergent thinking helps children formulate their own questions about poetry. Aesthetic learning comes from experiences provided by teachers where the poem is understood in the deepest way possible, with the mind and the heart. (2003, 59)

## PRACTITIONER PERSPECTIVE

*Poetry is so personal on so many levels. It seems to get right to the point of what the writer is feeling in his or her soul, yet other times poetry creates more questions than answers. Poetry is so different from fiction. It is not trying to create a story with a plot to follow; it is simply stating feelings and experiences. It is just amazing how so much can come from so few words. To share this with students, I think you definitely need to let them know you care about them and care about their feelings—whether they are reading poetry or writing poetry. That a teacher or librarian cares to ask what they think of something, and for there not to be a wrong answer, is a big deal. Some kids today do not have anyone to ask them what they think or how they feel. What a great opportunity this affords kids, especially high-risk kids! If we start out with some poetry and let children know right off the bat that what they think is important, we just might get them hooked for the year for the other classroom tasks and hooked for life as poetry readers and writers! It just seems that poetry can be such a catalyst for building a supportive, nurturing, trusting classroom or library environment.*

Rhonda Brockett, librarian
Ponder Elementary School, Ponder, Texas

In poetry sharing, the emphasis should be balanced between the poem and the response, allowing for time to read, time to think, time to talk. Not every question will generate spontaneous responses. Some trial and error is involved in finding questions that are comfortable to you. And not every child will respond verbally. Some of the quietest children may experience the poem deeply but not ask or respond to questions in a group setting. That is OK. And none of the follow-up questions should overwhelm the poem itself. A few minutes is often enough to open the door to discussion. Just be sure that you are not doing most of the talking. Ask your question and wait for the response. Do not answer your own question. Do not bombard children with too many questions. Do not interrupt the poem reading with questions or explanations. One or two questions can often be enough to follow up a single poem. When this dynamic is in place time after time, children will become comfortable with follow-up questions and will often volunteer their own responses before you can ask your questions because they know you are already open to their opinions! In *Tigers, Lilies, Toadstools, and Thunderbolts: Engaging K–8 Students with Poetry*, Iris McClellan Tiedt reminds us that "children's reactions to poetry at all ages will be influenced greatly by your presentation as their interpreter of poetry, for attitudes and values are reflected in your voice as you read, in the way you introduce the poem, and in your enthusiasm" (2002, 18). Often the best way to end a poetry-sharing session is to follow up a few questions and responses with a return to the poem: "Shall we read it again?"

## Fostering Response and Discussion

Asking questions is only part of what we do after sharing a poem. Opening the floor to discussion is also a critical step. Manning and Manning remind us:

> Discussing poems after they are read helps children develop critical thinking skills. By responding to poems, children make decisions about their likes and dislikes. Allowing children to select poems for oral reading also helps develop their evaluative skills. It also makes the children feel that their opinions are valued, and encourages them to participate. (1997, 100–101)

**PRACTITIONER PERSPECTIVE**

*I was student teaching a third-grade class in a farming community in Kyle, Texas. Suddenly, the principal announced over the intercom that we had a Kansas Alert. That was code meaning that a tornado was coming, and we were to take cover immediately. One of the boys spied the storm out the window and yelled, "I see a tornado coming!" Chaos ensued. Children began panicking and crying all around me. Amazingly, I was able to stay calm and take the children to our designated safe spot, a one-person, disabled-access bathroom. Let me tell you, it was a tight squeeze! The children had to take turns standing and sitting so we would all fit. Two actually had to sit on the toilet! I had grabbed* Where the Sidewalk Ends *from the shelf as we filed into the restroom. The kids were still crying, sniffling, and hugging each other. To calm everyone down and really get their minds off of the situation, I stood crammed in the corner by the sink and began to read from the book in a very silly fashion. Little by little, the sniffling stopped and the heartbeats slowed. I began taking requests and the laughter echoed (loudly) in our small space. We just kept going and they never got tired of it. Eventually, after over an hour (I had forgotten to pay attention to the time), the teacher from next door opened the door to the bathroom. She looked at us incredulously and said, "The all-clear came half an hour ago!" We had not been able to hear the intercom from the restroom. Upon finding we were coming out, the children groaned a chorus of "Awwww!" "Can we do this again?" "Can we keep reading?" were the questions I heard as we made our way back to our desks. Later, as I prepared to leave, I saw that the tornado had literally ripped through the field adjacent to the school. I was shaky when I realized the seriousness of the situation. We came very close to disaster, but we had our minds on other things—poetry.*

Melanie Letendre, librarian
Pike Middle School, Justin, Texas

Alternative grouping may be even more helpful than asking the right questions. Ask children to turn to a partner and talk with her or him about what the poet is saying. Children are often more comfortable sharing their opinions with one peer or poetry partner rather than with the whole group. Or small groups or poetry circles can also function well for digging deeper into a poem's meaning.

One colleague, June Jacko, used art projects done in small groups to help children explore multicultural poetry. Each group had a different poem, and after all the poems had been introduced, read by the teacher, and performed by the class, each group created a mini-mural to illustrate their poem. Then they explained their murals to the class as a whole. This kind of response activity helps children think deeply about a poem, talk critically with classmates about the words and ideas, make connections to the lesson's content, and express themselves creatively about their own interpretations of the poem's meaning.

Poetry circles, patterned along the line of literature circles, offer a wonderful collaborative opportunity for children to share preferences, read aloud, and talk about poems. Poetry circles, like book clubs or book groups, usually allow children to bond with the same peers over time, and the small-group atmosphere establishes a safety level that encourages the sharing of more personal reactions, positive and negative. One librarian I know holds a Poetry at Lunch group. The students bring their lunches and poetry to the library and share their favorite poems and poetry books. The meetings are fairly informal and unstructured but very successful. Another colleague, Janet Hilbun, ran the Poetry and Pop-Tarts Club before the day started at her middle school. She provided the Pop-Tarts and juice drink, and kids read their favorite poems or poems they had written themselves. It was a big draw for these tweens. Notice something else? Combining poetry and food is a good way for gathering group activities. "Recipe" poetry books like *Sopa de frijoles / Bean Soup*, *Arroz con leche / Rice Pudding*, and *Guacamole: Un poema para cocinar / A Cooking Poem*, all by Jorge Argueta, make it easy.

Poet and teacher Georgia Heard is often a poet in residence in the schools. She writes:

> Rather than standing up in the front of the room and asking questions about a poem I already know the answers to, I want to put my students in the position of learning about the poem for themselves. The key to learning how to enter the door of a difficult poem is to teach our students how to unlock the door themselves, and for them to find pleasure in this process. (1999, 43)

In her work with children, she recommends the following:

When you give a poem to your students, center it on a clean sheet of paper with a lot of white space around it so they can write directly on the sheet. . . . They can circle important or difficult words, write questions about parts they don't understand, or just write their thoughts about the poem—making the poem more accessible and less distant. (1999, 44)

If students can write, think, and share, they are mustering all their language resources to try to put their thoughts into words. Although this may take a few extra minutes or may even become the focus for the session, it is time well spent as we provide opportunity for children to respond to poems they find meaningful.

In their article "Talk about Poetry," Manning and Manning (1997) suggest that natural, front-porch-type discussions are the best method for enhancing children's enjoyment and understanding of poetry. They found that responses

**PRACTITIONER PERSPECTIVE**

*One of the questions I like to ask students after we enjoy a poem together is "What did you see in your mind while you listened?" Since poetry is largely about imagery, this gets students accustomed to anticipating the pictures poets try to paint for their audience. Their responses often surprise me—they're usually quite diverse and different from what I expect. Their mental images are also very telling about them as individuals, which helps me get to know them better. I also usually ask what their favorite part of the poem is and why, which can lead into discussions about the sounds words make, the emotions poetry can bring out, and the importance of word choice. With my older students, I sometimes ask specifically what emotion they feel during a particular poem. I find that with the younger students, I just hear "happy," but the older ones are better able to articulate a wide range of feelings. We even have a couple of posters showing different faces labeled with the corresponding feelings. I see them glancing at it sometimes to find just the one they want to respond to my question. It's a good springboard, and then we talk about which words, lines, or techniques the poet utilized to inspire that emotion. My hope is that in discussing these aspects, it will help them when they are writing their own poetry.*

Tracy LaHue, elementary school librarian
Mansfield, Texas

often cluster around the reader and his or her personal enjoyment of the poem and its rhyme (if the poem rhymes), the topic of the poem, or the word choice. Manning and Manning recommend using questions as a guide to encourage open discussions about poetry but advise against asking all of them or feeling limited to asking them in any particular order. In fact, the ideal approach may be displaying the guiding questions on a large poster and allowing children to select the question they want to address within their small-group settings. For further guidance, you can assign each member of a four-person group a distinctive role in facilitating the group dynamics. In this way, each person is sure to participate in some capacity and to feel included in the group activity. The roles in a four-person poetry circle might include the following:

- Reader—reads the poem out loud to the group
- Writer—writes down the group's responses
- Researcher—looks up other poems, other books, or other information as needed
- Reporter—shares the group's response with the whole class or large group

Or small groups can be used in other creative ways. For example, children could work together in small groups to introduce new poetry books, with each group examining a different book and presenting a book talk or poetry performance of it for the large group. Children could also work in small groups to consider multiple works by the same poet, with each group member examining a different title and then presenting the poet and all of his or her works to the large group. For an even more ambitious use of group discussion, try organizing a learning center, with each group participating in a different poetry experience, such as a featured poet center, an audiobook center of commercially produced poetry to listen to, a jam-session center with equipment for children to record their own poem readings, and a poetic arts center where children create art to accompany designated poems, a digital center to create poetry mini-movies or slideshows. When each group has completed its center, they can report on their experiences to the larger group. After trying this approach, older children might enjoy planning similar centers for the future.

As we move from sharing poetry to encouraging children to respond to poetry, we can rely on poetry partners or small groups for a variety of other activities. As we offer options in drama, music, art, crafts, and other areas, we often find that allowing children to express themselves with a friend or small group increases their comfort level with the task at hand.

---

**POET PROFILE**

## In His Own Words

### DAVID L. HARRISON

The tom-tom beat of poetry begins in the womb tucked below mother's heart. Our first one-way conversations with baby are poems of love.

I love you, pretty baby.
Just look at those eyes.
Such perfect tiny toes
sweet enough to eat.

Little wonder that most children, before they learn fear, can do anything. Words are toys to play with, rearrange, make up, jump rope to, yell, or joyfully shriek. In school, poetry continues to course through the veins of children's daily lives. They sing it, chant it, dance it, draw it, hear and read it without worrying about what it is or what it's called.

Sooner or later, of course, we name it. Everything must have a name so we'll know it when we see it. Some names sound friendly: *soup*. Some, ominous: *storm*. Some stir vague feelings of inadequacy: *poetry*. The older we are, the further removed from the innocent powers of youth, the more challenging poetry may sound.

That's why the best time to learn to love poetry is in elementary school, when imagination, though unfocused and untrained, is also unfettered by the cumulative clutter of learned restrictions. Here are two kid-tested techniques that open doors and invite students into what Frost called the game of words.

## Word-of-the-Month Poetry Challenge

Every word contains the seeds of stories, essays, novels, songs, and poems. Each month I post a word on my blog (http://davidlharrison.wordpress.com). The challenge is to think about the word until something about it inspires a poem. This is a risk-free opportunity to write a poem and share it. Children (and adults) who write poems this way focus first on what they want to say. Style and polish come later. And that's the right order. Here's a sample from the month when the word was *time*.

## Pictures

Tick, tock, tick, tock
goes the clock of
Father Time. Pictures
start whizzing by.

The first car was
invented. There go
the Wright Brothers
now contented. See
the rocket set off
to explore? Later on,
I was born.

Tick, tock, tick, tock
goes the clock of
Father Time. Pictures
stop flashing by.

*by Rachel Heinrichs, fourth grade, Pennsylvania (used with permission)*

## Partner Poems

On a New York City school playground I once observed two kids standing face-to-face, taking turns yelling. He would yell, she would laugh; she would yell, he would laugh. Why yelling brought forth such gales of glee I don't know. But they were partners in a very loud onomatopoeic poem. At a lower decibel level this is another way to involve young people in writing poems:

- Make a list of favorite subjects: family, pets, friends, school.
- Choose a writing partner.
- Have a brief conversation about the chosen topic.
- Record the conversation.
- Keep the lines short.
- Arrange the lines to form a beginning, a middle, and an end.
- Read the rough draft aloud with suitable expression.
- Sand down the rough edges.
- Perform for an audience.
- Celebrate the accomplishment.

Is it pure poetry? Maybe. Maybe not. Is it fun? You bet. Worth another try? Very likely. A sample:

---

## MaMa Mia Pizzaria

| *(First voice)* | *(Second voice)* |
|---|---|
| I love pizza! | |
| | Crunchy, munchy, crust. |
| Hot cheese | |
| yummy, yummy. | |
| | Spicy, spicy pepperoni. |
| Mushroom, yucky! | |
| | Cheese, yummy! |
| Pepperoni, delicious | |
| | Broccoli pizza, disgusting |
| I love pizza | |
| | Everyday! |

*by third grade students, New Jersey (used with permission)*

Every school-visiting poet relies on favorite techniques and prompts to hook kids on poetry. We need plenty if we are to appeal to all the learning styles. My favorite has three parts: keep it fun; keep it fun; keep it fun. Serious will come soon, unless we're on guard.

## The Perfect Word
*by David L. Harrison*

Don't say chartreuse
If the apple's green!
Words are picky
With what they mean,
They don't like it
When you guess,
The wrong word
Can make a mess.
Milk is milk,
Cream is cream,
The Amazon
Is not a stream.
It all depends
On what you use
So do be careful
When you choose.
Every word
Can be just fine,
In the right place,
In the right line.

*© 2012 by David L. Harrison. Used with permission.*

**CLASS EXERCISE** Harrison's poem begs for a word-choosing exercise like using magnetic poetry to create a simple poem placing each word just so. Or write key vocabulary (appropriate to the level of the students) on index cards, one word per card, then string a clothesline across the room and pin the words in a poetic order to create a one-line poem. And be sure to try Harrison's "Word-of-the-Month Poetry Challenge" and "Partner Poems" activities, too.

---

## Dramatizing Poetry

What happens after you share a poem? In my experience, talking about the poem naturally occurs first. But there are also other possibilities for engaging children in activities that expand their responses to a poem they have heard or read. This includes connecting drama and poetry. Dramatic activities include a wide spectrum—from the informal and improvisational to the more planned and structured. Resources like *Creative Drama in the Classroom and Beyond*, by Nellie McCaslin (2000), provide a multitude of ideas for connecting poetry and drama, including the following:

- Try physicalization (acting out motions, movements, gestures).
- Use pantomime (movement without speech).
- Create sound and voice effects.
- Plan and participate in a tableau (a moment of a poem frozen and posed as a scene).
- Role-play (taking on the persona of a character to speak the related lines).
- Perform monologues or dialogues.
- Use improvisation.
- Orchestrate scripted performances.

As we bring drama into poetry, we can allow children to exercise their natural wiggliness in acting out poems full of descriptions of motion and movement, such as "A Circle of Sun," by Rebecca Kai Dotlich, from *The 20th-Century Children's Poetry Treasury*, compiled by Jack Prelutsky. Or we can challenge them to use mime to perform the movements suggested in a poem without speaking at all. A poem that lends itself well to mime is "Hiccup Cure," by Shel Silverstein, from *A Light in the Attic*. Add sound back into poetry reading with sound or voice effects for poems such as "The Mosquitoes," by Douglas Florian, from *Insectlopedia*. And use "I, Too," by Langston Hughes, from *I, Too, Am America*, illustrated by Bryan Collier, as a powerful poem for staging a tableau. Set a table as if for dinner and seat a guest in every chair. The poem's reader stands aside, reading the poem. Photograph or film the tableau to share it more widely.

For role-playing, choose a poem with a strong point of view. For example, "Moon, Have You Met My Mother?", by Karla Kuskin, from the book of the same title, asks a question that could be addressed by a reader of any age, culture, or gender. Use different readers to convey different perspectives on the mother-child relationship. Individual or paired readers can also be used to perform poems written in monologue or dialogue. For example, "I Brought a Worm," by Kalli Dakos, from *If You're Not Here, Please Raise Your Hand*, lends itself to a solo reading (along with a gummy-worm prop!). For those brave enough to try it, improvisation can be a dramatic tool for poetry sharing. Children with a spontaneous and dramatic flair can have a lot of fun acting out a poem's meaning on the spot. For example, Judith Viorst's "Credit," from *Sad Underwear and Other*

## PRACTITIONER PERSPECTIVE

*My first exposure to poetry was in first grade. I had a teacher who asked her students to memorize a poem a week. Eager to please, I chose my favorite, which was and still is "The Night before Christmas." My teacher, knowing that I was determined and that my choice was certainly longer than the usual first-grade poem, allowed me to take longer than a week to memorize it. She was extremely supportive. To top off this experience, I was chosen to recite the poem in front of the entire school during the annual Christmas assembly! This was an exciting accomplishment for a first grader. I can still recite the poem and love to share it with the different classrooms I teach in. I am sorry to say that my memorization of poetry is limited to that one selection. However, my first-grade experience has given me lots of confidence in other areas. In the past I have had to perform several monologues for which memorization skills were an absolute necessity. My ability to memorize has also boosted my test-taking skills. As I reflect back, I am amazed at what one poem can do!*

Pam McWhorter, third-grade teacher
Pasco, Washington

*Complications,* is a short poem about a child's frustration about an unidentified "it." The child actor can improvise what "it" might be. And finally, for those who want to orchestrate a full-blown dramatic interpretation, I urge you to invite children to work with you to choose and script a favorite poem for performance. Seek out a drama coach or drama teacher, incorporate local actors or children's theater companies, and help children learn the process of taking poetry public. One poem that lends itself to a full performance is "Harriet Tubman," by Eloise Greenfield, from *Honey, I Love*. It has a strong narrative, vivid imagery, and even a refrain. In addition, it is a true story from history!

Never underestimate the possibilities drama offers for making poetry come alive. I have found that we grown-ups are often a bit shy and hesitant about hamming it up, but children usually are not. The world of pretending comes quite naturally to children, and extending that world to include poetry makes sense. So start with short, humorous poetry at first, and make it active and participatory. When kids do poetry, the experience is often deep and meaningful and creates a memory that lasts for a long, long time.

## Music and Poetry

Poetry and music have a strong, natural relationship, given how rhythmic much of poetry is and how poetic many song lyrics are. Children enjoy the steady beat of nursery rhymes, Mother Goose, and many light and humorous poems. They can clap or move to the beat, responding to the music of the rhyme. If you collaborate with music teachers or local musicians, it is even possible to use musical instruments to accompany poems with strong rhyme or rhythm and plan other poetry-music connections. Or try choosing music to play as a backdrop for the oral reading of a special poem. And with older children, writing down song lyrics, looking at line breaks, and separating out the words and the musical notes are effective approaches to poetry appreciation. Songs in book form can help young children see how language is used to tell a story poetically. So many songs and poems from different cultures are now available in book form. And some poems with strong meter can be put to the tune of a familiar song and sung (as described in the strategies in chapter 5). Whether we beat a poem's rhythm, sing a poem, unpack song lyrics, seek out a song poem picture book, or create a poem performance that incorporates words and music, we can help children enjoy the sound of poetry when we look for ways to connect poetry and music.

**Books of Poetry and Songs for Children**

Julie Andrews and Emma Walton Hamilton, eds., *Julie Andrews'
    Collection of Poems, Songs, and Lullabies*
Joseph Bruchac, *Four Ancestors: Stories, Songs, and Poems from Native North
    America*
Ashley Bryan, *All Night, All Day: A Child's First Book of African-
    American Spirituals*
Lulu Delacre, ed., *Arrorró, mi niño: Latino Lullabies and Gentle Games*
———, ed., *Arroz con leche: Popular Songs and Rhymes from Latin
    America*
Dan Fox, ed., *A Treasury of Children's Songs: Forty Favorites to Sing and Play*
Kathy Henderson, ed., *Hush, Baby, Hush! Lullabies from Around the World*
Frané Lessac, ed., *Camp Granada: Sing-Along Camp Songs*
José-Luis Orozco, ed., *"De colores" and Other Latin American Folk Songs for
    Children*
———, ed., *Diez deditos / Ten Little Fingers and Other Play Rhymes
    and Action Songs from Latin America*
———, ed., *Fiestas: A Year of Latin American Songs of Celebration*
Alvin Schwartz, ed., *And the Green Grass Grew All Around: Folk
    Poetry from Everyone*

## Art and Poetry

Poetry and art go hand in hand, since poems are full of imagery and poetry books
are often full of illustrations. As a result, there are many possibilities for using art
activities following the reading of poetry. Obviously, children can draw a picture
to accompany a favorite poem or use a variety of other media (such as clay, paint,
fabric) to create art to pair with poems. They can also experiment with some of
their artistic styles and media used to illustrate their favorite poetry books, such
as collage, pen and ink, computer-generated art, or photography. Consult with
art teachers, art students, or local artists to learn more about various techniques.

Children can also create posters, bookmarks, or book covers to promote
favorite poetry books. These can be displayed alongside the usual poetry promotion materials. Children can richly illustrate homemade poetry anthologies as
gifts for loved ones on special occasions.

And do not forget to introduce poetry books that incorporate art explicitly. For example, the classic poetry book *Hailstones and Halibut Bones*, by Mary O'Neill, introduces primary and secondary colors through individual poems that conjure up all kinds of sensory associations for pink, black, yellow, and so forth. *Red Sings from Treetops: A Year in Colors*, by Joyce Sidman, and *Color Me a Rhyme: Nature Poems for Young People*, by Jane Yolen, offer additional perspectives on color in nature. There are also several poetry anthologies that are illustrated by fine art. These mini–art museums can help children compare how artists and poets have expressed themselves through the ages.

Look at contemporary poetry books for additional examples of distinctive art and crafts. For example, Kristine O'Connell George's book *Fold Me a Poem* links poetry with origami, the Japanese art of paper folding. Or consider the poetry collections of Douglas Florian, a recipient of both illustration and poetry awards for his unique paintings, collages, and poems. His book *Unbeelievables* even incorporates rubber stamps in its illustrations. Concrete poems also display an artistic connection since they take the shape of their subject. Seek out some of the books of concrete poetry by Joan Bransfield Graham, Betsy Franco, John Grandits, J. Patrick Lewis, or Paul B. Janeczko to see how poem and shape work together. Children can take other poems (or write their own) and copy them into the shapes of their subjects, illustrating in any way they choose.

Another way to reexperience a poem is by manipulating its layout. Using technology to do the manipulating offers another opportunity for children to express themselves. They can tape themselves reading their favorite poems or capture the voices of friends, family members, or others reading poems, much like Robert Pinsky's Favorite Poem Project. Children may also use digital or video photography, which allows them to add more artistic elements. Children can create a short film for their favorite poem, with voice-over readings accompanying the images they choose to evoke their poem. A PowerPoint slide show can achieve a similar result using still photography and audiotape of voice, music, or sound effects. Older students could conduct a poetry webcast or TV poetry café or create an online student poetry magazine or zine. And any of these productions can be broadcast on school or community audio or cable networks or presented at special occasions, such as open houses, community meetings, or Poetry Month celebrations. Most children enjoy experimenting with technological tools, and many are very savvy about creative ways to express themselves. Using these tools to encourage children to share their responses to poetry can have powerful results.

## Poetry Books That Showcase Fine Art

Barbara Brenner, ed., *Voices: Poetry and Art from around the World*

Jan Greenberg, ed., *Heart to Heart: New Poems Inspired by Twentieth-Century American Art*

————, ed., *Side by Side: New Poems Inspired by Art from around the World*

J. Patrick Lewis and Jane Yolen, *Self-Portrait with Seven Fingers: A Life of Marc Chagall in Verse*

Naomi Shihab Nye, ed., *The Space between Our Footsteps: Poems and Paintings from the Middle East*

————, ed., *The Tree Is Older Than You Are: A Bilingual Gathering of Poems and Stories from Mexico with Paintings by Mexican Artists*

Nora Panzer, ed., *Celebrate America in Poetry and Art*

Belinda Rochelle, ed., *Words with Wings: A Treasury of African-American Poetry and Art*

Diane Siebert, *Tour America: A Journey through Poems and Art*

Charles Sullivan, ed., *Here Is My Kingdom: Hispanic-American Literature and Art for Young People*

# Magnetic Poetry

Nearly everyone has seen the low-tech but very inviting magnetic poetry kits that are now sold widely. The simple concept began with a guy named Dave who decided to glue words to pieces of magnets and stick them to a pizza tin as he was trying to write a song. He made the first kits himself and sold them locally. Since then, he has sold more than three million poetry kits. Clearly, the idea of manipulating words to create poems from a limited repertoire is a challenge that many enjoy. And the magnetic backing makes it possible to create poetry venues on refrigerators, file cabinets, cookie sheets, and any other metallic surface. Magnetic Poetry Inc. now has its own website (www.magneticpoetry.com) that offers a multitude of options, including Shakespeare, haiku, and foreign-language kits, as well as kits designed especially for children. The company website even publishes poetry created by adult or child magnetic poets.

A public library branch in my area has a place for magnetic poetry in its teen area. The staff made their own magnets using colored paper and different fonts, and creating magnetic poetry has become very popular. And I heard of another library in the area with an entire magnetic wall in their storytime room. What fun it would be to create gigantic words for that wall! Homemade alternatives need not be expensive and can be personalized to include words and names that are locally relevant. One librarian I know found that her magnetic poetry words were so popular that they kept disappearing little by little. As an alternative, she made a word bank on cards, strung clotheslines across a bulletin board, and left a bag of clothespins nearby—low tech, low budget, and it worked. The informality and spontaneity of magnetic (or nearly magnetic!) poetry makes creating poetry seem fun and easy, and it can serve as an appealing bridge to writing poetry—on paper.

---

**POET PROFILE**

# In Her Own Words

## NAOMI SHIHAB NYE

As a child, I started writing poems because my ears were filled with voices—the rich, musical voice of my mother, who sang us a string of wonderful lullabies every night to put us to sleep. The whimsical, graciously tender accent of my immigrant Palestinian father. The poems of Carl Sandburg on the public television station, which I still love more than thirty years later. The grave German tones of my grandparent and the mixed rhythms of all our neighbors.

Although the voice of my first-grade teacher did not like me very much, the voices of friends I made through children's-magazine poetry pages assured me, as did my father's folktales, that there was a larger world beyond our classroom. The young writers I read were my secret friends. When I started sending poems to magazines at age seven, the act was colored with no hope of proving any-thing—that my writing was "good" or "original"—but simply as a reaching out to those secret friends, a kind of correspondence. Where were they living? How would it change our lives to know one another? Because I read and wrote, the borders of everywhere always felt big. My brother and I visited the library every Saturday, balancing huge skyscrapers of books. In the library, everyone was rich.

My second-grade teacher, a legend at age seventy, *did* like me—thank good-ness. She liked everybody most of the time and bopped us on the heads with her bangle bracelets when we acted up. She was steeped in a deeper love of poetry and literature than any other teacher I would ever have. (This is hard, I realize later—to have the best teacher of your academic life in second grade. The rest of those years you keep hoping for someone to live up to him or her.) We memorized William Blake's "Songs of Innocence" in her class when we were seven years old. She did not worry about our not understanding Blake's mystical poems, or anything else. She said the human mind had plenty of room for mys-teries. If there was something we didn't understand, we could turn it over and over with our minds, like a lemon drop or a lozenge. She had faith in us. What we didn't know we were on our way to learning. Poetry gave us doors. "Swing it open!" she said. And we were swinging.

A long time later, working with students and their writing in Texas, I tried to remember all the reasons we have every day for needing to speak out on paper. Because sometimes paper listens better than people do. Because paper doesn't interrupt. Because our own stories will surprise us when we look at them like that, outside our minds. They will lead us, if we let them. One discovery will lead us to more than we can imagine from any given spot.

"In her own words" is excerpted from Naomi Shihab Nye, "Texas Authors: Naomi Shihab Nye," *The State of Reading* 1, no. 2 (1994): 77–79. Used with permission.

# Blue Bucket

*by Naomi Shihab Nye*

What if, instead of war,
we shared our buckets
of wind and worry?
Said, tell me the story
you carry there,
steeping in old pain
and future hope,
rich with fragrant
savory spices,
ginger, turmeric,
tarragon, find me
a spoon in one
of your pockets,
even if we don't
speak the same language,
I'll sip your dream,
and then, and then, say
this is what it looks like
to me—offering up a taste
of my own crazy past,
my own regret,
my regret on behalf of others,
and maybe
you hold my bucket
a while, see what
the handle feels like,
and I hold yours,
or maybe both buckets
are empty and
we trade them forever,
or maybe we

*(continued)*

just wanted to feel
noticed and hardworking
for a moment,
and that's why we were
swinging them so hard,
as we walked up
the lonely path
where we met,
and paused.

© 2012 by Naomi Shihab Nye. Used with permission. "Blue Bucket"
first appeared in *P*TAG: 31 Poems by 31 Poets for Teens*, edited by
Sylvia Vardell and Janet Wong (Princeton, NJ: Pomelo Books).

**CLASS EXERCISE** It would be ideal to find a blue bucket (or a bucket you can paint blue) and bring it to share along with the poem—in fact, place a copy of the poem in the bucket to remove for effect when reading the poem aloud. Then invite the students to write their own (anonymous) worry or dream on a piece of paper and drop it in the bucket. Decide together if this is private or to be shared, discussed, and turned into a new found poem.

## Writing Poetry

Children who hear poetry read aloud by an enthusiastic adult and browse through poetry books in their self-selected reading naturally turn to writing poetry when they have the chance. Poetry writing is one more type of writing that children of all ages should have the opportunity to experience. What may surprise you, however, is just how many models of poetry writing there are. What follows are several sources, forms, formulas, and activities that offer a fun introduction to poetic writing. Any of these can serve as a motivating springboard for a writing workshop. By collaborating with teachers, librarians can provide a great deal of support in promoting and developing poetry writing. But even with the sometimes-limited time available for activities or instruction in the library setting, we can incorporate poetry-writing opportunities there, too.

## THE BENEFITS OF WRITING POETRY WITH YOUNG PEOPLE

Poet Sara Holbrook offers these sound reasons for encouraging children's poetry writing efforts:

Writing poetry jogs the memory: "Working my memory over, I prioritize, make order out of chaos, rediscover details, and put events in sequence."

Writing poetry demands keen observation: "We want students to do more than watch—we want them to see."

Writing poetry requires precise language: "Poetry asks the important questions and forces us to define ourselves in concrete visual terms."

Writing poetry stimulates good communication skills: "What good is knowing something if we can't communicate our ideas to others?"

Writing poetry encourages reading fluency: "Poems want to be read again and again."

Writing poetry helps us learn about ourselves and our world: "Reading is trickle-down learning; writing is building our own learning curve."

Poetry—written, spoken, or read—is powerful language: "Poetry has been a jungle gym in my life, a place to stretch and flip, climb to the top for a look-see, and occasionally fall and skin my nose."

Source: Based on Sara Holbrook, *Practical Poetry; A Nonstandard Approach to Meeting Content-Area Standards* (Portsmouth, NH: Heinemann, 2005), 4–7.

It may be helpful to consider the advice of poets themselves when setting the stage for poetry writing. In several poetry collections for young people, a paragraph explaining the poet's sources of inspiration accompanies each poem.

Poet Georgia Heard (1994) reminds us how important listening is in the sharing and writing of poetry and relates specific anecdotes about children and their writing. She also suggests helpful questions to ask that guide but do not overwhelm children in *For the Good of the Earth and Sun: Teaching Poetry* (1994) and *Awakening the Heart: Exploring Poetry in Elementary and Middle School* (1999). She invites us to share what we notice about poems as we invite children to do the same. As we share more and more poetry, children will begin to point out the patterns and language that are interesting to them. These are the teachable moments that enable us to insert relevant mini-lessons. We can draw ideas from the previously presented question lists and group-discussion activities to set the stage for writing—whether individual, partner based, or group collaboration.

Working together with teachers or parents, we can provide aspiring young poets with the support and guidance they need to keep writing. We can listen and nudge, provide resources and opportunities, and offer empathy and encouragement. But keep in mind that not every child will be a poet, as Myra Cohn Livingston eloquently reminds us in *The Child as Poet: Myth or Reality?* (1984). Each child should have the opportunity to try poetry writing and have that outlet of self-expression, but not everyone aspires to write poetry professionally by any means. And that is OK. Experimenting with poetry writing gives us a greater appreciation for the poet's art and craft when we read published poetry.

## POETRY WITH COMMENTARY BY POETS

In the books below, the poets provide a few lines of explanation about where the ideas for the poems came from—fascinating and insightful, especially for aspiring poets:

Catherine Clinton, ed., *I, Too, Sing America: Three Centuries of African American Poetry*

Bernice Cullinan and Deborah Wooten, eds., *Another Jar of Tiny Stars: Poems by NCTE Award-Winning Poets*

Paul B. Janeczko, ed., *Seeing the Blue Between: Advice and Inspiration for Young Poets*

X. J. Kennedy and D. Kennedy, eds., *Knock at a Star: A Child's Introduction to Poetry*

Karla Kuskin, *Dogs and Dragons, Trees and Dreams*

JonArno Lawson, ed., *Inside Out: Children's Poets Discuss Their Work*

George Ella Lyon, *Where I'm From: Where Poems Come From*

Gary Soto, *A Fire in My Hands: A Book of Poems*

Sylvia Vardell and Janet Wong, eds., *PoetryTagTime: Poetry for Children*

Janet S. Wong, *A Suitcase of Seaweed and Other Poems*

**RESOURCES FOR TEACHING CHILDREN TO WRITE POETRY**

Full publishing information for the titles below can be found in the list of references:

Bob Barton and David Booth, *Poetry Goes to School: From Mother Goose to Shel Silverstein*

David Booth and Bill Moore, *Poems Please! Sharing Poetry with Children*

Jack Collom and Sheryl Noethe, *Poetry Everywhere: Teaching Poetry Writing in School and in the Community*

Betsy Franco, *Conversations with a Poet: Inviting Poetry into K–12 Classrooms*

Mary Kenner Glover, *A Garden of Poets: Poetry Writing in the Elementary Classroom*

David Ian Hanauer, *Poetry and the Meaning of Life: Reading and Writing Poetry in Language Arts Classrooms*

Georgia Heard, *Awakening the Heart: Exploring Poetry in Elementary and Middle School*

————, *For the Good of the Earth and Sun: Teaching Poetry*

S. L. Lipson, *Writing Success through Poetry: Create a Writers' Workshop*

Margriet Ruurs, *The Power of Poems: Teaching the Joy of Writing Poetry*

Iris McClellan Tiedt, *Tiger Lilies, Toadstools, and Thunderbolts: Engaging K–8 Students with Poetry*

## Poetic Form

Once children are immersed in poetry, they often begin to notice poems can take many different forms. They enjoy seeing the innovative ways poets have crafted poems. Chapter 3 introduced examples of published poetry books organized by poetic form, such as haiku, concrete poetry, and riddle poems. What poetry forms and techniques can children and young people learn to use? Poems can rhyme or not, be completely free flowing, or follow a specific form. Adults can introduce children to the various forms and techniques in context by using interesting examples from excellent poetry.

Paul B. Janeczko has a helpful picture-book resource for introducing poetic form in *A Kick in the Head: An Everyday Guide to Poetic Forms*. Jack Prelutsky invites young readers to try poem writing by offering prompts in *Read a Rhyme, Write a Rhyme*. Poet Helen Frost showcases several distinctive poetic forms, such as the sestina, sonnet, pantoum, acrostic, and haiku in her works *Keesha's House* and *Spinning through the Universe: A Novel in Poems from Room 214*, and she invents new forms in several of her other novels in poems. She includes back matter in each book that explains each poetic form as well as her reasons for choosing it. For tween and teen readers, two collections offer brief footnotes on the varying poem forms represented by each poem: *More Than Friends: Poems from Him and Her,* by Sara Holbrook and Allan Wolf, and *Dizzy in My Eyes*, by Pat Mora.

### *Poetic Forms from A to Z*

The alphabet has often been used as a framework for poetry. Avis Harley has written two picture books for middle grades that include a different poem and poetic form for each letter of the alphabet. They are *Fly with Poetry: An ABC of Poetry* and *Leap into Poetry: More ABCs of Poetry*. Paul B. Janeczko has a wonderful resource book for children and young adults filled with both serious and wacky poetry forms: *Poetry from A to Z: A Guide for Young Writers*. This can provide the background for expanding poetic repertoires. Children may enjoy discovering unusual forms of poetry or even trying their hands at writing them. Or working as a group, children can create their own alphabet book of poetry, with each child responsible for a letter to build a poem upon. Here are a few of the possibilities in poetic form (from Vardell 2012):

### Twenty Poem Possibilities
1. **Acrostic poem** (first letter of each line adds up to spell a word)
2. **Biopoem** (eleven-line biographical poem)
3. **Cinquain** (five-line poem with unrhymed lines of two, four, six, eight, and two syllables)
4. **Concrete, picture, or shape poetry** (lines arranged to suggest a poem subject visually)
5. **Diamante** (seven-line diamond-shape poem based on two contrasting ideas)

6. **Direct address** (poem that talks directly to another person or thing)

7. **Epitaph and elegy poems** (commemorating the passing or loss of someone or something)

8. **Found poetry** (rearranging words of exposition or prose to create a poem)

9. **Haiku** (Japanese poem of seventeen syllables with three lines of five, seven, and five syllables)

10. **How-to poem** (serious or silly directions with strong sequence words)

11. **Letter, note, or diary poem** (poem of address, apology, argument, explanation, or thanks to someone or something)

12. **Limerick** (humorous poem with five lines with the a/a/b/b/a rhyme scheme)

13. **List or litany poem** (organized list, usually in free verse)

14. **Persona or mask poem** (writing as if you were someone or something else)

15. **Question poem** (the poem asks a question, or each line is a question)

16. **Rap** (musical form featuring chanted rhyming lyrics with a strong rhythm)

17. **Rebus poem** (pictures substitute for key words)

18. **Riddle poem** (descriptive poem that requires one to guess at the subject)

19. **Sonnet** (fourteen-line verse form, such as Italian and Elizabethan)

20. **Tongue twister** (use of various devices to make poem lines difficult to pronounce)

## Biopoems

The biopoem is a popular format for children to try because it provides a framework to ease them into poetry writing and offers an opportunity for autobiographical writing—often a good place to begin. Thus, you can use biopoem writing at the beginning of a school year as a get-acquainted activity or pair biopoems with children's photographs or artwork for posting on special occasions. Actually, a biopoem does not have to be about the writer. It can be used to describe another person or even a literary character. The following biopoem

formula is adapted from the Biopoem Poetry Page, at http://library.thinkquest
.org/11883/data/biopoem.htm.

## The Biopoem Formula

Line 1: First name

Line 2: Three traits or adjectives that describe the person

Line 3: Relative status (e.g., brother, sister, husband, wife, son,
daughter) of _____

Line 4: Who loves _____ (three things or people that person loves)

Line 5: Who feels _____ (three items)

Line 6: Who needs _____ (three items)

Line 7: Who fears _____ (three items)

Line 8: Who gives _____ (one item fully explained)

Line 9: Who would like to see _____ (one item)

Line 10: Who lives _____ (place identified or described)

Line 11: Last name

Here is a sample biopoem I wrote about the protagonist of Natalie Babbitt's
classic fantasy novel *Tuck Everlasting* (Farrar, Straus, and Giroux, 1975):

Winnie

caring, curious, sensitive

companion of Mae, Tuck, Miles, Jesse

lover of family, friends, life

who feels afraid, adventurous, ambivalent

who needs an anchor, a challenge, a choice

who fears death, danger, decisions

who gives the gift of life with love

who would like to see the future

resident of Treegap

Foster

## Found Poems

Another poetic form that lends itself to practical application is found poetry.
Found poetry is created by taking text from other sources, such as newspaper

articles, ads, and picture books, and converting it into a poem. Fitch and Swartz (2008) recommend looking at novel excerpts, instructions, messages, recipes, and conversations, as well as newspaper articles, for text for creating found poetry. There are examples of found poems created by some of the best-known poets from a wide-variety of inspiring sources in Georgia Heard's anthology *The Arrow Finds Its Mark: A Book of Found Poems*. I enjoy using newspaper articles (or news from the Web) because such material is handy and offers current information that is often interesting and relevant to young people. Mining poems for words and ideas for a found poem helps children process the information and focus on key points for discussion. This activity can be conducted with a whole group, in small groups, or individually once children are familiar with the process. It begins with choosing a news article (or other text) of interest, then reading it, discussing it, and highlighting and writing the key words and ideas that seem particularly sharp, interesting, or relevant. From that list of words and ideas, you arrange a poem, eliminating unnecessary words and phrases and inserting a few others, if needed, for sense or meaning. What emerges is often interesting news plus powerful poetry. Then post the poem along with the news article and, if time allows, a drawing or photograph that the kids choose or create.

To illustrate, here is a sample news report from the Web:

### Peace One Day Commitments 2004

As one way of observing the Day, many peace-based NGOs and individuals representing a wide variety of religious and spiritual traditions are observing "International Day of Peace Vigils" with the following objective: "To encourage worldwide, 24-hour spiritual observations for peace and nonviolence on the International Day of Peace, 21 September 2004 in every house of worship and place of spiritual practice, by all religious and spiritually based groups and individuals and by all men, women and children who seek peace in the world." These global 24-hour observations for peace are meant to demonstrate the power of prayer and other spiritual observations in promoting peace and preventing violent conflict. They will also help raise public awareness of the International Day of Peace and can directly support the establishment of a global ceasefire. You can personally support this worldwide initiative by committing to conduct a spiritual observation and promulgating the Vigil idea among religious and peace-based groups in your community. (www.peaceoneday .org/bin/venda.plex?ex=co_disp-view&bsref=peaceoneday&page=2004)

Below is a sample poem that I created based on the words and ideas of the article (obviously, several different poems are possible from one news article, depending on the choices each poem finder makes):

## Peace One Day

One way
observing the Day
International Day of Peace
encourage
worldwide
24-hour
peace and nonviolence
21 September
in every house of worship
in every place of spiritual practice
individuals
all men, women, and children
who seek peace in the world
preventing violent conflict
raising public awareness
support a global cease-fire
this worldwide initiative
begins
in your community.

Once you develop the knack for using poetic formulas like biopoems and poetry-building exercises like the construction of found poems, you will begin to see other possibilities for creating original poems. Dave Morice provides even more options for creating poems in unusual formats in his book *The Adventures of*

*Dr. Alphabet: 104 Unusual Ways to Write Poetry in the Classroom and the Community* (2007). His suggestions are generally quite playful and unorthodox but can be lots of fun, too, including creating autumn leaf poems, writing postage-stamp poems, playing poetry checkers, building poetry mazes, and more.

## Poetry Journals

Keeping a poetry journal can be a meaningful exercise for children, especially for aspiring poets. A journal can take the form of a notebook or folder for storing copies of favorite poems; for recording one's responses to individual poems; for gathering favorite words, personal reflections, and one's own poetry writing—or for all three purposes. Poetry journals can assist children to participate actively in reading poetry, to record personal reactions and preferences, and to develop writing skills. This tool can be especially helpful for students learning English who struggle with new vocabulary and syntax in oral communication situations. Sometimes discussing possible journal content may serve as a powerful prewriting technique that prompts children toward more thoughtful responses in their journals. Journal entries may range from free writing to responses to prompts. Additionally, children may want to consider who will read their journals. They may write for an adult, may pair with peers or children of different ages or grade

**PRACTITIONER PERSPECTIVE**

*I think it's great that some people can admit that they miss some of the things their students pick up on. If we could all make such admissions more frequently, we might find it easier to use poems and literature from cultures other than our own. I think that many people, myself included, tend to stay away from the writings of other cultures because of our own fear factor. Simply put, it is scary to try to understand something unfamiliar, yet we ask our students to do exactly that with every new concept we introduce, regardless of possible differences in culture. I for one am finding myself ready to confront the challenge and at least try to incorporate more diversity into my poetry selections.*

Kirsten Murphy, librarian
Coder Elementary School, Aledo, Texas

levels, or may exchange thoughts with adult volunteers via buddy journals. One amusing mock journal that appears to be written and gathered by a child writer but is actually the creation of adult author Gary Crew and illustrator Craig Smith is the highly visual picture book *Troy Thompson's Excellent Peotry* [sic] *Book*. Sharon Creech creates another journal-like book with her verse novel *Love That Dog*. Both books are inspiring examples of a child's poetic voice (filtered through an adult author) and useful models of what a poetry journal might look and sound like.

## English-Language Learners and Poetry Writing

As children experience frequent poetry read-alouds and choral readings, the realization that they could write their own poetry emerges as a natural extension. And although some English-language learners may have limited linguistic proficiency, several poetry-writing formats are ideally suited to them. Because lists are simple and familiar to everyone, for example, the list poem (or catalog verse) is an excellent introduction to the writing of poetry at any age or proficiency level. Simple completion prompts such as "I wish . . ." or "I remember . . ." can lead to funny or poignant student-authored poems. Read-alouds and choral reading activities lay the foundation for composing by providing models of poem structure such as color poetry (e.g., "green is . . .") or five-senses poetry ("winter smells like / feels like / tastes like / looks like / sounds like"). After hearing various models, children can collaborate to generate similar poems of their own, discussing format, word choice, and style issues. Three resource books for choosing poems and designing activities include *A Chorus of Cultures: Developing Literacy through Multicultural Poetry*, by Alma Flor Ada, Violet Harris, and Lee Bennett Hopkins; *Writing in Rhythm: Spoken Word Poetry in Urban Classrooms*, by Maisha Fisher; and *Living Voices: Multicultural Poetry in the Middle School Classroom*, by Jaime Wood. Generally speaking, children are ready to solo only after they have worked on a poem with others in a class or group. But do not be surprised if your English-language learners impress you with their fresh ideas and use of words. Often their developing English vocabulary makes them even more resourceful with word choice and placement. I realized recently that the roots for my own obsession with poetry are buried deep. For me, poetry was part of the music of learning English, too. (I grew up in a German-speaking household.) It was the rhyme and rhythm of nursery rhymes and playground rhymes in English that helped me learn to speak—and then read—my new language, too. Something to keep in mind when we think non-English speakers can't "handle" poetry until they are fluent.

## Publishing Children's Writing

Children who enjoy writing are often interested in seeing their work in print. One informal approach is to type, print, and post their poetry. Or you can create a photocopied anthology of the poetry of many child writers. But for children who are truly dedicated and ambitious, submitting a poem for publication is a worthy goal. And there are several web and print resources that print children's original poetry. Help child poets become familiar with the protocol for submitting manuscripts (style, format, and so forth), and prepare them for the competitive process and for possible rejection. Let them choose which poems they are most proud of, keep copies of everything submitted, and get parent permission. Then celebrate with them when their work is accepted and appears in print. Congratulate them, publicly showcase their accomplishment, and spread

**RESOURCES FOR YOUNG PEOPLE ON POETRY WRITING**

Kathi Appelt, *Poems from Homeroom: A Writer's Place to Start*

Ralph J. Fletcher, *Poetry Matters: Writing a Poem from the Inside Out*

———, *A Writing Kind of Day: Poems for Young Poets*

Paul B. Janeczko, *How to Write Poetry*

———, *Poetry from A to Z: A Guide for Young Writers*

Nancy Loewen, *Words, Wit, and Wonder: Writing Your Own Poem*

Jack Prelutsky, *Pizza, Pigs, and Poetry: How to Write a Poem*

Laura Purdie Salas, *Write Your Own Poetry*

———, *Picture Yourself Writing Poetry: Using Photos to Inspire Writing*

Allan Wolf, *Immersed in Verse: An Informative, Slightly Irreverent, and Totally Tremendous Guide to Living the Poet's Life* the word. Success inspires success. And, of course, if their work is rejected, offer support and encouragement. The following are among the longest-running publications and websites that feature children's writing:

**CHILDREN'S LITERATURE WEB GUIDE:**
**CHILDREN'S WRITING** *www.ucalgary.ca/~dkbrown/writings.html*
This web page provides links to a variety of websites where children can see their own writing and art published and enjoy writing and art created by other children. Included are an encyclopedia written by children; a diary project; writing contests; and poetry, storybooks, and art by children of all ages, from elementary school through high school.

**MERLYN'S PEN** *www.merlynspen.com*
Middle school students can see their writing published in this print magazine. *11 South Angell St., Suite 301; Providence, RI 02906*

**NEW MOON: THE MAGAZINE**
**FOR GIRLS AND THEIR DREAMS** *www.newmoon.com*
An advertising-free magazine for girls age eight and up that publishes writing by girls alongside regular features. *34 E. Superior St., Suite 200; Duluth, MN 55802*

**POEM EXPRESS** *www.poem-express.com*
An international program involving children around the world in creating original posters and poems.

**POTATO HILL POETRY** *www.potatohill.com*
This website includes poetry-writing contests for kids, poems written by children of all ages, and teacher resources and workshop information. *PO Box 125; Natick, MA 01760*

**SKIPPING STONES** *www.skippingstones.org*
This multicultural and international nonprofit magazine publishes children's writing in multiple languages. *PO Box 3939; Eugene, OR 97403*

**STONE SOUP MAGAZINE**                    *www.stonesoup.com*

This print publication specializes in showcasing the original art and writing, including poetry, of children from eight to thirteen years of age. *PO Box 83; Santa Cruz, CA 95063*

## Conclusion

As we work to help children verbalize their responses to poetry and expand their poetry-based experiences through drama, music, art, and writing, we establish a pattern of connecting poetry with our lives in varied ways. We begin by learning how to ask appropriate questions and how to help children help themselves understand poetry. We help children internalize poems through genuine poetry talk. We invite them to extend their experiences of poetry by providing opportunities for verbal and artistic expression. And we open the door to self-expression by giving them opportunities to write their own poetry. As Susan Wooldridge reminds us in her book *Poemcrazy: Freeing Your Life with Words*, "The symbolic language of poetry allows us to express and begin to understand not only our feelings, but our idiosyncrasies, problems, and fears" (1996, 17). That give-and-take between the poem presenter and poem participants provides a shared experience that can create memorable moments as well as bonds that last a lifetime.

*Poetry is the synthesis of hyacinths and biscuits.*

—Carl Sandburg, poet

# One Final Word

**M**ARY ANN HOBERMAN WROTE THE POEM BELOW FOR the ceremony at which she was given the 2003 National Council of Teachers of English Award for Excellence in Poetry for Children. It then appeared in *Horn Book Magazine* (vol. 81, no. 3 [May–June 2005]: 255) and is used with her permission. She notes that this poem, "Take Sound," pays homage to the great children's poet David McCord, the first recipient of the NCTE award, by echoing the title and cadence of his poem "Take Sky." It is a lovely tribute to a long tradition of smart, rhythmic, evocative poetry for children—and a fitting end to this book about the pleasures of sharing the sounds and words of poetry with children.

## Take Sound
*by Mary Ann Hoberman*

Each word a poem.
Take sound—
Its mysteries abound:
To hear a sound;

*(continued)*

To sound to find;
Or to be sound
In body, mind;
A stretch of water
Wide and clear;
To register
Upon the ear—
Each separate meaning
Hovers, tense
Above the more
Intended sense.
Each part of speech
Another trope,
A turn
In the kaleidoscope.
And in this lovely
Layered thing,
The origins
Of language sing,
Alive, ambiguous, absurd—
*In the beginning was the word.*

# Poems Cited in "Ten Strategies for Sharing Poetry Out Loud"

Full publication information for the following resources can be found in appendix C.

## 1. Modeling: The Adult Reads the Poem Aloud

Janet Wong, "Our Daily Bread," in *A Suitcase of Seaweed and Other Poems*

Marilyn Singer, "Valentine's Day," in *Every Day's a Dog's Day: A Year in Poems*

John Ciardi, "Mummy Slept Late and Daddy Fixed Breakfast," in *You Read to Me, I'll Read to You*

Shel Silverstein, "Sarah Cynthia Sylvia Stout Would Not Take the Garbage Out," in *Where the Sidewalk Ends*

Calef Brown, "Allicatter Gatorpillar," in *Flamingos on the Roof*

Karla Kuskin, "Untitled" (begins "Three wishes"), in *Near the Window Tree: Poems and Notes*

Karen B. Winnick, "Quiet Morning," in *I Am the Book*, edited by Lee Bennett Hopkins

JonArno Lawson, "My Needs," in *Think Again*

Gary Soto, "Ode to Family Photographs," in *Neighborhood Odes*

## 2. Unison: Everyone Reads the Poem Together at the Same Time

Douglas Florian, "My Monster," in *Bing Bang Boing*

Marilyn Singer, "Porcupines," in *Twosomes: Love Poems from the Animal Kingdom*

David Elliott, "The Giraffe," in *In the Wild*

Langston Hughes, "Dreams," in *The Dreamkeeper and Other Poems*

Eloise Greenfield, "Education," in *Nathaniel Talking*

Karla Kuskin, "I Woke Up This Morning," in *Moon, Have You Met My Mother? The Collected Poems of Karla Kuskin*

## 3. Refrain: Children Join In on a Repeated Line, Stanza, or Word

Jack Prelutsky, "Homework, Oh Homework," in *The New Kid on the Block*

Eloise Greenfield, "Things," in *Honey, I Love and Other Love Poems*

Kristine O'Connell George, "Trespass," in *Emma Dilemma: Big Sister Poems*

Rebecca Kai Dotlich, "Amazing Face," in *Amazing Faces*, edited by Lee Bennet Hopkins

Joyce Sidman, "Welcome to the Night," in *Dark Emperor and Other Poems of the Night*

Ivy O. Eastwick, "Look in a Book," in *I Like It Here at School,* compiled by Jack Prelutsky

Kalli Dakos, "If My Hand Didn't Get So Tired," in *Don't Read This Book, Whatever You Do!*

Douglas Florian, "The Boa," in *Beast Feast*

Jack Prelutsky, "Louder Than a Clap of Thunder!" in *The New Kid on the Block*

Frank Asch, "Sunflakes," in *Ring Out, Wild Bells: Poems about Holidays and Seasons,* collected by Lee Bennett Hopkins

Karla Kuskin, "Snow," in *Snowy Day: Stories and Poems*, edited by Caroline Feller Bauer

Jack Prelutsky, "Countdown," in *It's Halloween*

Douglas Florian, "Weather It," in *Bing Bang Boing*

## 4. Movement: Children Read in Unison Using Motions or Gestures

Shel Silverstein, "Boa Constrictor," in *Where the Sidewalk Ends*

Douglas Florian, "The Bully," in *Bing Bang Boing*

Bobbi Katz, "Medusa," in *The Monsterologist: A Memoir in Rhyme*

Kristine O'Connell George, "Toasting Marshmallows" in *Toasting Marshmallows: Camping Poems*

Rebecca Kai Dotlich, "A Circle of Sun," in *The 20th-Century Children's Poetry Treasury*, selected by Jack Prelutsky

Jack Prelutsky, "I Am Running in a Circle," in *The New Kid on the Block*

Anonymous, "August Heat," in *The Sky Is Full of Song*, selected by Lee Bennett Hopkins

## 5. Call-and-Response: Two Groups Read Alternating (Not Simultaneous) Lines or Stanzas

Douglas Florian, "Worker Bees," in *Unbeelievables*

Sara Holbrook, "Copycat," in *Which Way to the Dragon! Poems for the Coming-on-Strong*

Carol Diggory Shields, "Clock-Watching," in *Lunch Money and Other Poems about School*

Shel Silverstein, "The Meehoo with an Exactlywatt," in *A Light in the Attic*

Jack Prelutsky, "I'm Thankful," in *The New Kid on the Block*

Janet Wong, "Speak Up," in *Good Luck Gold and Other Poems*

"Two Plus Two, or Why Indians Flunk," in *Through Indian Eyes: The Native American Experience in Books for Children*, edited by Beverly Slapin and Doris Seale

## 6. Groups: Multiple Groups Read Various Lines or Stanzas

Janet Wong, "Face It," in *A Suitcase of Seaweed and Other Poems*

Joyce Sidman, "The Season's Campaign," in *Song of the Water Boatman and Other Pond Poems*

Lee Bennett Hopkins, "Spring," in *Sharing the Seasons*

Karla Kuskin, "The Question," in *Dogs and Dragons, Trees and Dreams*

Shel Silverstein, "Smart," in *Where the Sidewalk Ends*

Carol Diggory Shields, "And the Answer Is . . . ?" in *Lunch Money and Other Poems about School*

## 7. Solos: Individual Children Read Individual Lines

Shel Silverstein, "Whatif?" in *A Light in the Attic*

Anna Grossnickle Hines, "Where I Live," in *Peaceful Pieces: Poems and Quilts about Peace*

Carol Diggory Shields, "Pledge," in *Lunch Money and Other Poems about School*

Laura Purdie Salas, "Top Ten Rules for Our Zoo Field Trip," in *The Arrow Finds Its Mark: A Book of Found Poems*, edited by Georgia Heard

Georgia Heard, "Recipe for Writing an Autumn Poem," in *The Arrow Finds Its Mark: A Book of Found Poems*

Myra Cohn Livingston, "April Fool," in *Celebrations*

Eloise Greenfield, "By Myself," in *Honey, I Love and Other Love Poems*

Mary O'Neill, in "What Is Red?" *Hailstones and Halibut Bones: Adventures in Color*

## 8. Two Voices: Two People Read Two Parts, Sometimes with Simultaneous but Different Lines

Paul Fleischman, "Honeybees" and "Book Lice," in *Joyful Noise: Poems for Two Voices*

———, *I Am Phoenix: Poems for Two Voices*

———, *Big Talk: Poems for Four Voices*

Mary Ann Hoberman, You Read to Me, I'll Read to You series

Lee Bennett Hopkins, *Side by Side: Poems to Read Together*

Betsy Franco, *Messing around the Monkey Bars and Other School Poems for Two Voices*

Joyce Shipley, "Pianoball," in *And the Crowd Goes Wild! A Global Gathering of Sports Poems*, edited by Carol-Ann Hoyte and Heidi Bee Roemer

Marilyn Singer, "In the Hood," in *Mirror, Mirror*

Jennifer Clement, "Árbol de limón / Lemon Tree," translated by Consuelo de Aerenlund, in *The Tree Is Older Than You Are: A Bilingual Gathering of Poems and Stories from Mexico with Paintings by Mexican Artists*, edited by Naomi Shihab Nye

## 9. Canon: Two Groups Read the Same Poem, with One Group Delaying Its Start until the Other Reaches a Predetermined Point

Robert Weinstock, "Can You Dig It?" in *Can You Dig It?*

Jane Yolen, "Oh Fly," in *Bug Off! Creepy Crawly Poems*

Judith Viorst, "No," in *If I Were in Charge of the World and Other Worries: Poems for Children and Their Parents*

Jack Prelutsky, "I'm Much Too Tired to Play Tonight," in *Something Big Has Been Here*

## 10. Singing: Children Sing Poems Set to Familiar Tunes

Douglas Florian, "School Cafeteria," in *Bing Bang Boing*

Laura Purdie Salas, "Calling All Readers," in *BookSpeak!*

Sara Holbrook, "The Dog Ate My Homework," in *The Dog Ate My Homework*

Calef Brown, "Birthday Lights," in *Flamingos on the Roof*

Jack Prelutsky, "Allosaurus," in *Tyrannosaurus Was a Beast: Dinosaur Poems*

Judith Viorst, "Someday Someone Will Bet That You Can't Name All Fifty States," in *Sad Underwear and Other Complications: More Poems for Children and Their Parents*

### Combining Strategies

Douglas Florian, "Delicious Wishes," in *Bing Bang Boing*

Judith Viorst, "It's a Wonderful World, but They Made a Few Mistakes," in *Sad Underwear and Other Complications: More Poems for Children and Their Parents*

"I Rise, I Rise," in *Dancing Teepees: Poems of American Indian Youth*, collected by Virginia Driving Hawk Sneve

Miroslav Holub, "Napoleon," translated by Kaca Polackova, in *This Same Sky: A Collection of Poems from around the World*, selected by Naomi Shihab Nye

# Noteworthy Poets Writing for Young People

Links and websites are subject to change. Poets' personal websites are listed, when known.

Arnold Adoff, www.arnoldadoff.com

Jaime Adoff, www.jaimeadoff.com

Jon Agee, www.jonagee.com

Kathi Appelt, www.kathiappelt.com

Jorge Argueta, http://jorgeargueta.com

Linda Ashman, www.lindaashman.com

Jeannine Atkins, www.jeannineatkins.com

Brod Bagert, http://brodbagert.com

Carmen T. Bernier-Grand, www.carmenberniergrand.com

Calef Brown, www.polkabats.com

Liz Brownlee, www.poetlizbrownlee.co.uk

Jen Bryant, www.jenbryant.com

Leslie Bulion, www.lesliebulion.com

Stephanie Calmenson, www.stephaniecalmenson.com

James Carter, www.jamescarterpoet.co.uk

Thalia Chaltas, www.thaliachaltas.com

Sherryl Clark, www.poetry4kids.netindex.html

Jill Corcoran, http://jillcorcoran.com

Kalli Dakos, www.kalllidakos.com

Rebecca Kai Dotlich, www.rebeccakaidotlich.com

Margarita Engle, http://margaritaengle.com

Carole Gerber, www.carolegerber.com

Gene Fehler, http://genefehler.com

Paul Fleischman, www.paulfleischman.net

Ralph Fletcher, www.ralphfletcher.com

Douglas Florian, http://floriancafe.blogspot.com

Betsy Franco, www.betsyfranco.com

Helen Frost, www.helenfrost.net

Kristine O'Connell George, www.kristinegeorge.com

Charles Ghigna, http://charlesghigna.com

Nikki Giovanni, http://nikki-giovanni.com

Joan Bransfield Graham, www.joangraham.com

John Grandits, http://johngrandits.com

Nikki Grimes, www.nikkigrimes.com

Lorie Ann Grover, www.lorieanngrover.com

David L. Harrison, www.davidlharrison.com

Georgia Heard, http://georgiaheard.com

Juan Felipe Herrera, www.juanfelipe.org/pageone.html

Steven Herrick, www.stevenherrick.com.au

Anna Grossnickle Hines, www.aghines.com

Mary Ann Hoberman, http://maryannhoberman.com

Sara Holbrook, www.saraholbrook.com

Ellen Hopkins, www.ellenhopkins.com

Lee Bennett Hopkins, www.leebennetthopkins.com

Patricia Hubbell, www.kidspoet.commain.html

Paul B. Janeczko, www.paulbjaneczko.com

Alan Katz, www.alankatzbooks.com

Bobbi Katz, www.bobbikatz.com

X. J. Kennedy and Dorothy Kennedy, http://xjanddorothymkennedy.com

Bruce Lansky, www.gigglepoetry.com

Julie Larios, http://julielarios.blogspot.com

Constance Levy, www.constancelevy.com

Debbie Levy, www.debbielevybooks.com

J. Patrick Lewis, www.jpatricklewis.com

George Ella Lyon, www.georgeellalyon.com

Guadalupe Garcia McCall, http://guadalupegarciamccall.com

Patricia McCormick, www.pattymccormick.com

Ryan Mecum, www.ryanmecum.com

Pat Mora, www.patmora.com

Heidi Mordhorst, www.heidimordhorst.com

Walter Dean Myers, www.walterdeanmyers.net

Kenn Nesbitt, www.poetry4kids.com

José-Luis Orozco, www.joseluisorozco.com

Linda Sue Park, www.lspark.com

Ann Whitford Paul, www.annwhitfordpaul.net

Andrew Fusek Peters, www.twopeters.com

Jack Prelutsky, http://jackprelutsky.com

Mary Quattlebaum, www.maryquattlebaum.com

Adam Rex, http://adamrex.com

Jame Richards, www.jamerichards.com

Heidi Bee Roemer, http://heidibroemer.com

Michael Rosen, www.michaelrosen.co.uk

Michael J. Rosen, www.fidosopher.com

Deborah Ruddell, www.deborahruddell.com

Laura Purdie Salas, http://laurasalas.com

Michael Salinger, www.michaelsalinger.com

Joyce Sidman, www.joycesidman.com

Shel Silverstein, www.shelsilverstein.com

Marilyn Singer, http://marilynsinger.net

Charles R. Smith Jr., www.charlesrsmithjr.com

Hope Anita Smith, http://hopeanitasmith.com

Sonya Sones, www.sonyasones.com

Gary Soto, www.garysoto.com

Eileen Spinelli, www.eileenspinelli.com

Maria Testa, www.mariatesta.com

Joyce Carol Thomas, www.joycecarolthomas.com

Amy Ludwig VanDerwater, www.amylv.com

Lee Wardlaw, www.leewardlaw.com

Charles Waters, www.charleswaters.net

April Halprin Wayland, www.aprilwayland.com

Carole Boston Weatherford, http://cbweatherford.com

Robert Weinstock, www.callmebob.com

Robert Paul Weston, www.robertpaulweston.com

Jenny Whitehead, http://jennywhitehead.com

Karma Wilson, http://karmawilson.com

Steven Withrow, http://cracklesofspeech.blogspot.com

Allan Wolf, www.allanwolf.com

Janet S. Wong, www.janetwong.com

Joyce Lee Wong, http://joyceleewong.com

Jane Yolen, www.janeyolen.com

Tracie Vaughn Zimmer, www.tracievaughnzimmer.com

## NOTABLE POETS FROM MANY CULTURES

### African American Poetry for Young People

| | |
|---|---|
| Jaime Adoff | Langston Hughes |
| Gwendolyn Brooks | Patricia McKissack |
| Ashley Bryan | Walter Dean Myers |
| Lucille Clifton | Marilyn Nelson |
| Curtis Crisler | Greg Neri |
| Countee Cullen | Charles R. Smith Jr. |
| Paul Laurence Dunbar | Hope Anita Smith |
| Nikki Giovanni | Joyce Carol Thomas |
| Eloise Greenfield | Carole Boston Weatherford |
| Nikki Grimes | |

### Latino and Latina Poetry for Young People

| | |
|---|---|
| Francisco X. Alarcón | Juan Felipe Herrera |
| Jorge Argueta | Guadalupe Garcia McCall |
| Carmen T. Bernier-Grand | Pat Mora |
| Lulu Delacre | José-Luis Orozco |
| Margarita Engle | Gary Soto |

### Asian–Pacific American Poetry for Young People

| | |
|---|---|
| Minfong Ho | Linda Sue Park |
| Michio Mado | Janet Wong |
| Kam Mak | Joyce Lee Wong |

### Native American Poetry for Young People

| | |
|---|---|
| Shonto Begay | Hettie Jones |
| Joseph Bruchac | Virginia Driving Hawk Sneve |

## International Poetry in English for Young People
## (from Canada, the Caribbean, Britain, and Beyond)

| | |
|---|---|
| John Agard | JonArno Lawson |
| Liz Brownlee | Dennis Lee |
| James Carter | Grace Nichols |
| Graham Denton | Andrew Fusek Peters |
| Monica Gunning | Pamela Porter |
| Avis Harley | Michael Rosen |
| Steven Herrick | Robert Paul Weston |
| Lynn Joseph | |

# Bibliography of Children's Poetry Books

A comprehensive list of all the poetry books cited in the text (and suggested pairings of fiction and nonfiction books), as well as additional recommended books of poetry for young readers.

Abeel, Samantha. 1993. *Reach for the Moon.* Duluth, MN: Pfeifer-Hamilton.

Ada, Alma Flor. 1997. *Gathering the Sun.* New York: Lothrop, Lee, and Shepard.

Ada, Alma Flor, and Isabel Campoy, eds. 2003. *¡Pío peep! Traditional Spanish Nursery Rhymes.* New York: HarperCollins.

———. 2011. *Ten Little Puppies / Diez perritos.* New York: Rayo/HarperCollins.

Adedjouma, D. 1996. *The Palm of My Heart: Poetry by African American Children.* New York: Lee and Low.

Adoff, Arnold, ed. 1968. *I Am the Darker Brother: An Anthology of Modern Poems by Negro Americans.* New York: Macmillan.

———. 1973. *Black Is Brown Is Tan.* New York: Harper and Row.

———, ed. 1974/1994. *My Black Me: A Beginning Book of Black Poetry.* New York: Dutton.

———. 1982. *All the Colors of the Race.* New York: Lothrop, Lee, and Shepard.

———. 1986. *Sports Pages.* New York: HarperCollins.

———. 1991. *In for Winter, Out for Spring.* San Diego: Harcourt Brace.

———. 1995. *Street Music: City Poems.* New York: HarperCollins.

———. 1997. *Love Letters.* New York: Scholastic.

———. 2000. *Touch the Poem.* New York: Blue Sky.

———. 2011. *Roots and Blues: A Celebration.* New York: Houghton Mifflin Harcourt.

Adoff, Jaime. 2008. *The Death of Jayson Porter.* New York: Jump at the Sun/ Hyperion Books for Children.

Agard, John, and Grace Nichols, eds. 1994. *A Caribbean Dozen: Poems from Caribbean Poets.* Cambridge, MA: Candlewick.

———. 1995. *No Hickory, No Dickory, No Dock: Caribbean Nursery Rhymes.* Cambridge, MA: Candlewick.

Akaza, Norihisa. 1994. *Smell of the Rain, Voices of the Stars.* Orlando, FL: Harcourt Brace.

Alarcón, Francisco X. 1997. *Laughing Tomatoes and Other Spring Poems / Jitomates risueños y otros poemas de primavera.* San Francisco: Children's Book Press.

———. 1998. *From the Bellybutton of the Moon and Other Summer Poems / Del ombligo de la luna y otros poemas de verano.* San Francisco: Children's Book Press.

———. 1999. *Angels Ride Bikes and Other Fall Poems / Los ángeles andan en bicicleta y otros poemas de otoño.* San Francisco: Children's Book Press.

———. 2001. *Iguanas in the Snow and Other Winter Poems / Iguanas en la nieve y otros poemas de invierno.* San Francisco: Children's Book Press.

———. 2005. *Poems to Dream Together / Poemas para soñar juntos.* New York: Lee and Low.

———. 2008. *Animal Poems of the Iguazú / Animalario del Iguazú.* San Francisco: Children's Book Press.

Amon, Aline. 1981. *The Earth Is Sore: Native Americans on Nature.* New York: Atheneum.

Andrews, Julie, and Emma Walton Hamilton, eds. 2009. *Julie Andrews' Collection of Poems, Songs, and Lullabies.* Illustrated by James McMullan. New York: Little, Brown.

Angelou, Maya. 1993. *Life Doesn't Frighten Me.* New York: Stewart, Tabori, and Chang.

Anholt, Catherine, and Laurence Anholt. 1998. *Big Book of Families.* Cambridge, MA: Candlewick.

Appelt, Kathi. 2002. *Poems from Homeroom: A Writer's Place to Start.* New York: Henry Holt.

———. 2004. *My Father's Summers: A Daughter's Memoirs.* New York: Henry Holt.

Arbuthnot, May Hill. 1961. *The Arbuthnot Anthology of Children's Literature: Single-Volume Edition of Time for Poetry, Time for Fairy Tales, and Time for True Tales.* Chicago: Scott Foresman.

Argueta, Jorge. 2009. *Sopa de frijoles / Bean Soup.* Illustrated by Rafael Yockteng. Toronto: Groundwood.

———. 2010. *Arroz con leche / Rice Pudding.* Illustrated by Fernando Vilela. Toronto: Groundwood.

———. 2012. *Guacamole: Un poema para cocinar / A Cooking Poem.* Illustrated by Margarita Sada. Toronto: Groundwood.

Asch, Frank. 1996. *Sawgrass Poems: A View of the Everglades.* San Diego: Harcourt Brace.

———. 1998. *Cactus Poems.* San Diego: Harcourt Brace.

———. 1999. *Song of the North.* San Diego: Harcourt Brace.

Atwood, Ann. 1971. *Haiku: The Mood of Earth.* New York: Scribner's.

Bagert, Brod. 1991. *Steel Cables: Love Poems from Adam Rib.* New Orleans: Juliahouse.

———. 1992. *Let Me Be the Boss: Poems for Kids to Perform.* Honesdale, PA: Wordsong/Boyds Mills.

———. 1993. *Chicken Socks and Other Contagious Poems.* Honesdale, PA: Wordsong/Boyds Mills.

———. 1997. *The Gooch Machine: Poems for Children to Perform.* Honesdale, PA: Wordsong/Boyds Mills.

———. 2007. *Shout! Little Poems That Roar.* New York: Dial Books for Young Readers.

———. 2008. *School Fever.* New York: Dial Books for Young Readers.

Bangs, Edward. 1976. *Steven Kellogg's Yankee Doodle.* New York: Parent's Magazine Press.

Baring-Gould, William, and Ceil Baring-Gould. 1962. *The Annotated Mother Goose: Nursery Rhymes Old and New.* New York: C. N. Potter.

Bartoletti, Susan Campbell. 2005. *Hitler Youth: Growing Up in Hitler's Shadow.* New York: Scholastic.

Bates, Katharine Lee. 1994. *O Beautiful for Spacious Skies.* Illustrated by Wayne Thiebaud. San Francisco: Chronicle.

———. 2003. *America the Beautiful.* Illustrated by Wendell Minor. New York: Putnam.

Bauer, Caroline Feller, ed. 1986. *Snowy Day: Stories and Poems.* New York: Harper-Collins.

Bedard, Michael. 1992. *Emily.* New York: Doubleday.

Begay, Shonto. 1995. *Navajo: Visions and Voices across the Mesa.* New York: Scholastic.

Behn, Harry, ed. and trans. 1964. *Cricket Songs: Japanese Haiku.* New York: Harcourt, Brace, and World.

———, trans. 1971. *More Cricket Songs: Japanese Haiku Translated by Harry Behn.* New York: Harcourt, Brace, Jovanovich.

Benjamin, Floella, ed. 1995. *Skip across the Ocean: Nursery Rhymes from around the World.* New York: Orchard.

Berry, James. 1991. I*sn't My Name Magical? Sister and Brother Poems.* New York: Simon and Schuster.

Bierhorst, John, ed. 1994. *On the Road of Stars: Native American Night Poems and Sleep Charms.* New York: Macmillan.

———. 1998. *In the Trail of the Wind: American Indian Poems and Ritual Orations.* Rev. ed. New York: Farrar, Straus, and Giroux.

Blackaby, Susan. 2010. *Nest, Nook, and Cranny.* Illustrated by Jamie Hogan. Watertown, MA: Charlesbridge.

Blake, Quentin, ed. 1995. *The Penguin Book of Nonsense Verse.* New York: Penguin.

Blume, Judy. 2002. *Superfudge.* New York: Puffin.

Bober, Natalie S. 1991. *A Restless Spirit: The Story of Robert Frost.* New York: Henry Holt.

Bogan, Louise, and William Jay Smith, eds. 1990. *The Golden Journey: Poems for Young People.* Chicago: Contemporary.

Bontemps, Arna, ed. 1941. *Golden Slippers: An Anthology of Negro Poetry for Young Readers.* New York: Harper and Row.

Booth, David. 1990. *Voices on the Wind: Poems for All Seasons.* New York: Morrow.

Bouchard, David. 1995. *If You're Not from the Prairie . . .* New York: Atheneum.

———. 1996. *Voices from the Wild.* San Francisco: Chronicle.

Brenner, Barbara. 1994. *The Earth Is Painted Green: A Garden of Poems about Our Planet.* New York: Scholastic.

———. 2000. *Voices: Poetry and Art from around the World.* Washington, DC: National Geographic.

Brooks, Gwendolyn. 1956/1984. *Bronzeville Boys and Girls.* New York: HarperCollins.

Brown, Calef. 1998. *Polkabats and Octopus Slacks*. Boston: Houghton Mifflin.

———. 2000. *Dutch Sneakers and Flea Keepers*. Boston: Houghton Mifflin.

———. 2006. *Flamingos on the Roof*. Boston: Houghton Mifflin.

———. 2008. *Soup for Breakfast*. Boston: Houghton Mifflin.

———. 2010. *Hallowilloween: Nefarious Silliness*. Boston: Houghton Mifflin.

Brown, Dale S. 1995. *I Know I Can Climb the Mountain*. Columbus, OH: Mountain Books and Music.

Brown, H. Jackson, Jr. 1991. *Live and Learn and Pass It On*. Nashville, TN: Rutledge Hill.

———. 1995. *Live and Learn and Pass It On*. Vol. 2. Nashville, TN: Rutledge Hill.

Brown, Monica. 2011. *Pablo Neruda*. Illustrated by Julie Paschkis. New York: Henry Holt.

Bruchac, Joseph. 1992. *Thirteen Moons on Turtle's Back: A Native American Year of Moons*. New York: Philomel.

———. 1995. *The Earth under Sky Bear's Feet: Native American Poems of the Land*. New York: Philomel.

———. 1996. *Between Earth and Sky: Legends of Native American Sacred Places*. San Diego: Harcourt Brace.

———. 1996. *The Circle of Thanks*. Mahwah, NJ: BridgeWater.

———. 1996. *Four Ancestors: Stories, Songs, and Poems from Native North America*. Mahwah, NJ: BridgeWater.

Bryan, Ashley, ed. 1978. *I Greet the Dawn: Poems by Paul Laurence Dunbar*. New York: Atheneum.

———. 1992. *Sing to the Sun*. New York: HarperCollins.

———. 1997. *Ashley Bryan's ABC of African American Poetry*. New York: Atheneum.

———. 2003. *All Night, All Day: A Child's First Book of African-American Spirituals*. New York: Atheneum.

Bryant, Jen. 2004. *The Trial*. New York: Knopf.

———. 2006. *Pieces of Georgia*. New York: Knopf.

———. 2008. *Ringside 1925: Views from the Scopes Trial*. New York: Knopf.

———. 2008. *A River of Words: The Story of William Carlos Williams*. Grand Rapids, MI: Eerdmans.

———. 2009. *Kaleidoscope Eyes*. New York: Knopf.

Burleigh, Robert. 1997. *Hoops*. San Diego: Silver Whistle.

———. 2004. *Langston's Train Ride*. New York: Scholastic.

Burt, Mary Elizabeth. 1904/1971. *Poems That Every Child Should Know: A Selection of the Best Poems of All Times for Young People.* Freeport, NY: Books for Libraries.

Bush, Timothy. 2000. *Ferocious Girls, Steamroller Boys, and Other Poems in Between.* New York: Orchard.

Calmenson, Stephanie. 2002. *Welcome, Baby! Baby Rhymes for Baby Times.* New York: HarperCollins.

———, ed. 2005. *Kindergarten Kids: Riddles, Rebuses, Wiggles, Giggles, and More!* New York: HarperCollins.

Carle, Eric. 1989. *Animals, Animals.* New York: Scholastic.

Carlson, Lori M., ed. 1994. *Cool Salsa: Bilingual Poems on Growing Up Latino in the United States.* New York: Henry Holt.

———. 1998. *Sol a Sol: Bilingual Poems.* New York: Henry Holt.

———. 2005. *Red Hot Salsa.* New York: Henry Holt.

Carlstrom, Nancy White. 1996. *Let's Count It Out, Jesse Bear.* New York: Simon and Schuster.

Carroll, Lewis. 2004. *Jabberwocky.* Illustrated by Stéphane Jorisch. Tonawanda, NY: Kids Can Press.

Carson, Jo. 1991. *Stories I Ain't Told Nobody Yet: Selections from the People Pieces.* New York: Theatre Communications Group.

Castillo, Ana. 2000. *My Daughter, My Son, the Eagle, the Dove: An Aztec Chant.* New York: Dutton.

Chandra, Deborah. 1993. *Rich Lizard and Other Poems.* New York: Farrar, Straus, and Giroux.

Cheng, Andrea. 2008. *Where the Steps Were.* Honesdale, PA: Wordsong/Boyds Mills.

Christensen, Bonnie. 2001. *Woody Guthrie: Poet of the People.* New York: Knopf.

Ciardi, John. 1962/1987. *You Read to Me, I'll Read to You.* Philadelphia: Lippincott. New York: HarperTrophy, 1987.

———. 1966/1991. *The Monster Den; or, Look What Happened at My House—and to It.* Philadelphia: Lippincott. Honesdale, PA: Wordsong/Boyds Mills, 1991.

———. 1970. *Someone Could Win a Polar Bear.* Philadelphia: Lippincott.

———. 1970. *You Know Who.* Philadelphia: Lippincott.

Clifton, Lucille. 1970. *Some of the Days of Everett Anderson.* New York: Holt, Rinehart, and Winston.

———. 1983. *Everett Anderson's Goodbye.* New York: Henry Holt.

Clinton, Catherine, ed. 1993/1998. *I, Too, Sing America: Three Centuries of African American Poetry.* Boston: Houghton Mifflin.

———, ed. 2003. *A Poem of Her Own: Voices of American Women Yesterday and Today.* New York: Abrams.

Cohn, Amy L., ed. 1993. *From Sea to Shining Sea: A Treasury of American Folklore and Folk Songs.* New York: Scholastic.

Cole, Joanna, ed. 1989. *Anna Banana: 101 Jump-Rope Rhymes.* Illustrated by Alan Tiegreen. New York: HarperTrophy.

Cole, Joanna, and Stephanie Calmenson, eds. 1995. *Yours Till Banana Splits: Autograph Rhymes.* New York: Morrow Junior Books.

Cooling, Wendy, ed. 2004. *Come to the Great World.* New York: Holiday House.

———. 2010. *All the Wild Wonders: Poems of Our Earth.* Illustrated by Piet Grobler. London: Frances Lincoln.

Coombs, Kate. 2012. *Water Sings Blue: Ocean Poems.* Illustrated by Meilo So. San Francisco: Chronicle.

Cooper, Floyd. 1994. *Coming Home: From the Life of Langston Hughes.* New York: Philomel.

Cooper, Kay. 2001. *"Too Many Rabbits" and Other Fingerplays about Animals, Nature, Weather, and Children.* New York: Cartwheel.

Creech, Sharon. 2001. *Love That Dog.* New York: HarperCollins.

———. 2004. *Heartbeat.* New York: HarperCollins.

———. 2008. *Hate That Cat.* New York: HarperCollins.

Crew, Gary. 2003. *Troy Thompson's Excellent Peotry* [sic] *Book.* La Jolla, CA: Kane/Miller.

Crews, Nina. 2004. *The Neighborhood Mother Goose.* New York: Greenwillow.

———. 2011. *The Neighborhood Sing-Along.* New York: HarperCollins.

Crist-Evans, Craig. 1999. *Moon over Tennessee: A Boy's Civil War Journal.* Boston: Houghton Mifflin.

Cullinan, Bernice, and Deborah Wooten, eds. 2009. *Another Jar of Tiny Stars: Poems by NCTE Award-Winning Poets.* Honesdale, PA: Wordsong/Boyds Mills.

Cumpian, Carlos. 1994. *Latino Rainbow: Poems about Latino Americans.* Chicago: Children's Press.

Curry, Jennifer. 2002. *Animal Poems.* New York: Scholastic.

Curtis, Christopher Paul. 1999. *Bud, Not Buddy.* New York: Delacorte.

Cyrus, Kurt. 2001. *Oddhopper Opera: A Bug's Garden of Verses.* San Diego: Harcourt Brace.

————. 2005. *Hotel Deep: Light Verse from Dark Water.* Orlando, FL: Harcourt.

Dakos, Kalli. 1990. *If You're Not Here, Please Raise Your Hand: Poems about School.* New York: Four Winds.

————. 1993. *Don't Read This Book, Whatever You Do! More Poems about School.* New York: Trumpet Club.

————. 1995. *Mrs. Cole on an Onion Roll and Other School Poems.* New York: Trumpet Club.

————. 1996. *The Goof Who Invented Homework and Other School Poems.* New York: Dial.

————. 2003. *Put Your Eyes Up Here and Other School Poems.* New York: Simon and Schuster.

————. 2011. *A Funeral in the Bathroom and Other School Bathroom Poems.* Chicago: Albert Whitman.

Deem, James M. 2008. *Bodies from the Ice: Melting Glaciers and the Recovery of the Past.* Boston: Houghton Mifflin.

De Fina, Allan A. 1997. *When a City Leans against the Sky.* Honesdale, PA: Boyds Mills.

De Gerez, Toni, ed. 1984. *My Song Is a Piece of Jade: Poems of Ancient Mexico in English and Spanish / Mi canción es un pedazo de jade: Poemas del México antiguo en inglés y español.* Boston: Little, Brown.

De Regniers, Beatrice Schenk, Mary Michaels White, Eva Moore, and Jan Carr, eds. 1988. *Sing a Song of Popcorn: Every Child's Book of Poems.* New York: Scholastic.

————, eds. 1988. *The Way I Feel Sometimes.* New York: Clarion.

Delacre, Lulu, ed. 1992. *Arroz con leche: Popular Songs and Rhymes from Latin America.* New York: Scholastic.

————, ed. 1992. *Las navidades: Popular Christmas Songs from Latin America.* New York: Scholastic.

————, ed. 2004. *Arrorró, mi niño: Latino Lullabies and Gentle Games.* New York: Lee and Low.

Demi, ed. 1986. *Dragon Kites and Dragonflies: A Collection of Chinese Nursery Rhymes.* San Diego: Harcourt Brace Jovanovich.

————, ed. 1994. *In the Eyes of the Cat: Japanese Poetry for All Seasons.* Translated by Tze-si Huang. New York: Henry Holt.

dePaola, Tomie. 1985. *Tomie dePaola's Mother Goose.* New York: Putnam.

Dotlich, Rebecca Kai. 1998. *Lemonade Sun and Other Summer Poems.* Honesdale, PA: Wordsong/Boyds Mills.

———. 2001. *When Riddles Come Rumbling: Poems to Ponder.* Honesdale, PA: Wordsong/Boyds Mills.

———. 2003. *In the Spin of Things: Poetry of Motion.* Honesdale, PA: Wordsong/Boyds Mills.

———. 2004. *Over in the Pink House: New Jump-Rope Rhymes.* Honesdale, PA: Wordsong/Boyds Mills.

Dunbar, Paul L. 1999. *Jump Back, Honey: The Poems of Paul Laurence Dunbar.* New York: Hyperion.

Dunning, Stephen, Edward Luders, and Hugh Smith. 1966. *Reflections on a Gift of Watermelon Pickle.* New York: Scholastic.

Elliott, David. 2010. *In the Wild.* Somerville, MA: Candlewick.

Engle, Margarita. 2006. *The Poet Slave of Cuba: A Biography of Juan Francisco Manzano.* New York: Holt.

———. 2008. *The Surrender Tree.* New York: Holt.

———. 2009. *Tropical Secrets: Holocaust Refugees in Cuba.* New York: Holt.

———. 2010. *The Firefly Letters: A Suffragette's Journey to Cuba.* New York: Henry Holt.

———. 2011. *Hurricane Dancers: The First Caribbean Pirate Shipwreck.* New York: Henry Holt.

———. 2012. *The Wild Book.* Boston: Houghton Mifflin.

Esbensen, Barbara. 1984. *Cold Stars and Fireflies: Poems of the Four Seasons.* New York: Crowell.

———. 1986. *Words with Wrinkled Knees.* New York: Crowell.

———. 1992. *Who Shrank My Grandmother's House? Poems of Discovery.* New York: HarperCollins.

———. 1995. *Dance with Me.* New York: HarperCollins.

———. 1995. *The Dream Mouse: A Lullaby Tale from Old Latvia.* Boston: Little, Brown.

———. 1996. *Echoes for the Eye: Poems to Celebrate Patterns in Nature.* New York: HarperCollins.

———. 1999. *Jumping Day.* Honesdale, PA: Boyds Mills.

Farrar, Sid. 2012. *The Year Comes Round: Haiku through the Seasons.* Illustrated by Ilse Plume. Chicago: Albert Whitman.

Feelings, Tom. 1993. *Soul Looks Back in Wonder.* New York: Dial.

Field, Edward. 1998. *Magic Words: Poems.* San Diego: Gulliver Books/Harcourt Brace.

Fisher, Aileen. 1980. *Out in the Dark and Daylight*. New York: Harper and Row.

———. 1991. *Always Wondering: Some Favorite Poems of Aileen Fisher*. New York: HarperCollins.

———. 2002. *I Heard a Bluebird Sing: Children Select Their Favorite Poems by Aileen Fisher*. Honesdale, PA: Boyds Mills.

Fleishman, Paul. 1988. *Joyful Noise: Poems for Two Voices*. New York: Harper and Row.

———. 1985. *I Am Phoenix: Poems for Two Voices*. New York: Harper and Row.

———. 2000. *Big Talk: Poems for Four Voices*. Cambridge, MA: Candlewick.

Fletcher, Ralph J. 1994. *I Am Wings: Poems about Love*. New York: Bradbury.

———. 1997. *Ordinary Things: Poems from a Walk in Early Spring*. New York: Atheneum.

———. 2002. *Poetry Matters: Writing a Poem from the Inside Out*. New York: HarperTrophy.

———. 2005. *A Writing Kind of Day: Poems for Young Poets*. Honesdale, PA: Wordsong/Boyds Mills.

Floca, Brian. 2009. *Moonshot: The Flight of Apollo 11*. New York: Atheneum.

Florian, Douglas. 1993. *Monster Motel: Poems and Paintings*. San Diego: Harcourt Brace Jovanovich.

———. 1994. *Beast Feast: Poems and Paintings*. San Diego: Harcourt Brace.

———. 1994. *Bing Bang Boing: Poems and Drawings*. San Diego: Harcourt Brace.

———. 1996. *On the Wing: Bird Poems and Paintings*. San Diego: Harcourt Brace.

———. 1997. *In the Swim: Poems and Paintings*. San Diego: Harcourt Brace.

———. 1998. *Insectlopedia: Poems and Paintings*. San Diego: Harcourt Brace.

———. 1999. *Laugh-eteria: Poems and Drawings*. San Diego: Harcourt Brace.

———. 1999. *Winter Eyes: Poems and Paintings*. New York: Greenwillow.

———. 2000. *Mammalabilia: Poems and Paintings*. San Diego: Harcourt.

———. 2002. *Summersaults: Poems and Paintings*. New York: Greenwillow.

———. 2003. *Autumnblings: Poems and Paintings*. New York: Greenwillow.

———. 2004. *Omnibeasts: Animal Poems and Paintings*. Orlando, FL: Harcourt.

———. 2005. *See for Your Self*. Katonah, NY: Richard C. Owen.

———. 2005. *Zoo's Who: Poems and Paintings*. Orlando, FL: Harcourt.

———. 2006. *Handsprings: Poems and Paintings*. New York: Greenwillow.

———. 2009. *Dinothesaurus: Prehistoric Poems and Paintings*. New York: Atheneum.

———. 2012. *Unbeelievables: Honeybee Poems and Paintings.* New York: Beach Lane.

Foreman, Michael. 2002. *Michael Foreman's Playtime Rhymes.* Cambridge, MA: Candlewick.

Foster, John, ed. 1988. *Another Third Poetry Book.* New York: Oxford University Press.

———, ed. 1997. *Let's Celebrate: Festival Poems.* New York: Oxford University Press.

Fox, Dan, ed. 2003. *A Treasury of Children's Songs: Forty Favorites to Sing and Play.* New York: Henry Holt.

Frame, Jeron Ashford. 2003. *Yesterday I Had the Blues.* Berkeley, CA: Tricycle.

Francis, Lee, ed. 1999. *When the Rain Sings: Poems by Young Native Americans.* New York: Simon and Schuster.

Franco, Betsy. 1999. *Counting Caterpillars and Other Math Poems.* New York: Scholastic.

———. 2003. *Mathematickles!* New York: Simon and Schuster.

———. 2004. *Counting Our Way to the 100th Day! 100 Poems.* New York: Margaret K. McElderry.

———, ed. 2008. *Falling Hard: 100 Love Poems by Teenagers.* Somerville, MA: Candlewick.

———. 2009. *A Curious Collection of Cats.* Illustrated by Michael Wertz. San Francisco: Tricycle.

———. 2009. *Messing around the Monkey Bars and Other School Poems for Two Voices.* Illustrated by Jessie Hartland. Somerville, MA: Candlewick.

———. 2011. *A Dazzling Display of Dogs.* Illustrated by Michael Wertz. San Francisco: Tricycle.

Frank, Josette. 1977. *Poems to Read to the Very Young.* New York: Random House.

Frost, Helen. 2003. *Keesha's House.* New York: Farrar, Straus, and Giroux.

———. 2004. *Spinning through the Universe: A Novel in Poems from Room 214.* New York: Farrar, Straus, and Giroux.

———. 2006. *The Braid.* New York: Farrar, Straus, and Giroux.

———. 2008. *Diamond Willow.* New York: Farrar, Straus, and Giroux.

———. 2009. *Crossing Stones.* New York: Farrar, Straus, and Giroux.

———. 2011. *Hidden.* New York: Farrar, Straus, and Giroux.

———. 2012. *Step Gently Out.* Illustrated by Rick Lieder. Somerville, MA: Candlewick.

Frost, Robert. 1978/2001. *Stopping by Woods on a Snowy Evening.* Illustrated by Susan Jeffers. New York: Dutton, 2001.

Geis, Jacqueline. 1992. *Where the Buffalo Roam.* Nashville, TN: Ideals Children's Books.

George, Kristine O'Connell. 1997. *The Great Frog Race and Other Poems.* New York: Clarion.

———. 1998. *Old Elm Speaks: Tree Poems.* New York: Clarion.

———. 2001. *Toasting Marshmallows: Camping Poems.* New York: Clarion.

———. 2002. *Little Dog and Duncan.* New York: Clarion.

———. 2002. *Swimming Upstream: Middle School Poems.* New York: Clarion.

———. 2004. *Hummingbird Nest: A Journal of Poems.* New York: Harcourt.

———. 2005. *Fold Me a Poem.* San Diego: Harcourt Brace.

———. 2011. *Emma Dilemma: Big Sister Poems.* Illustrated by Nancy Carpenter. New York: Clarion.

Gherman, Beverly. 1996. *Robert Louis Stevenson: Teller of Tales.* New York: Atheneum.

Ghigna, Charles. 1995. *Riddle Rhymes.* New York: Hyperion.

Giovanni, Nikki. 1971. *Spin a Soft Black Song.* New York: Hill and Wang.

———. 1981. *Vacation Time: Poems for Children.* New York: Morrow.

———. 1996. *The Sun Is So Quiet.* New York: Henry Holt.

———, ed. 2008. *Hip Hop Speaks to Children.* Naperville, IL: Sourcebooks.

Glaser, Isabel Joshlin, ed. 1995. *Dreams of Glory: Poems Starring Girls.* New York: Atheneum.

Glenn, Mel. 1982. *Class Dismissed! High School Poems.* New York: Clarion.

———. 1991. *My Friend's Got This Problem, Mr. Candler: High School Poems.* New York: Clarion.

———. 1996. *Who Killed Mr. Chippendale?* New York: Lodestar/Dutton.

———. 1997. *Jump Ball: A Basketball Season in Poems.* New York: Lodestar/Dutton.

———. 1997. *The Taking of Room 114: A Hostage Drama in Poems.* New York: Lodestar/Dutton.

———. 1999. *Foreign Exchange: A Mystery in Poems.* New York: Morrow Junior Books.

Goldstein, Bobbye S., ed. 1992. *Inner Chimes: Poems on Poetry.* Honesdale, PA: Boyds Mills.

———, ed. 1993. *Birthday Rhymes, Special Times.* New York: Bantam Doubleday.

Gollub, Matthew. 1998. *Cool Melons—Turn to Frogs! The Life and Poems of Issa.* New York: Lee and Low.

Gonzalez, Ray, ed. 1999. *Touching the Fire: Fifteen Poets of Today's Latino Renaissance.* New York: Anchor/Doubleday.

Gordon, Ruth, ed. 1995. *Pierced by a Ray of Sun: Poems about the Times We Feel Alone.* New York: HarperCollins.

Graham, Joan Bransfield. 1994. *Splish Splash.* Boston: Houghton Mifflin.

———. 1999. *Flicker Flash.* Boston: Houghton Mifflin.

Grandits, John. 2004. *Technically, It's Not My Fault: Concrete Poems.* New York: Clarion.

———. 2007. *Blue Lipstick: Concrete Poems.* New York: Clarion.

Greenberg, Jan, ed. 2001. *Heart to Heart: New Poems Inspired by Twentieth-Century American Art.* New York: Abrams.

———, ed. 2008. *Side by Side: New Poems Inspired by Art from around the World.* New York: Abrams.

Greenfield, Eloise. 1977/1992. *Africa Dream.* New York: John Day. New York: HarperTrophy, 1992.

———. 1978. *Honey, I Love and Other Love Poems.* New York: HarperCollins.

———. 1988. *Nathaniel Talking.* New York: Black Butterfly Children's Books.

———. 1988. *Under the Sunday Tree.* New York: Harper and Row.

———. 1996/1999. *Night on Neighborhood Street.* New York: Puffin Pied Piper. Jacksonville, IL: Bound to Stay Bound.

———. 2006. *The Friendly Four.* Illustrated by Jan Spivey Gilchrist. New York: HarperCollins.

———. 2008. *Brothers and Sisters: Family Poems.* New York: Amistad/HarperCollins.

Grimes, Nikki. 1994. *Meet Danitra Brown.* New York: Lothrop, Lee, and Shepard.

———. 1996. *Come Sunday.* Grand Rapids, MI: Eerdmans.

———. 1997. *It's Raining Laughter: Poems.* New York: Dial.

———. 1998. *Jazmin's Notebook.* New York: Dial.

———. 1999. *Hopscotch Love: A Family Treasury of Love Poems.* New York: Lothrop, Lee, and Shepard.

———. 1999. *My Man Blue: Poems.* New York: Dial.

———. 2000. *Is It Far to Zanzibar? Poems about Tanzania.* New York: Lothrop, Lee, and Shepard.

———. 2000. *Shoe Magic.* New York: Orchard.

———. 2000. *Stepping Out with Grandma Mac.* New York: Simon and Schuster.

———. 2002. *Bronx Masquerade.* New York: Dial.

———. 2002. *Danitra Brown Leaves Town.* New York: HarperCollins.

———. 2005. *Danitra Brown, Class Clown.* New York: HarperCollins/Amistad.

———. 2005. *Dark Sons.* New York: Hyperion.

———. 2011. *Planet Middle School.* New York: Bloomsbury.

Gunning, Monica. 1993. *Not a Copper Penny in Me House.* Honesdale, PA: Wordsong/Boyds Mills.

———. 1998. *Under the Breadfruit Tree: Island Poems.* Honesdale, PA: Wordsong/Boyds Mills.

———. 2004. *America, My New Home.* San Francisco: Children's Book Press.

Hague, Michael. 1997. *Teddy Bear, Teddy Bear: A Classic Action Rhyme.* New York: Morrow Junior Books.

Hale, Glorya, ed. 1997. *Read-Aloud Poems for Young People: An Introduction to the Magic and Excitement of Poetry.* New York: Black Dog and Leventhal.

Hale, Sarah Josepha. 1990. *Mary Had a Little Lamb.* Illustrated by Bruce McMillan. New York: Scholastic.

Hall, Donald, ed. 1999. *The Oxford Illustrated Book of American Children's Poems.* New York: Oxford University Press.

Hallworth, Grace, ed. 1996. *Down by the River: Afro-Caribbean Rhymes, Games, and Songs for Children.* New York: Scholastic.

Harley, Avis. 2000. *Fly with Poetry: An ABC of Poetry.* Honesdale, PA: Wordsong/Boyds Mills.

———. 2001. *Leap into Poetry: More ABCs of Poetry.* Honesdale, PA: Wordsong/Boyds Mills.

———. 2008. *The Monarch's Progress: Poems with Wings.* Honesdale, PA: Wordsong/Boyds Mills.

———. 2009. *African Acrostics: A Word in Edgeways.* Illustrated by Deborah Noyes. Somerville, MA: Candlewick.

Harrison, David L. 1993. *Somebody Catch My Homework.* Honesdale, PA: Wordsong/Boyds Mills.

———. 1996. *A Thousand Cousins: Poems of Family Life.* Honesdale, PA: Wordsong/Boyds Mills.

———. 2004. *Connecting Dots: Poems of My Journey.* Honesdale, PA: Wordsong/Boyds Mills.

———. 2007. *Bugs: Poems about Creeping Things.* Honesdale, PA: Wordsong/ Boyds Mills.

———. 2008. *Pirates.* Illustrated by Dan Burr. Honesdale, PA: Wordsong/Boyds Mills.

———. 2009. *Vacation: We're Going to the Ocean.* Illustrated by Rob Shepperson. Honesdale, PA: Wordsong/Boyds Mills.

———. 2012. *Cowboys.* Honesdale, PA: Wordsong/Boyds Mills.

Hass, Robert, ed. 1998. *Poet's Choice: Poems for Everyday Life.* Hopewell, NJ: Ecco.

Hastings, Scott E. 1990. *Miss Mary Mac All Dressed in Black: Tongue Twisters, Jump-Rope Rhymes, and Other Children's Lore from New England.* Little Rock, AR: August House.

Haverlah, B. J. 1993. P*oems from the Heart of Cow Country.* Maljamar, NM: Double Diamond.

Heard, Georgia. 1992. *Creatures of Earth, Sea, and Sky.* Honesdale, PA: Wordsong/ Boyds Mills.

———, ed. 2000. *Songs of Myself: An Anthology of Poems and Art.* New York: Mondo.

———, ed. 2002/2006. *This Place I Know: Poems of Comfort.* Somerville, MA: Candlewick.

———, ed. 2009. *Falling Down the Page: A Book of List Poems.* New York: Roaring Brook.

———, ed. 2012. *The Arrow Finds Its Mark: A Book of Found Poems.* New York: Macmillan.

Henderson, Kathy. 2011. *Hush, Baby, Hush! Lullabies from around the World.* Seattle: Frances Lincoln.

Henkes, Kevin. 2004. *Kitten's First Full Moon.* New York: Greenwillow.

Herrera, Juan Felipe. 1998. *Laughing Out Loud, I Fly: Poems in English and Spanish.* New York: HarperCollins.

Herrick, Steven. 2008. *Naked Bunyip Dancing.* Honesdale, PA: Wordsong/Boyds Mills.

Hesse, Karen. 1997. *Out of the Dust.* New York: Scholastic.

———. 2001. *Witness.* New York: Scholastic.

———. 2003. *Aleutian Sparrow.* New York: Margaret K. McElderry.

Hines, Anna Grossnickle. 2001. *Pieces: A Year in Poems and Quilts.* New York: Greenwillow.

———. 2011. *Peaceful Pieces: Poems and Quilts about Peace.* New York: Henry Holt.

Hirschfelder, Arlene B., and Beverly Singer, eds. 1992. *Rising Voices: Writings of Young Native Americans.* New York: Scribner's.

Ho, Minfong. 1996. *Maples in the Mist: Poems for Children from the Tang Dynasty.* New York: Lothrop, Lee, and Shepard.

Hoberman, Mary Ann. 1991. *Fathers, Mothers, Sisters, Brothers: A Collection of Family Poems.* Boston: Joy Street.

———. 1994. *My Song Is Beautiful: Poems and Pictures in Many Voices.* Boston: Little, Brown.

———. 1997. *The Seven Silly Eaters.* San Diego: Harcourt Brace.

———. 1998. *The Llama Who Had No Pajama: 100 Favorite Poems.* San Diego: Harcourt.

———. 1998. *Miss Mary Mack: A Hand-Clapping Rhyme.* New York: Scholastic.

———. 2001. *Very Short Stories to Read Together.* Boston: Little, Brown.

———. 2009. *All Kinds of Families.* New York: Little, Brown.

———, ed. 2012. *Forget-Me-Nots: Poems to Learn by Heart.* Illustrated by Michael Emberley. New York: Little, Brown.

Hoberman, Mary Ann, and Linda Winston, eds. 2009. *The Tree That Time Built: A Celebration of Nature, Science, and Imagination.* Naperville, IL: Sourcebooks.

Holbrook, Sara. 1996. *Am I Naturally This Crazy?* Honesdale, PA: Boyds Mills.

———. 1996. *The Dog Ate My Homework.* Honesdale, PA: Boyds Mills.

———. 1996. *I Never Said I Wasn't Difficult.* Honesdale, PA: Boyds Mills.

———. 1996. *Which Way to the Dragon! Poems for the Coming-on-Strong.* Honesdale, PA: Boyds Mills.

———. 2003. *By Definition: Poems of Feelings.* Honesdale, PA: Wordsong/Boyds Mills.

———. 2003. *Wham! It's a Poetry Jam: Discovering Performance Poetry.* Honesdale, PA: Wordsong/Boyds Mills.

———. 2011. *Weird? (Me, Too!) Let's Be Friends.* Illustrated by Karen Sandstrom. Honesdale, PA: Wordsong/Boyds Mills.

Holbrook, Sara, and Allan Wolf. 2008. *More Than Friends: Poems from Him and Her.* Honesdale, PA: Wordsong/Boyds Mills.

Holman, Felice. 1985. *The Song in My Head.* New York: Scribner's.

Hopkins, Lee Bennett, ed. 1983. *The Sky Is Full of Song.* New York: Harper and Row.

———, ed. 1984. *Surprises.* New York: HarperTrophy.

———, ed. 1987. *Click, Rumble, Roar: Poems about Machines.* New York: Crowell.

————, ed. 1988. *Side by Side: Poems to Read Together.* New York: Simon and Schuster.

————, ed. 1990/2000. *Good Books, Good Times!* New York: Trumpet. New York: HarperTrophy.

————, ed. 1992. *Ring Out, Wild Bells: Poems about Holidays and Seasons.* New York: Harcourt Brace.

————, ed. 1992. *Through Our Eyes: Poems and Pictures about Growing Up.* New York: Trumpet.

————, ed. 1993. *It's About Time.* New York: Simon and Schuster.

————. 1993. *The Writing Bug.* Katonah, NY: Richard C. Owen.

————, ed. 1994. *Hand in Hand: An American History through Poetry.* New York: Simon and Schuster.

————, ed. 1994. *Weather: Poems for All Seasons.* New York: HarperTrophy.

————. 1995. *Been to Yesterdays: Poems of a Life.* Honesdale, PA: Wordsong/Boyds Mills.

————, ed. 1995. *Blast Off: Poems about Space.* New York: HarperCollins.

————, ed. 1995. *Dinosaurs.* New York: Random House.

————. 1995. *Good Rhymes, Good Times: Original Poems.* New York: HarperCollins.

————. 1995. *Pauses: Autobiographical Reflections of 101 Creators of Children's Books.* New York: HarperCollins.

————, ed. 1995. *Small Talk: A Book of Short Poems.* San Diego: Harcourt Brace.

————, ed. 1996. *Opening Days: Sports Poems.* San Diego: Harcourt Brace.

————, ed. 1996. *School Supplies: A Book of Poems.* New York: Simon and Schuster.

————, ed. 1997. *Marvelous Math: A Book of Poems.* New York: Simon and Schuster.

————, ed. 1997. *Song and Dance.* New York: Simon and Schuster.

————, ed. 1998. *Around the Neighborhood.* New York: Sadlier-Oxford.

————, ed. 1998. *Climb into My Lap: First Poems to Read Together.* New York: Simon and Schuster.

————, ed. 1998. *Families, Families.* New York: Sadlier-Oxford.

————, ed. 1998. *Me, Myself, and I!* New York: Sadlier-Oxford.

————, ed. 1998. *Places to Visit, Places to See.* New York: Sadlier-Oxford.

————, ed. 1999. *Lives: Poems about Famous Americans.* New York: HarperCollins.

————, ed. 1999. *Mother Goose and Her Animal Friends.* New York: Sadlier-Oxford.

———, ed. 1999. *Spectacular Science: A Book of Poems.* New York: Simon and Schuster.

———, ed. 1999. *Sports! Sports! Sports!* New York: HarperCollins.

———, ed. 2000. *My America: A Poetry Atlas of the United States.* New York: Simon and Schuster.

———, ed. 2002. *Hoofbeats, Claws, and Rippled Fins: Creature Poems.* New York: HarperCollins.

———, ed. 2005. *Days to Celebrate: A Full Year of Poetry, People, Holidays, History, Fascinating Facts, and More.* New York: Greenwillow.

———, ed. 2007. *Behind the Museum Door.* New York: Abrams.

———, ed. 2008. *America at War.* New York: Margaret K. McElderry.

———. 2009. *City I Love.* Illustrated by Marcellus Hall. New York: Abrams.

———, ed. 2009. *Incredible Inventions.* Illustrated by Julia Sarcone-Roach. New York: HarperCollins.

———, ed. 2009. *Sky Magic.* Illustrated by Mariusz Stawarski. New York: Dutton.

———, ed. 2010. *Amazing Faces.* Illustrated by Chris Soentpiet. New York: Lee and Low.

———, ed. 2010. *Give Me Wings.* Illustrated by Ponder Goembel. New York: Holiday House.

———, ed. 2010. *Sharing the Seasons.* New York: Margaret K. McElderry.

———, ed. 2011. *I Am the Book.* New York: Holiday House.

———, ed. 2012. *Nasty Bugs.* Illustrated by Will Terry. New York: Dial.

Hoyte, Carol-Ann, and Heidi Bee Roemer, eds. 2012. *And the Crowd Goes Wild! A Global Gathering of Sports Poems.* Illustrated by Kevin Sylvester. Victoria, BC: Friesens Press.

Hudson, Wade, ed. 1993. *Pass It On: African American Poetry for Children.* New York: Scholastic.

Hughes, Langston. 1994. *The Dreamkeeper and Other Poems.* New York: Knopf.

———. 1994. *The Sweet and Sour Animal Book.* New York: Oxford University Press.

———. 2012. *I, Too, Am America.* Illustrated by Bryan Collier. New York: Simon and Schuster.

Hummon, David. 1999. *Animal Acrostics.* Nevada City, CA: Dawn Publications.

Izuki, Steven. 1994. *Believers in America: Poems about Americans of Asian and Pacific Islander Descent.* Chicago: Children's Press.

Jacobs, Leland B. 1993. *Just around the Corner: Poems about the Seasons.* New York: Henry Holt.

Janeczko, Paul B., ed. 1987. *This Delicious Day.* New York: Orchard.

———, ed. 1988. *The Music of What Happens: Poems That Tell Stories.* New York: Orchard.

———, ed. 1991. *Preposterous: Poems of Youth.* New York: Orchard.

———. 1993. *Stardust Hotel.* New York: Orchard.

———, ed. 1994/2009. *A Kick in the Head: An Everyday Guide to Poetic Forms.* Cambridge, MA: Candlewick.

———, ed. 1994. *Poetry from A to Z: A Guide for Young Writers.* New York: Bradbury.

———. 1999. *How to Write Poetry.* New York: Scholastic.

———. 1998. *That Sweet Diamond: Baseball Poems.* New York: Atheneum.

———, ed. 2000. *Stone Bench in an Empty Park.* New York: Orchard.

———, ed. 2001. *A Poke in the I: A Collection of Concrete Poems.* Cambridge, MA: Candlewick.

———, ed. 2002. *Seeing the Blue Between: Advice and Inspiration for Young Poets.* Cambridge, MA: Candlewick.

———. 2004. *Worlds Afire.* Cambridge, MA: Candlewick.

———, ed. 2009. *A Foot in the Mouth: Poems to Speak, Sing, and Shout.* Illustrated by Chris Raschka. Somerville, MA: Candlewick.

———. 2011. *Requiem: Poems of the Terezin Ghetto.* Somerville, MA: Candlewick.

Jenkins, Steve. 2004. *Actual Size.* Boston: Houghton Mifflin.

Johnson, Angela. 1998. *The Other Side: Shorter Poems.* New York: Orchard.

Johnson, Dave, ed. 2000. *Movin': Teen Poets Take Voice.* New York: Orchard.

Johnson, James Weldon. 1995. *Lift Ev'ry Voice and Sing.* New York: Scholastic.

Johnson, Lindsay Lee. 2002. *Soul Moon Soup.* Asheville, NC: Front Street.

Johnston, Tony. 1996. *My Mexico / México mío.* New York: Putnam's Sons.

———. 1999. *An Old Shell: Poems of the Galapagos.* New York: Farrar, Straus, and Giroux.

Jones, Hettie, ed. 1971. *The Tree Stands Shining: Poetry of the North American Indian.* New York: Dial.

Joseph, Lynn. 1990. *Coconut Kind of Day: Island Poems.* New York: Lothrop, Lee, and Shepard.

Josephson, Judith Pinkerton. 2000. *Nikki Giovanni: Poet of the People.* Berkeley Heights, NJ: Enslow.

Katz, Alan. 2001. *Take Me out of the Bathtub and Other Silly Dilly Songs.* New York: Margaret K. McElderry.

———. 2005. *Where Did They Hide My Presents? Silly Dilly Christmas Songs.* New York: Margaret K. McElderry.

———. 2008. *Oops!* Illustrated by Edward Koren. New York: Margaret K. McElderry.

———. 2009. *Going, Going, Gone! and Other Silly Dilly Sports Songs.* New York: Simon and Schuster.

———. 2011. *Mosquitoes Are Ruining My Summer! and Other Silly Dilly Camp Songs.* New York: Margaret K. McElderry.

———. 2011. *Poems I Wrote When No One Was Looking.* Illustrated by Edward Koren. New York: Simon and Schuster.

Katz, Bobbi, ed. 1992. *Puddle Wonderful: Poems to Welcome Spring.* New York: Random House.

———. 2000. *We the People: Poems.* New York: Greenwillow.

———. 2001. *A Rumpus of Rhymes: A Book of Noisy Poems.* New York: Dutton.

———, ed. 2004. *Pocket Poems.* Illustrated by Deborah Zemke. New York: Dutton.

———. 2006. *Once around the Sun.* Illustrated by LeUyen Pham. San Diego: Harcourt.

———. 2007. *Trailblazers: Poems of Exploration.* New York: Greenwillow.

———. 2009. *The Monsterologist: A Memoir in Rhyme.* Illustrated by Adam McCauley. New York: Sterling.

———, ed. 2009. *More Pocket Poems.* Illustrated by Deborah Zemke. New York: Dutton.

Kellogg, Steven. 1976. *Steven Kellogg's Yankee Doodle.* New York: Parent's Magazine Press. Reprinted as Yankee Doodle. New York: Simon and Schuster, 1996.

Kennedy, Dorothy M., ed. 1993. *I Thought I'd Take My Rat to School: Poems for September to June.* New York: Little, Brown.

———, ed. 1998. *Make Things Fly: Poems about the Wind.* New York: Margaret K. McElderry.

Kennedy, X. J. 1975. *One Winter Night in August and Other Nonsense Jingles.* New York: Scribner's.

———. 2002. *Exploding Gravy: Poems to Make You Laugh.* Boston: Little, Brown.

Kennedy, X. J., and Dorothy Kennedy, eds. 1982. *Knock at a Star: A Child's Introduction to Poetry.* Boston: Little, Brown.

———, eds. 1992. *Talking like the Rain: A Read-to-Me Book of Poems.* Boston: Little, Brown.

Kerley, Barbara. 2004. *Walt Whitman: Works for America.* New York: Scholastic.

Knudson, R. Rozanne, and May Swensen, eds. 1988. *American Sports Poems.* New York: Orchard.

Koertge, Ron. 2003. *Shakespeare Bats Cleanup.* Cambridge, MA: Candlewick.

Korman, Gordon, and Bernice Korman. 1992. *The D+ Poems of Jeremy Bloom: A Collection of Poems about School, Homework, and Life (Sort Of).* New York: Scholastic.

Koss, Amy Goldman. 1987. *Where Fish Go in Winter, and Answers to Other Great Mysteries.* Los Angeles: Price Stern Sloan.

Kurtz, Jane. 2000. *River Friendly, River Wild.* New York: Simon and Schuster.

Kuskin, Karla. 1975. *Near the Window Tree: Poems and Notes.* New York: HarperCollins.

———. 1980. *Dogs and Dragons, Trees and Dreams: A Collection of Poems.* New York: HarperCollins.

———. 1985. *Something Sleeping in the Hall: Poems.* New York: Harper and Row.

———. 1995. *Thoughts, Pictures, and Words.* Katonah, NY: Richard C. Owen.

———. 2003. *Moon, Have You Met My Mother? The Collected Poems of Karla Kuskin.* New York: HarperCollins.

Lai, Thanhha. 2011. *Inside Out and Back Again.* New York: HarperCollins.

Lansky, Bruce, ed. 1994. *A Bad Case of the Giggles: Kids' Favorite Funny Poems.* Deephaven, MN: Meadowbrook.

———, ed. 1997. *No More Homework! No More Tests! Kids' Favorite Funny School Poems.* Minnetonka, MN: Meadowbrook.

———, ed. 1998. *Miles of Smiles: Kids Pick the Funniest Poems, Book #3.* New York: Scholastic.

Lasky, Kathryn. 2003. *A Voice of Her Own: The Story of Phillis Wheatley, Slave Poet.* Cambridge, MA: Candlewick.

Lawrence, Jacob. 1968. *Harriet and the Promised Land.* New York: Simon and Schuster.

Lawson, JonArno. 2006. *Black Stars in a White Night Sky.* Illustrated by Sherwin Tjia. Toronto: Pedlar Press.

————. 2008. *Inside Out: Children's Poets Discuss Their Work*. London: Walker.

————. 2008. *A Voweller's Bestiary, from Aardvark to Guineafowl (and H)*. Erin, ON: Porcupine's Quill.

————. 2010. *Think Again*. Toronto: Kids Can Press.

Lear, Edward. 1991. *The Owl and the Pussycat*. Illustrated by Jan Brett. New York: Putnam.

————. 1998. *The Owl and the Pussycat*. Illustrated by James Marshall. New York: HarperCollins.

Lear, Edward, and Daniel Pinkwater. 2011. *His Shoes Were Far Too Tight*. Illustrated by Calef Brown. San Francisco: Chronicle.

Lee, Dennis. 1991/1999. *The Ice Cream Store*. New York: Scholastic. New York: HarperCollins.

Lessac, Frané, ed. 2003. *Camp Granada: Sing-Along Camp Songs*. New York: Henry Holt.

Levy, Constance. 1998. *A Crack in the Clouds*. New York: Margaret K. McElderry.

————. 2002. *Splash! Poems of Our Watery World*. New York: Orchard.

Levy, Debbie. 2010. *The Year of Goodbyes: A True Story of Friendship, Family, and Farewells*. New York: Hyperion.

Lewis, J. Patrick. 1990. *A Hippopotamusn't and Other Animal Verses*. New York: Dial.

————. 1995. *Black Swan White Crow*. New York: Atheneum.

————. 1995. *Ridicholas Nicholas: More Animal Poems*. New York: Dial.

————. 1996. *Riddle-icious*. New York: Scholastic.

————. 1998. *Boshblobberbosh: Runcible Poems for Edward Lear*. Mankato, MN: Creative Editions; San Diego: Harcourt.

————. 1998. *Doodle Dandies: Poems That Take Shape*. New York: Atheneum.

————. 1998. *Riddle-lightful*. New York: Knopf.

————. 1999. *The Bookworm's Feast: A Potluck of Poems*. New York: Dial.

————. 2000. *Freedom Like Sunlight: Praisesongs for Black Americans*. Mankato, MN: Creative Editions.

————. 2002. *Arithme-Tickle: An Even Number of Odd Riddle-Rhymes*. San Diego: Harcourt.

————. 2002. *A World of Wonders: Geographic Travels in Verse and Rhyme*. New York: Dial.

————. 2004. *Scien-trickery: Riddles in Science*. Orlando, FL: Harcourt.

————. 2005. *Monumental Verses*. Washington, DC: National Geographic.

————. 2005. *Please Bury Me in the Library.* Orlando, FL: Gulliver/Harcourt.

————. 2005. *Vherses: A Celebration of Outstanding Women.* Mankato, MN: Creative Editions.

————. 2009. *Countdown to Summer: A Poem for Every Day of the School Year.* Illustrated by Ethan Long. New York: Little, Brown.

————. 2009. *Spot the Plot! A Riddle Book of Book Riddles.* Illustrated by Lynn Munsinger. San Francisco: Chronicle.

————. 2009. *The Underwear Salesman and Other Jobs for Better or Verse.* Illustrated by Serge Bloch. New York: Simon and Schuster/Atheneum.

————, ed. 2012. *Book of Animal Poetry.* Washington, DC: National Geographic.

————. 2012. *Edgar Allan Poe's Pie: Math Puzzlers in Classic Poems.* New York: Houghton Mifflin Harcourt.

————. 2012. *If You Were a Chocolate Mustache.* Illustrated by Matt Cordell. Honesdale, PA: Wordsong/Boyds Mills.

————. 2012. *When Thunder Comes: Poems for Civil Rights Leaders.* San Francisco: Chronicle.

Lewis, J. Patrick, and Paul B. Janeczko. 2006. *Wing Nuts: Screwy Haiku.* New York: Little, Brown.

Lewis, J. Patrick, and Jane Yolen. 2011. *Self Portrait with Seven Fingers: A Life of Marc Chagall in Verse.* Mankato, MN: Creative Editions.

————. 2012. *Take Two! A Celebration of Twins.* Illustrated by Sophie Blackall. Somerville, MA: Candlewick.

Lewis, Richard, ed. 1971. *I Breathe a New Song: Poems of the Eskimo.* New York: Simon and Schuster.

————. 1988. *In the Night Still Dark.* New York: Atheneum.

Lillegard, Dee. 2000. *Wake Up House! Rooms Full of Poems.* New York: Knopf.

Lindbergh, Reeve. 1990. *Johnny Appleseed.* Boston: Joy Street.

Little, Jean. 1989. *Hey World, Here I Am!* New York: Harper and Row.

Little, Lessie Jones. 1988/2000. *Children of Long Ago: Poems.* New York: Lee and Low, 2000.

Livingston, Myra Cohn. 1959/2007. *Calendar.* New York: Holiday House.

————. 1982. *A Circle of Seasons.* New York: Holiday House.

————. 1985. *Celebrations.* New York: Holiday House.

————, ed. 1989. *Halloween Poems.* New York: Holiday House.

————. 1990. *Climb into the Bell Tower: Essays on Poetry.* New York: Harper and Row.

———. 1991. *Poem-Making: Ways to Begin Writing Poetry.* New York: HarperCollins.

———. 1992. *Let Freedom Ring: A Ballad of Martin Luther King Jr.* New York: Holiday House.

———. 1993. *Abraham Lincoln: A Man for All the People; A Ballad.* New York: Holiday House.

———, ed. 1993. *Roll Along: Poems on Wheels.* New York: Margaret K. McElderry.

———. 1994. *Animal, Vegetable, Mineral: Poems about Small Things.* New York: HarperCollins.

———. 1996. *Festivals.* New York: Holiday House.

———. 1998. *Space Songs.* New York: Holiday House.

Loewen, Nancy. 2009. *Words, Wit, and Wonder: Writing Your Own Poem.* Minneapolis, MN: Picture Window Books.

Longfellow, Henry Wadsworth. 1984. *Hiawatha's Childhood.* Illustrated by Errol Le Cain. New York: Farrar, Straus, and Giroux.

———. 1990. *Paul Revere's Ride.* Illustrated by Ted Rand. New York: Dutton.

———. 2001. *The Midnight Ride of Paul Revere.* Illustrated by Christopher Bing. New York: Handprint.

Lowe, Ayana, ed. 2008. *Come and Play: Children of Our World Having Fun.* New York: Bloomsbury.

Lowry, Lois. 1989. *Number the Stars.* Boston: Houghton Mifflin.

Lyne, Sandford, ed. 1996. *Ten-Second Rainshowers: Poems by Young People.* New York: Simon and Schuster.

———, ed. 2004. *Soft Hay Will Catch You: Poems by Young People.* New York: Simon and Schuster.

Lyon, George Ella. 1999. *Where I'm From: Where Poems Come From.* Spring, TX: Absey.

MacLachlan, Patricia. 1995. *What You Know First.* New York: HarperCollins.

Mado, Michio. 1992. *The Animals: Selected Poems.* New York: Margaret K. McElderry.

———. 1998. *The Magic Pocket.* New York: Margaret K. McElderry.

Mak, Kam. 2001. *My Chinatown: One Year in Poems.* New York: HarperCollins.

Manguel, Alberto, ed. 1990. *Seasons.* New York: Doubleday.

Marsalis, Wynton. 2005. *Jazz A·B·Z: An A to Z Collection of Jazz Portraits.* Illustrated by Paul Rogers. Somerville, MA: Candlewick.

Martin, Bill Jr., and Michael Sampson, eds. 2008. *The Bill Martin Jr. Big Book of Poetry.* New York: Simon and Schuster.

Mayo, Margaret. 2002. *Wiggle Waggle Fun: Stories and Rhymes for the Very Very Young.* Cambridge, MA: Candlewick.

McCall, Guadalupe Garcia. 2011. *Under the Mesquite.* New York: Lee & Low.

McCord, David. 1986. *One at a Time: His Collected Poems for the Young.* Boston: Little, Brown.

———. 1999. *Every Time I Climb a Tree.* New York: Little, Brown.

McKissack, Patricia. 2011. *Never Forgotten.* Illustrated by Leo and Diane Dillon. New York: Schwartz and Wade.

McLaughlin, Timothy, ed. 2012. *Walking on Earth and Touching the Sky: Poetry and Prose by Lakota Youth at Red Cloud Indian School.* New York: Abrams.

Mecum, Ryan. 2008. *Zombie Haiku.* Cincinnati, OH: How Books.

Medearis, Angela Shelf. 1995. *Skin Deep and Other Teenage Reflections: Poems.* New York: Macmillan.

Medina, Jane. 1999. *My Name Is Jorge on Both Sides of the River: Poems.* Honesdale, PA: Boyds Mills.

———. 2004. *The Dream on Blanca's Wall / El sueño pegado en la pared de Blanca: Poems in English and Spanish.* Illustrated by Robert Casilla. Honesdale, PA: Boyds Mills.

Meltzer, Milton. 1968/1997. *Langston Hughes: A Biography.* New York: Crowell. Brookfield, CT: Millbrook.

———. 1999. *Carl Sandburg: A Biography.* Brookfield, CT: Twenty-First Century.

———. 2002. *Walt Whitman: A Biography.* Brookfield, CT: Twenty-First Century.

———, ed. 2003. *Hour of Freedom: American History in Poetry.* Honesdale, PA: Wordsong/Boyds Mills.

———. 2004. *Emily Dickinson: A Biography.* Brookfield, CT: Twenty-First Century.

Merriam, Eve. 1962. *There Is No Rhyme for Silver.* New York: Scribner.

———. 1964. *It Doesn't Always Have to Rhyme.* New York: Atheneum.

———. 1970. *Finding a Poem.* New York: Atheneum.

———. 1995. *Bam Bam Bam.* New York: Henry Holt.

———. 1996. *You Be Good and I'll Be Night.* New York: HarperTrophy.

Michael, Pamela, ed. 2008. *River of Words.* Minneapolis, MN: Milkweed.

Michelson, Richard. 2000. *Ten Times Better.* New York: Marshall Cavendish.

Millen, C. M. 2010. *The Ink Garden of Brother Theophane.* Illustrated by Andrea Wisnewski. Watertown, MA: Charlesbridge.

Milne, A. A. 1928. *The House at Pooh Corner.* London: Methuen.

———. 1958. *The World of Christopher Robin: The Complete When We Were Very Young and Now We Are Six.* New York: Dutton.

———. 1988. *When We Were Very Young.* New York: Dutton.

Milnes, Gerald. 1990. *Granny Will Your Dog Bite and Other Mountain Rhymes.* New York: Knopf.

Mitchell, Stephen. 2003. *The Wishing Bone and Other Poems.* Cambridge, MA: Candlewick.

Molloy, Paul, ed. 1968. *Poetry U.S.A.* New York: Scholastic.

Monahan, Sean. 1992. *Multivoice Magic: Poetry as Shared Reading.* Melbourne, Australia: Longman Cheshire.

Montgomery, Sy. 2004. *The Tarantula Scientist.* Boston: Houghton Mifflin, 2004.

Moore, Lilian, ed. 1992. *Sunflakes: Poems for Children.* New York: Clarion.

———. 1997. *Poems Have Roots: New Poems.* New York: Atheneum.

———. 2001. *I'm Small and Other Verses.* Cambridge, MA: Candlewick.

———. 2004. *Mural on Second Avenue and Other City Poems.* Somerville, MA: Candlewick.

———. 2006. *Beware, Take Care.* New York: Holt.

Mora, Pat. 1994. *The Desert Is My Mother / El desierto es mi madre.* Houston, TX: Piñata.

———. 1996. *Confetti: Poems for Children.* New York: Lee and Low.

———. 1996. *Uno, dos, tres / One, Two, Three.* New York: Clarion.

———. 1998. *Delicious Hullabaloo / Pachanga deliciosa.* Houston, TX: Piñata.

———. 1998. *This Big Sky.* New York: Scholastic.

———. 2000. *My Own True Name: New and Selected Poems for Young Adults, 1984–1999.* Houston, TX: Piñata.

———. 2001. *Love to Mama: A Tribute to Mothers.* New York: Lee and Low.

———. 2007. *Yum! Mmmm! ¡Qué rico! Americas' Sproutings.* New York: Lee and Low.

———. 2010. *Dizzy in My Eyes.* New York: Knopf.

Mordhorst, Heidi. 2005. *Squeeze: Poems from a Juicy Universe.* Honesdale, PA: Wordsong/Boyds Mills.

———. 2009. *Pumpkin Butterfly: Poems from the Other Side of Nature.* Honesdale, PA: Wordsong/Boyds Mills.

Morrison, Lillian, ed. 1992. *At the Crack of the Bat: Baseball Poems.* New York: Hyperion.

Morrison, Meighan. 1993. *Long Live Earth.* New York: Scholastic.

Moss, Jeff. 1997. *Bone Poems.* New York: Scholastic.

———. 1997. *The Dad of the Dad of the Dad of Your Dad.* New York: Ballantine.

Most, Bernard. 1990/1999. *Four and Twenty Dinosaurs.* New York: Harper and Row. San Diego: Voyager, 1999.

Murphy, Elspeth Campbell. 1988. *Recess: Prayer Meditations for Teachers.* Grand Rapids, MI: Baker Book House.

Murphy, Jim. 1993. *Across America on an Emigrant Train.* New York: Clarion.

Myers, Walter Dean. 1993. *Brown Angels: An Album of Pictures and Verse.* New York: HarperCollins.

———. 1995. *Glorious Angels: A Celebration of Children.* New York: HarperCollins.

———. 1997. *Harlem: A Poem.* New York: Scholastic.

———. 1998. *Angel to Angel.* New York: HarperCollins.

———. 2003. *Blues Journey.* New York: Holiday House.

———. 2004. *Here in Harlem: Poems in Many Voices.* New York: Holiday House.

———. 2006. *Jazz.* Illustrated by Christopher Myers. New York: Holiday House.

———. 2011. *We Are America: A Tribute from the Heart.* Illustrated by Christopher Myers. New York: HarperCollins.

Nelson, Kadir. 2011. *Heart and Soul.* New York: Balzer and Bray.

Nelson, Marilyn. 2004. *Fortune's Bones: The Manumission Requiem.* Asheville, NC: Front Street.

Neri, G., and Jesse Joshua Watson. 2007. *Chess Rumble.* New York: Lee and Low.

Nesbitt, Kenn. 2007. *Revenge of the Lunch Ladies: The Hilarious Book of School Poetry.* New York: Meadowbrook Press.

———. 2009. *My Hippo Has the Hiccups and Other Poems I Totally Made Up.* Naperville, IL: Sourcebooks.

———. 2010. *The Tighty Whitey Spider and More Wacky Animal Poems I Totally Made Up.* Naperville, IL: Sourcebooks.

Newcome, Zita. 2000. *Head, Shoulders, Knees, and Toes and Other Action Rhymes.* Cambridge, MA: Candlewick.

Newsome, Effie Lee. 1999. *Wonders: The Best Children's Poems by Effie Lee Newsome.* Honesdale, PA: Boyds Mills.

Nicholls, Judith, ed. 1993. *Earthways, Earthwise: Poems on Conservation.* Oxford: Oxford University Press.

Nichols, Grace. 1997. *Asana and the Animals: A Book of Pet Poems.* Cambridge, MA: Candlewick.

Niven, Penelope. 2003. *Carl Sandburg: Adventures of a Poet.* Orlando, FL: Harcourt.

*Nursery Rhyme Comics: 50 Timeless Rhymes from 50 Celebrated Cartoonists.* New York: First Second.

Nye, Naomi Shihab, ed. 1992. *This Same Sky: A Collection of Poems from around the World.* New York: Four Winds.

———, ed. 1995. *The Tree Is Older Than You Are: A Bilingual Gathering of Poems and Stories from Mexico with Paintings by Mexican Artists.* New York: Simon and Schuster.

———. 1998. *Fuel.* Rochester, NY: BOA Editions.

———, ed. 1998. *The Space between Our Footsteps: Poems and Paintings from the Middle East.* New York: Simon and Schuster.

———, ed. 1999. *What Have You Lost?* New York: Greenwillow.

———. 2000. *Come with Me: Poems for a Journey.* New York: Greenwillow.

———, ed. 2000. *Salting the Ocean: 100 Poems by Young Poets.* New York: Greenwillow.

———. 2005. *A Maze Me: Poems for Girls.* New York: Greenwillow.

———. 2008. *Honeybee.* New York: Greenwillow.

Nye, Naomi Shihab, and Paul B. Janeczko, eds. 1996. *I Feel a Little Jumpy around You: A Book of His and Her Poems Collected in Pairs.* New York: Simon and Schuster.

Ochoa, Annette Piña, Betsy Franco, and Traci L. Gourdine, eds. 2003. *Night Is Gone, Day Is Still Coming: Stories and Poems by American Indian Teens and Young Adults.* Somerville, MA: Candlewick.

O'Connell, Caitlin, and Donna M. Jackson. 2011. *The Elephant Scientist.* Boston: Houghton Mifflin.

Okutoro, Lydia Omolola, ed. 1999. *Quiet Storm: Voices of Young Black Poets.* New York: Hyperion.

Oliver, Mary. 1992. *New and Selected Poems.* Boston: Beacon.

O'Neill, Mary. 1968. *Take a Number.* Garden City, NY: Doubleday.

———. 1989. *Hailstones and Halibut Bones: Adventures in Color.* New York: Doubleday.

Opie, Iona, ed. 1996. *My Very First Mother Goose.* Cambridge, MA: Candlewick.

———, ed. 1997. *Wee Willie Winkie and Other Rhymes.* Cambridge, MA: Candlewick.

—————. 1999. *Here Comes Mother Goose.* Cambridge, MA: Candlewick.

Opie, Iona, and Peter Opie, eds. 1992. *I Saw Esau: The Schoolchild's Pocket Book.* Cambridge, MA: Candlewick.

Orozco, José-Luis, ed. 1994. *"De colores" and Other Latin American Folk Songs for Children.* New York: Dutton.

—————. 1994. *Fiestas: A Year of Latin American Songs of Celebration.* New York: Dutton.

—————. 2002. *Diez deditos / Ten Little Fingers and Other Play Rhymes and Action Songs from Latin America.* New York: Dutton.

Osofsky, Audrey. 1996. *Free to Dream: The Making of a Poet; Langston Hughes.* New York: Lothrop, Lee, and Shepard.

Panzer, Nora, ed. 1994. *Celebrate America in Poetry and Art.* New York: Hyperion.

Pappas, Theoni. 1991. *Math Talk: Mathematical Ideas in Poems for Two Voices.* San Carlos, CA: Wide World Publishing/Tetra.

Park, Linda Sue. 2001. *A Single Shard.* Boston: Clarion, 2001.

—————. 2007. *Tap Dancing on the Roof: Sijo (Poems).* New York: Clarion.

Paschen, Elise, and Dominique Raccah, eds. 2005. *Poetry Speaks to Children.* Naperville, IL: Sourcebooks.

—————, eds. 2010. *Poetry Speaks: Who I Am.* Naperville, IL: Sourcebooks.

Paul, A. W. 1999. *All by Herself: 14 Girls Who Made a Difference; Poems.* San Diego: Browndeer/Harcourt Brace.

Pearson, Susan, ed. 2002. *The Drowsy Hours.* New York: HarperCollins.

—————. 2004. *Squeal and Squawk: Barnyard Talk.* New York: Marshall Cavendish.

—————. 2005. *Grimericks.* New York: Marshall Cavendish.

—————. 2005. *Who Swallowed Harold? and Other Poems about Pets.* New York: Marshall Cavendish.

Peck, Jan, and David Davis, eds. 2011. *The Green Mother Goose: Saving the World One Rhyme at a Time.* Illustrated by Carin Berger. New York: Sterling.

Perdomo, Willie. 2002. *Visiting Langston.* New York: Henry Holt.

Peters, Lisa Westberg. 2003. *Earthshake: Poems from the Ground Up.* Illustrated by Cathie Felstead. New York: HarperCollins.

Peterson, Isabel, ed. 1954. *The First Book of Poetry.* New York: Franklin Watts.

Philip, Neil, ed. 1995. *Singing America: Poems That Define a Nation.* New York: Viking.

—————, ed. 1996. *Earth Always Endures: Native American Poems.* New York: Viking.

———, ed. 1996. *The New Oxford Book of Children's Verse.* Oxford: Oxford University Press.

———, ed. 1997. *In a Sacred Manner I Live: Native American Wisdom.* New York: Clarion.

———, ed. 2000. *It's a Woman's World: A Century of Women's Voices in Poetry.* New York: Dutton.

Poe, Edgar Allan. 2006. *The Raven.* Illustrated by Ryan Price. Toronto: Kids Can Press.

Pomerantz, Charlotte. 1982. *If I Had a Paka: Poems in Eleven Languages.* New York: Greenwillow.

Prelutsky, Jack. 1976/1993. *Nightmares: Poems to Trouble Your Sleep.* New York: Greenwillow. Reprinted New York: Mulberry, 1993.

———. 1977. *It's Halloween.* New York: Greenwillow.

———. 1980/1993. *Rolling Harvey Down the Hill.* New York: Mulberry, 1993.

———, ed. 1983. *The Random House Book of Poetry for Children.* New York: Random House.

———. 1984. *The New Kid on the Block.* New York: Greenwillow.

———, ed. 1986. *Read-Aloud Rhymes for the Very Young.* New York: Knopf.

———. 1986. *Ride a Purple Pelican.* New York: Greenwillow.

———. 1990. *Something Big Has Been Here.* New York: Scholastic.

———. 1993. *The Dragons Are Singing Tonight.* New York: Scholastic.

———. 1993. *Tyrannosaurus Was a Beast: Dinosaur Poems.* New York: Greenwillow.

———. 1994. *A Pizza the Size of the Sun.* New York: Greenwillow.

———. 1996. *Monday's Troll.* New York: Scholastic.

———, ed. 1997. *The Beauty of the Beast: Poems from the Animal Kingdom.* New York: Knopf.

———, ed. 1997. *Dinosaur Dinner with a Slice of Alligator Pie: Favorite Poems by Dennis Lee.* New York: Scholastic.

———, ed. 1999. *The 20th-Century Children's Poetry Treasury.* New York: Knopf.

———. 2000. *It's Raining Pigs and Noodles.* New York: Greenwillow.

———. 2002. *The Frog Wore Red Suspenders.* New York: Greenwillow.

———, ed. 2003. *I Like It Here at School.* New York: Scholastic.

———. 2004. *If Not for the Cat: Haiku.* Illustrated by Ted Rand. New York: Greenwillow.

———. 2005. *Read a Rhyme, Write a Rhyme.* New York: Random House.

———. 2006. *What a Day It Was at School!* New York: Greenwillow.

———. 2007. *It's Thanksgiving!* New York: HarperCollins.

———. 2008. *My Dog May Be a Genius.* New York: Greenwillow.

———. 2008. *Pizza, Pigs, and Poetry: How to Write a Poem.* New York: Greenwillow.

———. 2009. *The Swamps of Sleethe: Poems from beyond the Solar System.* Illustrated by Jimmy Pickering. New York: Knopf.

Raczka, Bob. 2010. *Guyku: A Year of Haiku for Boys.* Illustrated by Peter Reynolds. Boston: Houghton Mifflin.

Reef, Catherine. 1995. *Walt Whitman.* New York: Clarion.

———. 2000. *Paul Laurence Dunbar: Portrait of a Poet.* Berkeley Heights, NJ: Enslow.

Rich, Mary Perrotta, ed. 1998. *Book Poems: Poems from National Children's Book Week, 1959–1998.* New York: Children's Book Council.

Robb, Laura, ed. 1997. *Music and Drum: Voices of War and Peace, Hope and Dreams.* New York: Philomel.

Roberts, Elizabeth, and Elias Amidon. 1991. *Earth Prayers: 365 Prayers, Poems, and Invocations for Honoring the Earth.* San Francisco: HarperCollins.

———. 1996. *Life Prayers: 365 Prayers, Blessings, and Affirmations to Celebrate the Human Journey from around the World.* San Francisco: HarperCollins.

Rochelle, Belinda, ed. 2001. *Words with Wings: A Treasury of African-American Poetry and Art.* New York: HarperCollins.

Roemer, Heidi. 2004. *Come to My Party and Other Shape Poems.* New York: Henry Holt.

Rogasky, Barbara, ed. 1994. *Winter Poems.* New York: Scholastic.

———, ed. 2001. *Leaf by Leaf.* New York: Scholastic.

Rosen, Michael, ed. 1991. *A World of Poetry.* London: Kingfisher.

———. 1992. *Itsy-Bitsy Beasties: Poems from around the World.* Minneapolis, MN: Carolrhoda.

———, ed. 1995. *The Kingfisher Book of Children's Poetry.* London: Kingfisher.

———, ed. 1995. *Walking the Bridge of Your Nose.* London: Kingfisher.

———, ed. 1998. *Classic Poetry: An Illustrated Collection.* Cambridge, MA: Candlewick.

Rosen, Michael J. 2009. *The Cuckoo's Haiku and Other Birding Poems.* Illustrated by Stan Fellows. Somerville, MA: Candlewick.

———, ed. 1996. *Food Fight: Poets Join the Fight against Hunger with Poems about Their Favorite Foods.* San Diego: Harcourt Brace.

———, ed. 1992. *Home: A Collaboration of Thirty Distinguished Authors and Illustrators of Children's Books to Aid the Homeless.* New York: HarperCollins.

———. 2011. *The Hound Dog's Haiku and Other Poems for Dog Lovers.* Cambridge, MA: Candlewick.

———. 2012. *Running with Trains: A Novel in Poetry and Two Voices.* Honesdale, PA: Wordsong/Boyds Mills.

Rosenberg, Liz, ed. 1996. *The Invisible Ladder: An Anthology of Contemporary American Poems for Young Readers.* New York: Henry Holt.

———, ed. 1998. *Earth-Shattering Poems.* New York: Henry Holt.

———, ed. 2000. *Light-Gathering Poems.* New York: Henry Holt.

Rosenthal, Betsy R. 2004. *My House Is Singing.* Illustrated by Margaret Chodos-Irvine. New York: Harcourt.

Ryan, Pam Muñoz. 2010. *The Dreamer.* New York: Scholastic.

Rylant, Cynthia. 1984. *Waiting to Waltz: A Childhood.* Scarsdale, NY: Bradbury.

———. 1991. *Appalachia: The Voices of Sleeping Birds.* San Diego: Harcourt Brace Jovanovich.

———. 1996. *The Whales.* New York: Scholastic.

Sachar, Louis. 1998. *Holes.* New York: Farrar, Straus, and Giroux.

Salas, Laura Purdie. 2008. *Write Your Own Poetry.* Minneapolis, MN: Compass Point Books.

———. 2009. *Stampede! Poems to Celebrate the Wild Side of School!* New York: Clarion.

———. 2011. *BookSpeak!* Illustrated by Josée Bisaillon. New York: Clarion.

———. 2011. *Picture Yourself Writing Poetry: Using Photos to Inspire Writing.* Minneapolis, MN: Capstone.

Sandburg, Carl. 1998. *Grassroots: Poems by Carl Sandburg.* San Diego: Browndeer/Harcourt Brace.

Schertle, Alice. 1994. *How Now, Brown Cow?* San Diego: Browndeer/Harcourt Brace.

———. 1995. *Advice for a Frog.* New York: Lothrop, Lee, and Shepard.

———. 1999. *A Lucky Thing.* San Diego: Harcourt Brace.

———. 2007. *We.* New York: Lee and Low.

———. 2009. *Button Up! Wrinkled Rhymes.* Illustrated by Petra Mathers. New York: Harcourt.

Schickedanz, Judith, Mary Lynn Pergantis, Jan Kanosky, Annmarie Blaney, and Joan Ottinger. 1997. *Curriculum in Early Childhood: A Resource Guide for Preschool and Kindergarten Teachers.* Boston: Allyn and Bacon.

Schlitz, Laura Amy. 2007. *Good Masters! Sweet Ladies! Voices from a Medieval Village.* Somerville, MA: Candlewick.

Schmidt, Annie M. G. 1981. *Pink Lemonade: Poems for Children.* Translated and adapted from the Dutch by Henrietta ten Harmsel. Grand Rapids, MI: Eerdmans.

Schnur, Steven. 1999. *Spring: An Alphabet Acrostic.* New York: Clarion.

Schwartz, Alvin. 1992. *And the Green Grass Grew All Around: Folk Poetry from Everyone.* New York: HarperCollins.

Schwartz, David M., and Yael Schy. 2010. *What in the Wild? Mysteries of Nature Concealed . . . and Revealed.* Berkeley, CA: Tricycle.

Selznick, Brian. 2007. *The Invention of Hugo Cabret.* New York: Scholastic, 2007.

Sendak, Maurice. 1963. *Where the Wild Things Are.* New York: Harper.

Seuss, Dr. [Theodor Geisl]. 1996. *My Many Colored Days.* New York: Knopf.

Shakur, Tupac. 1999. *A Rose That Grew from Concrete.* New York: Pocket Books.

Shannon, George, ed. 1996. *Spring: A Haiku Story.* New York: Greenwillow.

Shaw, Alison, ed. 1995. *Until I Saw the Sea: A Collection of Seashore Poems.* New York: Henry Holt.

Shields, Carol Diggory. 1995. *Lunch Money and Other Poems about School.* New York: Dutton.

———. 2002. *BrainJuice: American History, Fresh Squeezed!* Brooklyn, NY: Handprint.

———. 2003. *Almost Late to School and More School Poems.* New York: Dutton.

———. 2003. *BrainJuice: Science, Fresh Squeezed!* Brooklyn, NY: Handprint.

Sidman, Joyce. 2003. *The World According to Dog: Poems and Teen Voices.* Boston: Houghton Mifflin.

———. 2005. *Song of the Water Boatman and Other Pond Poems.* Illustrated by Beckie Prange. Boston: Houghton Mifflin.

———. 2006. *Butterfly Eyes and Other Secrets of the Meadow.* Illustrated by Beth Krommes. Boston: Houghton Mifflin.

———. 2006. *Meow Ruff: A Story in Concrete Poetry.* Illustrated by Michelle Berg. Boston: Houghton Mifflin.

———. 2007. *This Is Just to Say: Poems of Apology and Forgiveness.* Illustrated by Pamela Zagarenski. Boston: Houghton Mifflin.

———. 2009. *Red Sings from Treetops: A Year in Colors.* Illustrated by Pamela Zagarenski. Boston: Houghton Mifflin.

———. 2010. *Dark Emperor and Other Poems of the Night.* Illustrated by Rick Allen. Boston: Houghton Mifflin.

———. 2010. *Ubiquitous: Celebrating Nature's Survivors.* Illustrated by Becky Prange. Boston: Houghton Mifflin.

Siebert, Diane. 1984. *Truck Song.* New York: Crowell.

———. 1988. *Mojave.* New York: Crowell.

———. 1989. *Heartland.* New York: Crowell.

———. 1990/1993. *Train Song.* New York: Crowell. New York: HarperCollins.

———. 1991. *Sierra.* New York: HarperCollins.

———. 2000. *Cave.* New York: HarperCollins.

———. 2006. *Tour America: A Journey through Poems and Art.* San Francisco: Chronicle.

Siegen-Smith, Nikki. 2001. *First Morning: Poems about Time.* New York: Barefoot Books.

Sierra, Judy. 1998. *Antarctic Antics: A Book of Penguin Poems.* New York: Scholastic.

———. 2005. *Gruesome Guide to World Monsters.* Somerville, MA: Candlewick.

———. 2005. *Schoolyard Rhymes: Kids' Own Rhymes for Rope Skipping, Hand Clapping, Ball Bouncing, and Just Plain Fun.* New York: Knopf.

Silverstein, Shel. 1974. *Where the Sidewalk Ends.* New York: Harper and Row.

———. 1981. *A Light in the Attic.* New York: Harper and Row.

———. 1996. *Falling Up: Poems and Drawings.* New York: HarperCollins.

———. 2011. *Every Thing On It.* New York: HarperCollins.

Simon, Seymour. 1995. *Star Walk.* New York: Morrow.

Singer, Marilyn. 1989. *Turtle in July.* New York: Macmillan.

———. 1996. *All We Needed to Say: Poems about School from Tanya and Sophie.* New York: Atheneum.

———. 2001. *Monster Museum.* New York: Hyperion.

———. 2004. *Creature Carnival.* New York: Hyperion.

———. 2005. *Monday on the Mississippi.* New York: Henry Holt.

———. 2010. *Mirror, Mirror.* New York: Dutton.

———. 2011. *Twosomes: Love Poems from the Animal Kingdom.* New York: Knopf.

———. 2012. *Every Day's a Dog's Day: A Year in Poems.* New York: Dial.

———. 2012. *A Strange Place to Call Home: The World's Most Dangerous Habitats and the Animals That Call Them Home*. Illustrated by Ed Young. San Francisco: Chronicle.

Sis, Peter. 2003. *The Tree of Life: Charles Darwin*. New York: Farrar, Straus, and Giroux.

Sklansky, Amy E. 2012. *Out of This World: Poems and Facts about Space*. Illustrated by Stacey Schuett. New York: Knopf.

Slapin, Beverly, and Doris Seale, eds. 1998. *Through Indian Eyes: The Native American Experience in Books for Children*. Berkeley, CA: Oyate.

Slier, Deborah, ed. 1991. *Make a Joyful Sound: Poems for Children by African American Poets*. New York: Checkerboard.

Smaridge, Norah. 1968. *Teacher's Pest*. New York: Hawthorn.

———. 1977. *School Is Not a Missile Range*. Nashville, TN: Abingdon.

Smith, Charles R. Jr. 2003. *Hoop Queens*. Somerville, MA: Candlewick.

———. 2004. *Hoop Kings*. Cambridge, MA: Candlewick.

———. 2007. *Twelve Rounds to Glory: The Story of Muhammad Ali*. Somerville, MA: Candlewick.

———. 2012. *Stars in the Shadows: The Negro League All-Star Game of 1934*. Illustrated by Frank Morrison. New York: Atheneum.

Smith, Hope Anita. 2003. *The Way a Door Closes*. New York: Henry Holt.

Smith, Lane. 2011. *Grandpa Green*. New York: Roaring Brook.

Smith, William Jay, ed. 1982. *A Green Place: Modern Poems*. New York: Delacorte.

Sneve, Virginia Driving Hawk, ed. 1989. *Dancing Teepees: Poems of American Indian Youth*. New York: Holiday House.

Sones, Sonya. 1999. *Stop Pretending: What Happened When My Big Sister Went Crazy*. New York: HarperCollins.

———. 2001. *What My Mother Doesn't Know*. New York: Simon and Schuster.

———. 2004. *One of Those Hideous Books Where the Mother Dies*. New York: Simon and Schuster.

Soto, Gary. 1990. *A Fire in My Hands: A Book of Poems*. New York: Scholastic.

———. 1992. *Neighborhood Odes*. San Diego: Harcourt Brace Jovanovich.

———. 1995. *Canto familiar*. San Diego: Harcourt Brace.

———. 2002. *Fearless Fernie: Hanging Out with Fernie and Me*. New York: Putnam.

———. 2005. *Worlds Apart: Fernie and Me*. New York: Putnam.

———. 2008. *Partly Cloudy: Poems of Love and Longing.* Boston: Houghton Mifflin Harcourt.

Spier, Peter. 1967. *London Bridge Is Falling Down!* Garden City, NY: Doubleday.

———. 1970. *The Erie Canal.* Garden City, NY: Doubleday.

———. 1973. *The Star-Spangled Banner.* Garden City, NY: Doubleday.

Spinelli, Eileen. 2007. *Where I Live.* New York: Dial.

Stepanek, Mattie J. T. 2001. *Journey through Heartsongs.* Alexandria, VA: VSP.

Steptoe, Javaka, ed. 1997. *In Daddy's Arms I Am Tall: African Americans Celebrating Fathers.* New York: Lee and Low.

Stevenson, James. 1995. *Sweet Corn: Poems.* New York: Greenwillow.

———. 1998. *Popcorn: Poems.* New York: Greenwillow.

Stevenson, Robert Louis. 1999. *A Child's Garden of Verses.* New York: Simon and Schuster.

———. 2005. *Block City.* Illustrated by Daniel Kirk. New York: Simon and Schuster.

Still, James. 1998. *An Appalachian Mother Goose.* Lexington: University Press of Kentucky.

Stone, Tanya Lee. 2009. *Almost Astronauts: 13 Women Who Dared to Dream.* Somerville, MA: Candlewick.

Strickland, Dorothy S., ed. 1982. *Listen, Children: An Anthology of Black Literature.* New York: Bantam Doubleday.

Strickland, Dorothy S., and Michael R. Strickland, eds. 1994. *Families: Poems Celebrating the African-American Experience.* Honesdale, PA: Wordsong/Boyds Mills.

Strickland, Michael R., ed. 1993. *Poems That Sing to You.* Honesdale, PA: Wordsong/Boyds Mills.

———. 1996. *African-American Poets.* Springfield, NJ: Enslow.

Strong, Amy. 2003. *Lee Bennett Hopkins: A Children's Poet.* New York: Franklin Watts.

Sullivan, Charles, ed. 1994. *Here Is My Kingdom: Hispanic-American Literature and Art for Young People.* New York: Abrams.

Swamp, Chief Jake. 1995. *Giving Thanks: A Native American Good Morning Message.* New York: Lee and Low.

Swann, Brian. 1998. *The House with No Door: African Riddle-Poems.* San Diego: Browndeer.

———. 1998. *Touching the Distance: Native American Riddle-Poems.* San Diego: Browndeer.

Sweet, Melissa. 2011. *Balloons over Broadway: The True Story of the Puppeteer of Macy's Parade*. Boston: Houghton Mifflin, 2011.

Sword, Elizabeth Hauge, and Victoria Flournoy McCarthy, eds. 1995/1998. *A Child's Anthology of Poetry*. New York: Franklin Watts. New York: Trumpet.

Tashjian, Virginia, ed. 1969. *Juba This and Juba That: Story Hour Stretches for Large or Small Groups*. Boston: Little, Brown.

Tedlock, Dennis. 1972. *Finding the Center: Narrative Poetry of the Zuni Indians*. New York: Dial.

Testa, Maria. 2002. *Becoming Joe DiMaggio*. Cambridge, MA: Candlewick.

Thayer, Ernest Lawrence. 2000. *Ernest L. Thayer's Casey at the Bat: A Ballad of the Republic Sung in the Year 1888*. Illustrated by Christopher Bing. San Francisco: Handprint.

Thomas, Joyce Carol. 1993. *Brown Honey in Broomwheat Tea: Poems*. New York: HarperCollins.

———. 1995. *Gingerbread Days*. New York: HarperCollins.

———. 1998. *I Have Heard of a Land*. New York: HarperCollins.

———. 2008. *The Blacker the Berry*. Illustrated by Floyd Cooper. New York: HarperCollins.

Thomas, Shelley Moore. 1998. *Somewhere Today: A Book of Peace*. Morton Grove, IL: Albert Whitman.

Thompson, Brian, ed. 1989. *Catch It If You Can*. London: Viking Kestral.

Thurston, Cheryl Miller. 1987. *Hide Your Ex-Lax under the Wheaties: Poems about Schools, Teachers, Kids, and Education*. Fort Collins, CO: Cottonwood.

Tran, Ngoc-Dung, ed. 1998. *To Swim in Our Own Pond / Ta ve ta tam ao ta: A Book of Vietnamese Proverbs*. Fremont, CA: Shen's Books.

Turner, Ann. 1993. *Grass Songs*. San Diego: Harcourt Brace Jovanovich.

———. 1997. *Mississippi Mud: Three Prairie Journals*. New York: HarperCollins.

Ulrich, George. 1995. *My Tooth Ith Loothe: Funny Poems to Read Instead of Doing Your Homework*. New York: Bantam Doubleday.

Untermeyer, Louis, ed. 1959. *The Golden Treasury of Poetry*. New York: Golden Press.

Vardell, Sylvia, and Janet Wong, eds. 2011. *Gift Tag*. Princeton, NJ: Pomelo Books.

———, eds. 2011. *PoetryTagTime*. Princeton, NJ: Pomelo Books.

———, eds. 2011. *P*TAG*. Princeton, NJ: Pomelo Books.

Viorst, Judith. 1972. *Alexander and the Terrible, Horrible, No Good, Very Bad Day*. New York: Atheneum.

———. 1981. *If I Were in Charge of the World and Other Worries: Poems for Children and Their Parents.* New York: Atheneum.

———. 1995. *Sad Underwear and Other Complications: More Poems for Children and Their Parents.* New York: Atheneum.

Volavkova, Hana, ed. 1993. *I Never Saw Another Butterfly: Children's Drawings and Poems from Terezin Concentration Camp, 1942–1944.* New York: Schocken.

Wardlaw, Lee. 2011. *Won Ton: A Cat Tale Told in Haiku.* Illustrated by Eugene Yelchin. New York: Henry Holt.

Warren, Robert Penn. 1946/1984. *All the King's Men.* Southern Living Gallery, 1984.

Wayland, April Halprin. 2002. *Girl Coming in for a Landing: A Novel in Poems.* New York: Knopf.

Weatherford, Carole Boston. 2002. *Remember the Bridge: Poems of a People.* New York: Philomel.

———. 2007. *Birmingham, 1963.* Honesdale, PA: Wordsong/Boyds Mills.

———. 2008. *Becoming Billie Holiday.* Honesdale, PA: Wordsong/Boyds Mills.

Weinstock, Robert. 2010. *Can You Dig It?* New York: Disney/Hyperion.

Westcott, Nadine Bernard. 1987. *Peanut Butter and Jelly: A Play Rhyme.* New York: Dutton.

———, ed. 1994. *Never Take a Pig to Lunch and Other Poems about the Fun of Eating.* New York: Orchard.

Weston, Robert Paul. 2008. *Zorgamazoo.* New York: Razorbill/Penguin.

Wheeler, Lisa. 2011. *Spinster Goose: Twisted Rhymes for Naughty Children.* Illustrated by Sophie Blackall. New York: Atheneum.

Whipple, Laura, ed. 1989. *Eric Carle's Animals, Animals.* New York: Scholastic.

———, ed. 1994. *Celebrating America: A Collection of Poems and Images of the American Spirit.* New York: Philomel.

Whitman, Walt. 1991. *I Hear America Singing.* New York: Philomel.

Wilbur, Richard. 1998. *The Disappearing Alphabet.* San Diego: Harcourt Brace.

Willard, Nancy. 1981. *A Visit to William Blake's Inn: Poems for Innocent and Experienced Travelers.* San Diego: Harcourt.

———. 1987. *The Voyage of the Ludgate Hill: Travels with Robert Louis Stevenson.* San Diego: Harcourt.

Williams, Vera B. 2001. *Amber Was Brave, Essie Was Smart.* New York: Greenwillow.

Winter, Jeanette. 2002. *Emily Dickinson's Letters to the World*. New York: Frances Foster Books/Farrar, Straus, and Giroux.

Winters, Kay. 2000. *Tiger Trail*. New York: Simon and Schuster.

Wise, William. 2000. *Dinosaurs Forever*. New York: Dial.

Wolf, Allan. 2003. *The Blood-Hungry Spleen and Other Poems about Our Parts*. Illustrated by Greg Clark. Cambridge, MA: Candlewick.

———. 2004. *New Found Land: Lewis and Clark's Voyage of Discovery*. Somerville, MA: Candlewick.

———. 2006. *Immersed in Verse: An Informative, Slightly Irreverent, and Totally Tremendous Guide to Living the Poet's Life*. New York: Sterling.

———. 2011. *The Watch That Ends the Night: Voices from the Titanic*. Somerville, MA: Candlewick.

Wong, Janet S. 1994. *Good Luck Gold and Other Poems*. New York: Margaret K. McElderry.

———. 1996. *A Suitcase of Seaweed and Other Poems*. New York: Margaret K. McElderry.

———. 1999. *Behind the Wheel: Poems about Driving*. New York: Margaret K. McElderry.

———. 1999. *The Rainbow Hand: Poems about Mothers and Children*. New York: Margaret K. McElderry.

———. 2000. *Night Garden: Poems from the World of Dreams*. New York: Margaret K. McElderry.

———. 2003. *Knock on Wood: Poems about Superstitions*. New York: Margaret K. McElderry.

———. 2003. *Minn and Jake*. New York: Farrar, Straus, and Giroux.

———. 2006. *Before It Wriggles Away*. Katonah, NY: Richard C. Owen.

———. 2007. *Twist: Yoga Poems*. New York: Margaret K. McElderry.

———. 2008. *Minn and Jake's Almost Terrible Summer*. New York: Farrar, Straus, and Giroux.

———. 2011. *Once upon a Tiger: New Beginnings for Endangered Animals*. OnceUponaTiger.com.

———. 2012. *Declaration of Interdependence: Poems for an Election Year*. PoetrySuitcase.com.

Wong, Joyce Lee. 2006. *Seeing Emily*. New York: Abrams.

Wood, Nancy. 1993. *Spirit Walker*. New York: Doubleday.

———. 1995. *Dancing Moons.* New York: Doubleday.

———. 1998. *Sacred Fire.* New York: Doubleday.

Woodson, Jacqueline. 2003. *Locomotion.* New York: Putnam.

Worth, Valerie. 1994. *All the Small Poems and Fourteen More.* New York: Farrar, Straus, and Giroux.

———. 2007. *Animal Poems.* Illustrated by Steve Jenkins. New York: Farrar, Straus, and Giroux.

Wyndham, Robert, ed. 1968. *Chinese Mother Goose Rhymes.* Cleveland: World. Reprinted New York: PaperStar, 1998.

Yep, Laurence, ed. 1993. *American Dragons: Twenty-Five Asian American Voices.* New York: HarperCollins.

Yolen, Jane. 1992. *A Letter from Phoenix Farm.* Katonah, NY: Richard C. Owen.

———, ed. 1992. *Street Rhymes from Around the World.* Honesdale, PA: Word-song/Boyds Mills.

———. 1995. *Water Music.* Honesdale, PA: Wordsong/Boyds Mills.

———. 1996. *Sacred Places.* San Diego: Harcourt Brace.

———, ed. 1997. *Once upon Ice and Other Frozen Poems.* Honesdale, PA: Word-song/Boyds Mills.

———. 1998. *Snow, Snow: Winter Poems for Children.* Honesdale, PA: Wordsong/Boyds Mills.

———. 2000. *Color Me a Rhyme: Nature Poems for Young People.* Honesdale, PA: Wordsong/Boyds Mills.

———. 2000. *How Do Dinosaurs Say Good Night?* New York: Blue Sky.

———. 2003. *Least Things: Poems about Small Natures.* Honesdale, PA: Word-song/Boyds Mills.

———. 2006. *Count Me a Rhyme: Animal Poems by the Numbers.* Honesdale, PA: Wordsong/Boyds Mills.

———. 2006. *This Little Piggy: Lap Songs, Finger Plays, Clapping Games, and Pantomime Rhymes.* With CD. Somerville, MA: Candlewick.

———. 2009. *My Uncle Emily.* New York: Philomel.

———. 2011. *Birds of a Feather.* Illustrated by Jason Stemple. Honesdale, PA: Wordsong/Boyds Mills.

———. 2012. *Bug Off! Creepy Crawly Poems.* Illustrated by Jason Stemple. Honesdale, PA: Wordsong/Boyds Mills.

Yolen, Jane, and Andrew Fusek Peters, eds. 2007. *Here's a Little Poem: A Very First Book of Poetry.* Somerville, MA: Candlewick.

Young, Ed. 1997. *Voices of the Heart.* New York: Scholastic.

Yu, Chin. 2005. *Little Green: Growing Up during the Chinese Cultural Revolution.* New York: Simon and Schuster.

Zehares, Wade. 2001. *Big, Bad, and a Little Bit Scary: Poems That Bite Back!* New York: Viking.

Ziefert, Harriet. 1997. *Mother Goose Math.* New York: Viking.

Zimmer, Tracie Vaughn. 2007. *Reaching for Sun.* New York: Bloomsbury.

———. 2009. *Steady Hands: Poems about Work.* New York: Clarion.

———. 2011. *Cousins of Clouds: Elephant Poems.* New York: Clarion.

# References

This list identifies professional reference tools for the adult who wants to learn more about sharing poetry with children. It also provides full publication information for the reference sources cited in the text.

Ada, Alma Flor, Violet Harris, and Lee Bennett Hopkins. 1993. *A Chorus of Cultures: Developing Literacy through Multicultural Poetry.* Carmel, CA: Hampton-Brown.

Anderson, Nancy A. 2006. *Elementary Children's Literature: The Basics for Teachers and Parents.* 2nd ed. New York: Pearson.

Bagert, Brod. 1992. "Act It Out: Making Poetry Come Alive." In *Invitation to Read: More Children's Literature in the Reading Program,* edited by Bernice Cullinan, 14–23. Newark, DE: International Reading Association.

Barton, Bob, and David Booth. 2004. *Poetry Goes to School: From Mother Goose to Shel Silverstein.* Markham, ON: Pembroke Publishers.

Bauer, Caroline Feller. 1995. *The Poetry Break: An Annotated Anthology with Ideas for Introducing Children to Poetry.* New York: H. W. Wilson.

Booth, David, and Bill Moore. 2003. *Poems Please! Sharing Poetry with Children.* 2nd ed. Markham, ON: Pembroke Publishers.

Brountas, Maria. 1995. "The Versatility of Poetry." *Teaching PreK–8* 25 (March): 40–42.

Bryant, P. E., L. Bradley, M. MacLean, and J. Crossland. 1989. "Nursery Rhymes, Phonological Skills, and Reading." *Journal of Child Language* 16: 407–28.

Burleson, Marcie Lynn. 2002. "Seeing the 'Sights' with Poetry." *Teaching PreK–8* 32 (April): 60–61.

Bush, Gail. 1997. "Speak, Muses." *School Library Journal* 43 (September): 139.

Chatton, Barbara. 2010. *Using Poetry across the Curriculum.* 2nd ed. Santa Barbara, CA: ABC-CLIO.

Collom, Jack, and Sheryl Noethe. 2005. *Poetry Everywhere: Teaching Poetry Writing in School and in the Community.* New York: Teachers and Writers Collaborative.

Copeland, Jeffrey S. 1993. *Speaking of Poets: Interviews with Poets Who Write for Children and Young Adults.* Urbana, IL: National Council of Teachers of English.

Copeland, Jeffrey S., and Vicky S. Copeland. 1995. *Speaking of Poets 2: More Interviews with Poets Who Write for Children and Young Adults.* Urbana, IL: National Council of Teachers of English.

Cullinan, Bernice. 1999. "Lessons from Mother Goose." *Instructor-Primary* 108 (March): 55.

Cullinan, Bernice, Marilyn Scala, and Virginia Schroder. 1995. *Three Voices: An Invitation to Poetry across the Curriculum.* York, ME: Stenhouse.

Fisher, C. J., and M. A. Natarella. 1982. "Young Children's Preferences in Poetry: A National Survey of First, Second, and Third Graders." *Research in the Teaching of English* 16 (4): 339–54.

Fisher, Maisha T. 2007. *Writing in Rhythm: Spoken Word Poetry in Urban Classrooms.* New York: Teachers College Press.

Fitch, Sheree, and Larry Swartz. 2008. *The Poetry Experience: Choosing and Using Poetry in the Classroom.* Markham, ON: Pembroke.

Fox, Mem. 2001. *Reading Magic: Why Reading Aloud to Our Children Will Change Their Lives Forever.* San Diego: Harcourt.

Franco, Betsy. 2005. *Conversations with a Poet: Inviting Poetry into K–12 Classrooms.* Katonah, NY: Richard C. Owen.

Glover, M. K. 1999. *A Garden of Poets: Poetry Writing in the Elementary Classroom.* Urbana, IL: National Council of Teachers of English.

Goforth, F. S. 1998. *Literature and the Learner.* Belmont, CA: Wadsworth.

Hadaway, Nancy, Sylvia M. Vardell, and Terrell Young. 2001. "Scaffolding Oral Language Development through Poetry for Students Learning English." *Reading Teacher* 54: 796–806.

———. 2002. *Literature-Based Instruction with English Language Learners.* New York: Allyn and Bacon.

Hanauer, David Ian. 2004. *Poetry and the Meaning of Life: Reading and Writing Poetry in Language Arts Classrooms.* Toronto: Pippin.

Heard, Georgia. 1994. *For the Good of the Earth and Sun: Teaching Poetry.* Portsmouth, NH: Heinemann.

———. 1999. *Awakening the Heart: Exploring Poetry in Elementary and Middle School.* Portsmouth, NH: Heinemann.

Heitman, Jane. 2003. *Rhymes and Reasons: Librarians and Teachers Using Poetry to Foster Literacy, Grades K–6.* Worthington, OH: Linworth.

Holbrook, Sara. 2002. *Wham! It's a Poetry Jam: Discovering Performance Poetry.* Honesdale, PA: Wordsong/Boyds Mills.

———. 2005. *Practical Poetry: A Nonstandard Approach to Meeting Content-Area Standards.* Portsmouth, NH: Heinemann.

Holbrook, Sara, and Michael Salinger. 2006. *Outspoken: How to Improve Writing and Speaking through Poetry Performance.* Portsmouth, NH: Heinemann.

Hopkins, Lee Bennett. 1986. *Pass the Poetry, Please!* 3rd ed. New York: HarperCollins.

———. 1995. *Pauses: Autobiographical Reflections of 101 Creators of Children's Books.* New York: HarperCollins.

Huck, Charlotte, Barbara Kiefer, Susan Hepler, and Janet Hickman. 2003. *Children's Literature in the Elementary School.* New York: McGraw Hill.

Jacobs, James, and Michael Tunnell. 2004. *Children's Literature, Briefly.* 3rd ed. New York: Merrill.

Janeczko, Paul B. 2011. *Reading Poetry in the Middle Grades: 20 Poems and Activities That Meet the Common Core Standards and Cultivate a Passion for Poetry.* Portsmouth, NH: Heinemann.

Korbeck, Sharon. 1995. "Children's Poetry: Journeying beyond the Road Less Traveled." *School Library Journal* 41 (April): 43–44.

Kordigel, M. 1995. "'Every Poet a Big Child': The Slovene Poet Boris A. Novak." *Bookbird* 33 (1): 36–37.

Kutiper, Karen, and Patricia Wilson. 1993. "Updating Poetry Preferences: A Look at the Poetry Children Really Like." *Reading Teacher* 47 (1): 28–34.

Lipson, S. L. 2006. *Writing Success through Poetry: Create a Writers' Workshop.* Waco, TX: Prufrock Press.

Livingston, Myra Cohn. 1984. *The Child as Poet: Myth or Reality?* Boston: Horn Book.

Manning, Maryann, and Gary Manning. 1997. "Talk about Poetry." *Teaching PreK–8* 27 (February): 100–101.

McCaslin, Nellie. 2000. *Creative Drama in the Classroom and Beyond.* 7th ed. New York: Addison Wesley Longman.

McClure, Amy. 1990. *Sunrises and Songs: Reading and Writing Poetry in an Elementary Classroom.* Portsmouth, NH: Heinemann.

Morice, Dave. 1996/2007. *The Adventures of Dr. Alphabet: 104 Unusual Ways to Write Poetry in the Classroom and the Community.* New York: Teachers and Writers Collaborative.

Nye, Naomi Shihab. 2005. "Spiral Staircase." *Horn Book Magazine* 81, no. 3 (May–June): 251–54.

O'Connor, John. 2004. *Wordplaygrounds: Reading, Writing, and Performing Poetry in the English Classroom.* Urbana, IL: National Council of Teachers of English.

Partington, Richie. 2009. *I Second That Emotion: Sharing Children's and Young Adult Poetry; A 21st Century Guide for Teachers and Librarians.* Salt Lake City, UT: Hi Willow.

Raymond, Allen. 1999. "Lee Bennett Hopkins Is Still the 'Little Kid from Newark.'" *Teaching PreK–8* 29 (January): 58–61.

Ruurs, Margriet. 2001. *The Power of Poems: Teaching the Joy of Writing Poetry.* Gainesville, FL: Maupin House.

Sloan, Glenna. 2003. *Give Them Poetry: A Guide for Sharing Poetry with Children K–8.* New York: Teachers College Press.

Steinbergh, Judith. 1994. *Reading and Writing Poetry: A Guide for Teachers.* New York: Scholastic.

Terry, Ann. 1974. *Children's Poetry Preferences: A National Survey of Upper Elementary Grades.* Urbana, IL: National Council of Teachers of English.

Thomas, Joseph T. Jr. 2007. *Poetry's Playground: The Culture of Contemporary American Children's Poetry.* Detroit, MI: Wayne State University Press.

Tiedt, Iris McClellan. 2002. *Tigers, Lilies, Toadstools, and Thunderbolts: Engaging K–8 Students with Poetry.* Newark, DE: International Reading Association.

Treviño, Rose Z. 2009. *Read Me a Rhyme in Spanish and English.* Chicago: American Library Association.

Vardell, Sylvia, and Janet Wong, eds. 2012. *The Poetry Friday Anthology K-5.* Princeton, NJ: Pomelo Books.

Vardell, Sylvia, and Janet Wong, eds. 2013. *The Poetry Friday Anthology for Middle School (Grades 6-8).* Princeton, NJ: Pomelo Books.

Vardell, Sylvia, and Janet Wong, eds. 2014. *The Poetry Friday Anthology for Science.* Princeton, NJ: Pomelo Books.

Vardell, Sylvia, Nancy Hadaway, and Terrell Young. 2002. "Choosing and Sharing Poetry with ESL Students." *Book Links* 11 (5): 51–56.

Vardell, Sylvia M. 2003. "Poetry for Social Studies: Poems, Standards, and Strategies." *Social Education* 67 (4): 206–11.

———. 2005. "Lift Ev'ry Voice and Sing: Multicultural Poetry for Children and Young Adults." *Versed* (Bulletin of the Office for Diversity, American Library Association) (March–April). www.ala.org/ala/diversity/versed/versedbackissues/march2005abc/mar05.htm.

———. 2007. *Poetry People: A Practical Guide to Children's Poets.* Englewood, CO: Libraries Unlimited.

———. 2009. "Everyday Poetry: Pairing Award Winners with Poetry." *Book Links* 18 (3): 44–45.

———. 2010. "Making Poetry Movies." *Book Links* 20 (1): 36–37.

———. 2011. "Everyday Poetry: Poetry Tag." *Book Links* 20 (3): 14–15.

———. 2012. *The Poetry Teacher's Book of Lists.* Seattle, WA: CreateSpace.

Vardell, Sylvia M., and June M. Jacko. 2005. "Folklore for Kids: Exploring the Rhymes, Songs, and Games of Childhood." *Book Links* 14 (4): 29–33.

Wilson, Patricia, and Karen Kutiper. 1994. "Beyond Silverstein and Prelutsky: Enhancing and Promoting the Elementary and Middle School Poetry Collection." *Youth Services in Libraries* (Spring 1994): 273–81.

Wood, Jaime R. 2007. *Living Voices: Multicultural Poetry in the Middle School Classroom.* Urbana, IL: National Council of Teachers of English.

Wooldridge, Susan Goldsmith. 1996. *Poemcrazy: Freeing Your Life with Words.* New York: Three Rivers Press.

Zipes, Jack, Lissa Paul, Lynne Vallone, Peter Hunt, and Gillian Avery. 2005. *The Norton Anthology of Children's Literature: The Traditions in English.* New York: Norton.

# Index

*Page numbers in italics indicate a profile of the poet.*